The Philosophical Traditions of India

BY THE SAME AUTHOR

Thought and Reality: Hegelianism and Advaita
Comparative Studies in Philosophy (Editor, with Dean Inge et al.)
Idealistic Thought of India
The Concept of Man: A Study in Comparative Philosophy
(Editor, with S. Radhakrishnan)

The Philosophical Traditions of India

P. T. RAJU

Professor of Philosophy and Indian Studies
at the College of Wooster, Wooster, Ohio

LONDON · GEORGE ALLEN & UNWIN LTD
Ruskin House Museum Street

First published in 1971

ISBN 0 04 181016 3

Printed in Great Britain
In 11 point Fournier
by Unwin Brothers Limited
Woking and London

Contents

Pronunciation of Sanskrit Words

The following is only a general guide to the pronunciation of Sanskrit terms and names. It is not the general practice to use diacritical marks for contemporary names of persons.

a	short as in 'particular'
ā	long as in 'father'
i	short as in 'pit'
ī	long as in 'police'
u	short as in 'put'
ū	long as in 'rude'
ṛ	short as in 'merrily'
e	as in 'pet'
ai	as in 'aisle'
au	as in 'house'
o	as in 'go'
g	as in 'go'
ṅ	as in 'sing'
c	as in 'chores'
ch	as in 'chur*chh*ouse'
ñ	as in 'singe'
ṭ	as in 'true'
ḍ	as in 'drum'
ṇ	as in 'tent'
t	as in 'thermos' without the h-sound
th	as in 'thunder'
d	as in 'this'
dh	as in 'this' with another h added
ś	as in 'sure'
ṣ	as in 'shine'
s	as in 'sit'

Introduction

AIM OF THE BOOK

The author of present work has a background of nearly forty years of teaching Indian philosophy to Indian students and of nearly twenty years of teaching Western students. The book attempts to overcome many of the difficulties which Western students encounter in studying Indian philosophy and also to remove many misunderstanding about it, such as that it is all pure mysticism without logic, that it is based upon some supernatural intuition, that it is only or mainly the philosophy of the worship of Śakti or Mother Goddess in the form of sexual energy, and that it has no academic side. The book tries to convey – within the scope of an elementary work which it is – that Indian philosophy has as intricate and complex metaphysical and epistemological theories as many others and that in fact these disciplines – epistemology and metaphysics – are an essential and necessary part of Indian philosophy, as they ought to be of any philosophy that claims to be a philosophy of life. And this claim of philosophy ought constantly to be kept before our minds. For if philosophy gives up the task of being a philosophy of life, there is no other subject to undertake the task. Hegel's view that a culture without philosophy – by which he means metaphysics – is like a temple without the holy of the holies applies well to Indian philosophy, which is the holy of the holies of India's culture and way of life. We may also remember Santayana's observation that there were only two metaphysical nations, the Greeks and the Indians. Metaphysics with all that it implies, particularly logic and epistemology, was a gift of nature to the Greeks and the Indians and points to the holy of the holies, however defined or described.

It is hoped that the book will be useful also as a basis for students and teachers of comparative philosophy, although it is meant mainly for beginners in Indian philosophy. However, Indian philosophy is studied in the West for mutual understanding and for purposes of comparison. Without implicit or explicit comparison, Western students cannot understand Indian thought. This book, it is hoped, can avoid the necessity of relying on prejudiced and one-sided presentations of Indian thought for comparisons. Comparisons based upon some superficial and apparent aspects of philosophies can only have superficial results – not to speak of prejudiced and cavalier presentations – if they do not grasp the conceptual frameworks of the systems. So the presentation of philosophies in this book gives importance to conceptual frameworks, albeit in an elementary way. Even those readers who are not interested in comparative philosophy should know the conceptual frameworks of the schools and systems and should not be content merely with oversimplifications and one-sided generalizations. Experience shows that, when Sanskrit technical terms are not adequately or are wrongly explained, enthusiastic Western students tend to jump to hasty conclusions and even wrong identifications with Western concepts.[1]

OURS AN AGE OF MUTUAL UNDERSTANDING

However, the confluence of several global currents – religious, social, political, and economic – both violent and peaceful, has turned our age into one of earnestness for mutual understanding. This necessitates presenting Indian philosophy to Indian and Western students in mutually understandable terms. It is also being recognized, though slowly, that we have to be self-critical as well as being critical of others. It is said by many great philosophers that the gap between Eastern and Western philosophies has to be bridged. But one hears also that Indian philosophies are mere religious doctrines and have little or nothing to contribute to metaphysics, ethics, logic and so forth. It is heard, furthermore, that every Indian philosopher contradicts whatever is said about Indian philosophy, thereby creating an impossible situation in research and evaluation. Such reaction to Indian philosophers is often due to lack of right acquaintance with Indian philosophies, which cannot be classified under any single concept except that of 'philosophies of life'. But philosophies of life can be many and no single metaphysical term can cover all. And evaluation has to be not in terms of any Western philosophy as the standard, but in terms of experience, truth, and reality. To classify Indian philosophies as religious can be, though not necessarily, as misleading as to classify them under a single epistemological or metaphysical term. Religion

[1] This often happens when Sanskrit terms themselves are used in the main text without the English equivalents and also when they are translated wrongly into some well-known English philosophical technical terms without properly grasping their implications.

for the Indians is not a revealed religion like Islam or Christianity; and if either of the two is taken as the standard, then Indian religion has to be pronounced defective. But in fact, neither should treat the other as *the* standard. We have on our hands, then, the question: What is the standard? Self-reflection, as a result, becomes necessary as reflection on the other. One may safely say that classical Indian philosophy is a handmaid to religion that is not understood as revealed, but as a religion of intuition and reflection on life and Being, on man's inwardness and outwardness. To teach it as some doctrinal theology can again be misleading; for theology in the West originated in a particular revelation and its dogmatics, and so distinctions are drawn among revealed theology, natural theology, philosophical theology, and philosophy of religion. But no such distinctions apply to Indian religious thought. One may say that, in the West, Greek philosophy is a direct handmaid to life, medieval philosophy to theology, and much of contemporary philosophy to science. And it is the latter trend of contemporary philosophy that has more or less forgotten about its roots in human life and existence, with the consequent protest of existence philosophies which tend to discard reason and science. The tension between philosophy and religion, religion and science, and science and philosophy has become characteristic of the West, which cannot be applied to Indian thought. During the author's student days, he heard it often asked by some professors: If metaphysics is not meant to show the ultimate truth which we have to become, what else is it meant for and what can be its purpose? One Sanskrit pundit, whose knowledge of English was little or nothing, asked the author: 'Is philosophy needed to tell me that the book I am holding is real? Do I not know it without philosophy?' He meant that philosophy is needed to tell us the implications of our life; the elucidation of the implications is metaphysics, and the realization of them in our life is religion. As metaphysics and religion are understood thus by the Indian thinkers, they never felt any tension between philosophy and religion, and philosophy and science. The elucidation of the implications of our existence is found in both science and philosophy and covers the whole field of thought's endeavour.

Whatever be the reason, Indian philsophy had a more complex and profound development than the Chinese, is older than the Western, and can compare favourably with the Western in many aspects up to about the time of the European Renaissance. As much patience, perseverance, and humility are needed to study and understand Indian philosophy as for studying and understanding Western philosophy. The advantages of a profound study of Indian thought can be as great for the Western philosopher as those of a profound understanding of Western thought for the Indian, provided neither adapts the dilemma, attributed to the Sultan of Baghdad, before burning the Alexandrian library: If the library says what the Koran says, it is unnecessary; if it says what the Koran does not say, it is false.

PHILOSOPHICAL TRADITIONS

'There is hardly any height of spiritual insight or rational philosophy attained in the world', wrote Radhakrishnan with a dissatisfaction with some western attitudes to Indian thought, 'that has not its parallel in the vast stretch that lies between the early Vedic seers and the modern Naiyāyikas.'[2] A suppressed reaction to this statement is that it makes too vast a claim. But Radhakrishnan does not mean that Indian philosophy contains the formal logic of Russell and Whitehead's *Principia Mathematica*, but *only that all the possible traditions of thought, which the thinking man's life generates, can be found in Indian thought* and that no cavalier over-simplification is true of it. And each of these traditions had a systematic and elaborate development from about the fourth century BC, to about the fifteenth or sixteenth century AD. Nearly two thousand years of systematizing and development – if we omit the early Vedic period – of philosophical ideas by a variety of philosophers cannot properly be characterized by a single term.

Philosophical traditions are continuations of the drives of formative thought generated by human life, and of its problems and questionings – perspectives or strands of the Platonic Eros – even if in contemporary times thought tends to forget its roots in human life and to forfeit its original claim to being a guide to life. To speak of traditions is *not* the same as to speak of traditionalism. The difference between the traditions of the traditionalists and philosophical traditions lies in the latter being avowedly self-reflective. Otherwise, even thorough-going logicalism will have to be called a type of traditionalism. Many thought-forms and their impulses are rooted in our life, and aim at throwing light on the different aspects of life. Sometimes they overlap and

[2] S. Radhakrishnan, *Indian Philosophy*, Vol. 1, p. 8 (George Allen and Unwin Ltd, London, 1948).

become confused. To remove the confusions, thought generates forms of self-reflection and creates traditions of methodology, epistemology, and logic like the Nyāya in India. These methodological traditions overlap other traditions, penetrate of necessity the metaphysical and ethical traditions, and create new problems; then philosophical thought may be pushed farther and farther from its origins. When the forms of philosophical thought do not lose contact with their origins and retain the consciousness of the originative forces that have been driving them on, thinkers in India speak of them as traditions (*sampradāyas*), and often as schools also.

The development of these perspectives of thought in time constitutes history of philosophy. Does Indian philosophy have a history? Both an affirmative and a negative answer seem to be possible. As Indian philosophy has stuck to the idea of traditions and as almost all Indian philosophers claim that they are developing an original tradition, it can be said that India has had no history of philosophy. But one German indologist, Dr Paul Hacker, said to the author that the Indians had been unfair to themselves in thinking that they had had no history of philosophy; for although they had only traditions, these were developed stage by stage in history – schools generating sub-schools – through self-criticism and mutual criticism; so, it could be said, there had been a historical development in time. In support of Hacker one may say that if Christianity has a history, then Indian philosophy has one. But a book showing this history has yet to be written. S. N. Dasputa calls his book *History of Indian Philosophy*; but it follows the usual pattern of presentation and is not divided into historical periods. The present work, being very elementary, follows the usual pattern, but in its own way.

The aim of the new arrangement of the chapters is first to remove the misunderstanding that India has no philosophy of action and second to show the relevance of the main traditions to one another. Whitehead said that Western philosophy is a series of footnotes of Plato. We may add that all post-Kantian philosophy up to the present is a series of footnotes to Kant. Similarly, Indian philosophy can be considered to be a series of footnotes to the Upaniṣads. That the different traditions are series of footnotes to some philosopher or his work may be acknowledged, unacknowledged, or even denied by some followers of the traditions. Some philosophers, for instance, may only elaborate a point of Plato or Kant, or may make it a new point of view and develop a whole philosophy out of it, or may criticize and reject it and in opposition develop a rival philosophy. Generally when this rival philosophy can have no standing except as an antidote or complementary to the first considered as a philosophy of the whole life, then such development can be treated as an indirect footnote to the original. However, ultimately all are footnotes to life and reason in different perspectives and become traditions to the overall observer. When this primary and basic nature of philosophies is recognized, unity of understanding and mutual understanding become possible. After all, all philosophies, Eastern and Western, are footnotes to the living Logos in its different aspects and dimensions.

Classical Indian philosophies may be characterized as philosophies of life. They form different traditions, representing different aspects and constituents of human nature, which form the many philosophical perspectives. The traditions are the articulations, direct or indirect, of man and the world in the different perspectives or from different points of view. They are needed for a complete understanding of man and his world or rather man in the world, and the deep underlying unity holding the two in its grip is the Logos in its philosophical meaning. Philosophy is meant – Kant said the same long ago – to understand what one is, what one can and ought to become in this world, how one can become it, and what the nature of the world is in which one has one's being and can attain the ideal of life. It is necessary to understand both oneself and the reality in which one has one's being; for one has to know whether the nature of oneself and of reality allow the achievement of the ideal. To these questions several answers are possible from the many standpoints. These questions and answers, and their implications determine the nature of the traditions of thought which human life has generated in its history of self-reflection.

If something is to be achieved, man in general thinks that it can be achieved only through action, i.e. by working for it. But action implies a pluralistic universe, the nature of which is to be explained in terms of action and in the philosophy for which action becomes the supreme principle. Such a philosophy is the Mīmāmsā. To understand reality, thought has to work methodically and logically without turning imagination and hopes into methods. Logic implies also a plurality; for if all is one, there is no need of thinking. The philosophy in which logic and methodology play the primary role belongs to the Nyāya; and the main defence of pluralism belongs to the philosophy of the

Vaiśeṣika. In the basic works of these two schools, logic and method are the main concern of the Nyāya and the defence of pluralism that of the Vaiśeṣika. The philosophy of action of the Mīmāmsā is also pluralistic; but its main purpose is the explanation of right action. Next, understanding oneself can be understanding oneself as apart from that which is not one's self and which can be regarded as one whole massive object. This understanding leads to a kind of qualitative dualism, which we find in the Sāṅkhya and the Yoga. But thought does not stop here. It asks: If the world, the alien object, is an other to oneself, how can one be sure that it permits the realization of one's ideals? Are the ideals empty hopes and longings or are they realizable? They can be realized only if there is a unity underlying oneself and the world. Man has to search for it. The philosophies of such unities are the Vedānta and later Buddhism. Early Buddhism and Jainism are somewhat similar to the Nyāya, the Vaiśeṣika and the Mīmāmsā in their conceptions of the world except for some differences of detail. And both Buddhism and Jainism rejected the Vedas as scriptural authorities. The Cārvāka system worked out its philosophy in opposition to scriptural authority and to every form of other-worldliness. It also is a significant and possible philosophical tradition, the significance of which can be seen in periods when the other-worldliness of an outlook reaches extremes, develops excesses, and man wastes his energies for other-worldly fancies and ignores this life and existence.

We may so understand these traditions, so far as they were formed in India: For life there has to be a tradition of action and of its metaphysical implications; that is the Mīmāmsā tradition. Then there has to be a tradition of the forms and methods of understanding and of their implications: such a tradition is that of the Nyāya, and the Vaiśeṣika. Next, there has to be a tradition of the self and of the methods of knowing the self: that is the Sāṅkhya, and the Yoga tradition. Lastly, there has to be a tradition for explaining the underlying unity of the self and the surrounding world: that is the tradition of the Vedānta. The others are reactions to some of the excesses and extremes of the Mīmāmsā in some form or other. The basic elements or concepts and doctrines of Indian philosophy can be understood the best in the context of these traditions.

But historically the traditions in India do not seem to have arisen and grown in the simple logical way mentioned above out of one another. They represent perpetual needs of man's life and thought, and their root ideas may have been present right from the beginning with or without recognized conflicts among them. In the schools and subschools there have been several permutations and combinations of the root, elemental ideas; and such schools and their subdivisions are quite many, as may be expected. The early Aryans who entered India believed in action for obtaining things of this world and the next; and the first two parts of the Veda contain their ideas, on which the Mīmāmsā philosophy is based. As these ideas are the earliest, the Mīmāmsā philsophy is given first in this book. This was originally the true orthodox tradition; to belittle it is to belittle half the Veda. The Cārvāka, Jainism, and Buddhism are reactions to the Mīmāmsā and are, therefore, given next. After them the Nyāya, the Vaiseṣika, the Sāṅkhya, and the Yoga, all of which more or less nominally accept the Vedic scriptural authority but rose and developed as traditions independent of the Vedas, are presented. The Vedānta, which is based on the last two parts of the Veda, is claimed – indeed the original Mīmāmsā rejects the claim – to be a completion and fulfilment of the Mīmāmsā and is really a development of its spiritual implications.[3] It represents also the final form of the philosophy of life for the majority of the men of thought in India. By the time the Vedānta was systematized into aphorisms (of Bādarāyaṇa), several paths or ways of life (*mārgas*, *yoga*) came to be recognised and the need for reconciling them was keenly felt. This reconciliation with the recognition that the ways in their isolation from one another are inadequate to the total life of man is presented by the epics and the ethical codes; and so the chapter on them is given next. In the end a general idea is given of contemporary philosophical developments.

PLAN OF THE WORK AND SOME CONVENTIONS

The chapters do not, therefore, follow a historical order. Most of the schools originated simultaneously and are not separated in time, if systematizations and mutual differentiations are taken into consideration. But all represent practically most of the main possible philosophical traditions which human life and mind can originate. In this sense, one may say that India had all the philosophical doctrines, some more and others less developed. As an elementary work, this book avoids the later complicated developments of the traditions, and presents only the

[3] In the author's opinion, the sequence of the chapters can be different.

essentials. But in a few cases, technicalities could only be reduced to the minimum and could not be avoided completely, as this book is one on philosophy, but not merely on culture. For instance, the Nyāya school was born to introduce technicalities and critical analysis, for making controversy and argument methodical and methodological. To omit even an elementary presentation of its technicalities is to omit the Nyāya. The reader will then know only the word 'Nyāya', but not what it means.

The author, though the book is elementary, has not combined the Nyāya and the Vaiśeṣika into one single chapter and the Sāṅkhya and the Yoga into another single one, although the amalgamations seem to have taken place about the tenth century. For the traditions started separately, but not jointly. Their original interests were different. The Nyāya was primarily interested in logic and epistemology and the Vaiśeṣika in a pluralistic metaphysics. The Sāṅkhya interest lay in fixing the categories and the Yoga wanted to systematise the practices of the body and mind for stopping the functions of 'reason' (*buddhi*).

The author has not avoided the use of Sanskrit terms in brackets in the text itself, giving at the same time the approximate English equivalents. To the Western student even occasional encounterings of Sanskrit terms, though within brackets, may be irksome; but they have to be given to constantly remind the reader that the corresponding ideas belong to Sanskrit philosophy. Too often the English words have their own significance and associations, which the student may read into Indian thought. Even in the translation of French and German works and in the exposition of their philosophies, French and German words are often given in brackets, although these languages are nearer to English than Sanskrit is. Some words like *ātman* and *Brahman* have entered English dictionaries; but using them without translations has not yet become the vogue. Words like *sattva* etc., ought to be used.

It was suggested to this author that the use of Sanskrit terms in the text can be avoided by using stars on the concerned English translations, and explaining them in the glossary. But this method can be followed only if it is advantageous and without risks. The author cannot find that it is either. Firstly, the same Sanskrit term has different meanings in different systems. Then translating it by the same English term will be misleading. For example, *buddhi* means consciousness, light of intelligence, for the Nyāya; but it means creative reason, something like the Logos with cosmic significance, for the Sāṅkhya.

If it is translated as 'understanding' even with an asterisk, the meaning does not fit either of the above meanings. Such troublesome words are many such as *ātman*, *jīva*, *vijñāna*, *prajñā*, and so on. Secondly, a writer using the asterisk method has to assume on his own part a thorough grasp of the significances of the words in the different systems, to do which, in the present writer's opinion, the time has not yet come so far as Indian thought and its exposition in Western philosophical terminology go. Modern research into Indian philosophy is not yet complete and the conceptual schemata are not yet made precise in every case. It is risky to make such an assumption and adopt the asterisk method. Thirdly, the new method is not less irksome than the one so far followed, if the reader has often to look at the glossary and select the relevant signification, even if all are given. The present author, therefore, feels that there can at present be no better method than to give the relevant English term in the running text so that the English term suits the system and add the Sanskrit term within brackets. However, a Glossary is added at the end.

Again, the tendency and temptation to give an original meaning to a term by taking its etymological meaning or a derivation from it as the meaning of the technical term and by giving the corresponding English word as the proper translation of the Sanskrit word is misleading. Surely, in some cases etymologies become helpful and even explanatory. But the reader will see that to rely on etymology exposes one to one of the fallacies (*nayābhāsās*) pointed out by Jainism. The English word selected thus may not fit the system that is being interpreted. One should not try to be too original in interpreting a philosophy propounded in a different language. The author remembers a German indologist – a serious and earnest student – saying that Śaṅkara did not understand the true meaning of the Vedic words *ātman* and *puruṣa* and even *brahman* in their origins and etymologies and that he has, therefore, to be reinterpreted.[4] But even if Śaṅkara committed such a

[4] Many books have been written on Indian philosophy both in India and the West. One can fairly distinguish among them books written by authors who are trained in both Western and Indian philosophies and have a feel and grasp of their conceptual frameworks, and insights into them, books written by authors who are trained mainly in Western philosophies, books written by Western theologians or those who have mainly the Western theological background, and books written by orientalists or indologists. The first kind is fairly reliable, as it can grasp both the similarities and differences insightfully; the second tends either to assimilate Indian thought to the Western, judging the former by the

mistake, our new interpretation will not be Śaṅkara's philosophy. But our aim is to understand his philosophy. We should remember that many Sanskrit technical terms have their own peculiar meanings, which sometimes include the meanings of cognate English terms but go beyond them. In many cases the meanings of English and Sanskrit terms mainly overlap but do not coincide. It is, therefore, safer to use the Sanskrit words as often as possible – provided they are not too long – at least within brackets in the text itself.

I have been finding it necessary to explain why I have been constantly using 'the' before *ātman*, Brahman, and the names of the schools. 'The' denotes a class, and to mean the class of *ātmans* the definite article is used. Again, 'Brahman' means in the systems the Absolute; etymologically, it means the 'ever-growing', the 'ever-increasing', the 'ever-expanding'; and philosophically, it means the 'ultimate', the 'unconditioned', and so on. I think that after the vast study devoted to Indian thought, we should consider it right to use the definite article before the word. Furthermore, words like *sāṅkhya*, *yoga*, and *nyāya* have not only the exclusive meanings of the systems of thought called by the terms, but also their general meanings like 'exact knowledge', 'yogic practice', and 'logic'. In the former meanings it is proper to use the definite article. There certainly is no strict rule to be followed. Before 'Prakṛti', which is compared to a woman by the Sāṅkhya, it sounds jarring to use 'the', as it does if used before Māyā and Avidyā. Besides, in these cases the distinction between the general meaning and the particular meaning is not very definite. And except where the word *ātman* means the Brahman, it is written as '*ātman*', without capitalizing the first 'a'.

I have not hesitated, whenever helpful and convenient, to use terms

latter or to read too much into Indian thought to be accurate; the third group tends to judge Indian philosophy as a religion or religious thought with Western theology as the standard, and further it tends to ignore the deeper philosophical technicalities of the Indian systems and is generally cavalier and touches only the surface; the fourth group tends to ignore the conceptual structure, which is essential for any philosophy, attends to single concepts as derived etymologically and overlooks the fact that even the single concepts may change their significance almost completely in the developing systems. There can be exceptions to each of these four types; but it is generally difficult for an author to shake off his confirmed habits of thought. Even in the case of some Indian authors of Indian philosophies, it seems that they missed the dynamics of the life of the concepts or of the patterns of the philosophies.

such as 'pragmatism', 'correspondence', 'syllogism' etc., in interpreting the Indian doctrines. Some philosophers and interpreters of Indian thought are opposed to this practice. In India itself I was acquainted with a controversy about the rightness and usefulness of comparative interpretations introducing such terms. To say that the Buddhists accepted the pragmatic criterion of truth may, indeed, make one jump to the false conclusion that they accepted William James' theory of the universe. One may, therefore, reject the use of the word 'pragmatism'. But the advantage in using the term is first that the reader can easily assimilate the Buddhist doctrine of truth and second that he will realize that the pragmatic criterion of truth can go very well with the Buddhist metaphysics of Vijñāna and Śūnya. I still remember an associate member at the 1964 East-West Philosophers Conference (Honolulu) asking me whether the Mīmāmsakas were Marxists, when he heard me speak of the activism and pragmatism of the Mīmāmsā philosophers, who were certainly not Marxists. One may point to this case also as an example of the disadvantage of using 'activism' and 'pragmatism'. But the advantage lies in noting that Marxism is not the only type of activism and pragmatism – is William James a Marxist? – and that the two lines of thinking can go well even with highly spiritual philosophies. Similarly, an idealistic metaphysics can go very well with realistic epistemology. For most of the sub-schools of even the Advaita (Non-dualism) of Śaṅkara are realistic in their epistemologies. The realization of this phenomenon in the world's philosophies – a realization that is possible only when we discard philosophical provincialisms and when we view such apparently strange features in the philosophies of the world brought together – is one of the necessary conditions for making East and West transparent to each other and for bridging the gulf between the two. The great traditions (isms) contain many strands of minor traditions (isms); and when we are able to see how the great traditions are constituted, they lose their strangeness, opaqueness, and outlandishness. Then only is mutual understanding possible. Otherwise, if we are to take the critic's objections earnestly, no translation even will be possible of philosophical texts, not to speak of their interpretation. For the majority of philosophical terms – in fact, most of the words that are generated during the course of the different cultural evolutions – are loaded with their own peculiar shades of meaning, and have their own peculiar tone, colour, and even significance.

What I have said in this Introduction and in the chapters that follow may or may not have the support of interpreters taken for some reason or other to be standards. The question at the proper occasion ought not to be: 'Who before you has interpreted this concept like you?' but 'What evidence do you have in the original sources in support of your interpretation?' Many wrong interpretations have now to be superseded. Interpretations of Indian thought have been due to many attitudes and have always had their opposites: condescending, cavalier, sympathetic, patronizing, admiring, and even flattering and the opposites of all of them. Along with the attitudes responsible for, and lying behind, such interpretations, reflection over and penetration into the Indian doctrines and concepts have also advanced and are progressing. Now, 'What is true?' ought to be a more important question than 'Who said it?'

This Introduction to the book is meant mainly for the teacher who may here and there find differences from the early accepted authorites. In the interpretation of the systems and doctrines I have tried to stick mainly to the original sources and the orthodox non-English-knowing authorities and to interpret them as carefully as possible, with constant anxiety lest I should use a misleading English term or give a misleading interpretation that does not fit. Yet, I am aware that not perfection, but an honest and careful approximation to it can be a human achievement. In an elementary work, much has to be left unsaid, and the omission may still be a source of misapprehension. Often not to speak the whole truth is to falsify it. I hope that I shall be able to give in a future work an exhaustive and yet propaedeutical presentation of Indian philosophy bringing out the insights, implied and overt, and avoiding the possible sources of misunderstanding so far as possible. Again, as this book is an elementary one meant to be completed by beginners in one semester or quarter in Western colleges and a year in the Indian, I have not given an exhaustive bibliography, but only suggestions for further readings and consultations. Students interested in philosophies may obtain the bibliography from Radhakrishnan and C. A. Moore: *A Source Book in Indian Philosophy* (Oxford University Press, Oxford, 1957); and those interested in Indian culture may consult similarly Wm. Theodore de Bary: *Sources of Indian Tradition* (Columbia University Press, London, 1960). It will give me satisfaction if this small book can give a clear idea of the basic doctrines of the Indian philosophical traditions to the western beginner without misleading him, and to the Indian student without confining and limiting him to the traditional conceptual schemata of understanding.

The persons to whom my thankful acknowledgements are due are too many to mention by name. But I should mention the name of Prof. H. W. Schneider who first gave me the idea of writing an elementary book on Indian philosophy, which can at the same time be reliable and understandable to western students and which can bring the Indian students close to Western philosophy for purposes of mutual understanding. He went also through the manuscript in its original shape and made valuable suggestions about forms of presentation and improvements in style. I am thankful to the students of the College of Wooster who have been guides to me for observing the merits and advantages of teaching the subject based on the manuscript and who gave me indirectly many useful suggestions for recasting and representing the material.

The College of Wooster,
Wooster, Ohio.

P. T. RAJU

Chapter I

NATURE AND DEVELOPMENT OF INDIAN THOUGHT

PHILOSOPHY AND RELIGION

Like any other philosophy, Indian philosophy grew out of religion. But to say so is to oversimplify and even to mislead, because the words philosophy and religion do not mean exactly the same to the Indian and to the western student. It may be interesting to note that even in the West philosophy does not mean the same to Plato and to the modern analytic philosopher. Philosophy etymologically means 'love of wisdom', but the philosophy that is transmitted, for instance, by Socrates to Plato is not the 'love of wisdom', but 'wisdom' itself in the form of ideas, doctrines and theories. So philosophy has come to mean all those theories about man, his world, his ideals and goals, and the rules of conduct for achieving them.

Now we find such theories in India also, and we call them Indian philosophy. Philosophy is evidently not an Indian word, and India's ancient and classical thinkers used many words to mean these theories, two of which, *darśana* and *mata* are important. *Darśana* means seeing, looking at, viewing, and therefore sight, look, view. The *darśana* of the Nyāya school means the 'view' of the Nyāya school, the perception of reality according to the Nyāya, and so the philosophical theory of the Nyāya. The school or system may be spiritual or materialistic, theistic or atheistic; yet it is a *darśana* or view or perception of reality. Perception here does not mean direct knowledge like the seeing of colours or the hearing of sounds, but a mental view on vision of reality, and therefore a theory of reality.

The other word *mata* means opinion, thought, and therefore a doctrine, theory. The *mata* of the Nyāya means the theory or doctrine according to the Nyāya. In this sense, the Western word philosophy means what the Indian words *darśana* and *mata* mean.

The concept 'religion' is more difficult to interpret than the concept of philosophy. It leads us back to the origins of our being. But if the origin is matter – as the materialists say – we do not call going back to matter by the name religion. But if it is Spirit, we call going back to or caring for our spiritual origins 'religion'. To understand religion in this way is philosophical. In order to be religious, man has, therefore, to believe that the basis or origin of the world is spiritual and that his goal is to realize it in his own being, not merely in his thought. Understood as such, religion includes a philosophical theory of reality and also a plan to guide man's life towards such a realization.

If religion is understood in the above sense, one finds it in India also. But the word is used in the West in a slightly different sense. Religion is a faith, it involves certain dogmas, unquestioningly accepted and followed, and it demands also the acceptance of the reality of a personal God as the creator, sustainer and possibly the destroyer of the world. But in India, these characteristics of belief are not regarded as necessary for religious life. If the Mīmāmsā interpretation demands faith in the Vedic scriptures, Jainism, Buddhism and even some followers of the Advaita Vedānta reject the demand. The Nyāya, the Yoga, and some Vedāntic schools accept a personal God, but the early Mīmāmsā, the Sāṅkhya, the Advaita Vedānta (in a way), Jainism and Buddhism deny the reality of God, and no dogmas are accepted by them except faith in experience and reason. Yet in all these schools are found the religious and spiritual philosophies of India. And it is a paradox that, in order to have a spiritual philosophy, it is not considered necessary to accept the reality of even the soul or spirit. Most of the Buddhist philosophies, for instance, reject the reality of spirit (*ātman*) and yet Buddhism is one of the greatest religions of the world.

What then does an Indian think of when one speaks of religion? The word that most nearly corresponds to 'religion' in its meaning is *yoga*, which means 'uniting'. The word *yoga* and the English word 'yoke' have the same Indo-Germanic root (*yuj*), meaning 'to join'. *Yoga* has, therefore, come to mean the practice – bodily and mental – that leads to our joining the origin of our being. Although this word corresponds to 'religion' in its general meaning, it is not used in India to mean religion. The word often used for religion is *Dharma*. *Dharma* is etymologically what sustains, supports. It is what supports life, and life is sustained only when it is not in discord with its basis, the origin of our being. *Dharma* has, therefore, come to mean the law, and then the law of life. Existence depends upon the laws of its being. If they are violated, existence becomes non-existence. *Dharma* is therefore the law of life, the way of life, that keeps it running in union with the foundations of our being. In this sense, *Dharma* is a way of life in accord with reality. We can speak of the *Cārvāka-dharma* also, although the Cārvāka teaching is thoroughly materialistic and atheistic, and does not believe in the reality of any spirit and any objective validity even of ethical laws.

The Indians have used the word *mata* also for religion. We can speak of Christian *mata* and Islamic *mata*, just as we speak of Christian *dharma* and Islamic *dharma*. But *mata* means, as mentioned above, opinion, doctrine, theory, view. So the Indian regards religion as a theory of reality guiding our life and also as a way or plan of life according to that theory.

It is useful to keep the above distinctions in mind in order to understand how Indian philosophy grew out of Indian religion, as otherwise one may think that Indian philosophy grew out of the beliefs or dogmas enunciated by some ancient religious leaders. It enables us also to appreciate why Indian philosophy still keeps its religious bias, which is actually a bias towards spirituality. Indian religion is a reflective way of life and therefore embodies philosophy also. In its purely academic formulations, which appeared later, this combination of philosophy and religion may not be so obvious, except when the problems of ethics and salvation are discussed; but it has continued to exist. Because religious life in India has always been reflective, it gave rise to different views and therefore to different philosophies, and one can find about as many philosophical traditions in India as in the West.

GROWTH OF INDIAN RELIGION

Religion in India is a way of life according to a conception of reality. And Indian religion means the various religions born in India, each one of which embodies such a way. Islam, Christianity, and Zoroastrianism are therefore not Indian religions according to this definition, although they are strong in India today and Zoroastrianism hardly exists anywhere except in India. However, for the purpose of tracing the growth of Indian religion and philosophy, we should omit them for the present.

The extant religious literature is mainly that of the Aryans, the so-called white races, who entered India by about 2000 BC. But elements of

Indian religion can be traced back to the pre-Aryan Mohenjo-daro civilization[1] in the Indus Valley of about 3000 BC or of even earlier times, which had a script that has not yet been deciphered. Excavations reveal that the people of the time had a meditative religion and worship of some Mother-goddess. The Aryans who entered India seem to have destroyed that civilization and perhaps attacked their religion also. The earliest known stage of Indian religion is that of the Mohenjo-daro civilization, about which unfortunately we know only very little. The second stage is that of the early Aryans, which is found in the Ṛgvedic hymns. The early Aryans worshipped the natural forces directly, without temples and symbols. They treated the natural forces as divine, offered sacrifices for propitiating them, and prayed for wealth and enjoyment. Theirs was a religion of sacrifices and hymns to varied spirits or 'shining' forces. The early Aryans, like the early Greeks, were reflective primitive peoples, but not philosophical in the sense of having acquired systems of conceptual and abstract thought. They worshipped the natural forces and beings like the sun, the moon, the wind, the sky, the earth, fire, water and the clouds, as if they were animated beings like men, and made no distinction between body and mind. Such a religion is called a 'nature religion'. It involves beliefs called 'animatism', as it deals with forces considered to be alive or animated.[2] But when men began to distinguish within themselves between body and spirit, they thought that the natural forces also had spirits presiding over them. They then began to worship these presiding or ruling spirits and called them '*adhi-devatās*' (presiding deities). When man conceived a general order in Nature, he felt the natural forces were governed by laws, and thought, therefore, that there must be a supreme governor that controlled all the others. But man was unable to decide exactly which power was supreme. Sometimes he thought it was the Sun; then he conceived a 'Maker of the Universe' (Viśvakarman), or of the 'Lord of Men' (Prajāpati) and others. And whenever he addressed such a god, he addressed him as *the* Supreme God, thereby exalting one God above the other gods in turn. Then man thought that the Supreme Deity must be the Supreme Spirit, akin to human spirit, intelligent and personal; and that all other deities were only his forms or manifestations and could, therefore, be controlled by

[1] Mortimer Wheeler, *The Indus Civilization* (Cambridge University Press, Cambridge, 1960).

[2] Cf. hylozoism, consubstantialism, etc.

Him, just as man controls his senses and organs. This stage of religious reflection is called monotheism. But then the doubt arose whether such an all-comprehensive Being could be a person. The idea of personality can be understood only when one person is distinguished from other persons and also from other objects. But the being of God includes everything and there can be nothing else besides such a universal Being. He must be greater than all the things put together, otherwise He cannot control them. And so some Aryans of India thought that the Supreme Being could not be a person, a one among many. This stage of thinking is called monism. Instead of God as the Supreme Person, an all-inclusive Supreme Being was conceived in which human persons had their life and being.

This process of development from pluralistic animatism and animism, through various types of theism to monism, did not occur as simply as we have described. The deities of the natural forces have to be given their places within the being of the Supreme Spirit and so have to be spiritualized. Spirit is inward being, and so the external gods have to be inwardized. The Supreme Spirit as Spirit has itself to be made inward to man. It cannot be seen outside man but deep down in the depths of his being. Then all gods give up their externality and become inward forces. The outward world becomes a manifestation of the inward. The essential truth or reality of the world can therefore be reached only by turning the consciousness inward, which is known as 'meditation'. The meditative religion, therefore, gained in prestige over the religion of sacrifices; and the light of the sun, which illumines the world, came to be identified with the light of the Spirit (Ātman) that illumines our minds. This philosophy took form by about the ninth century BC when the first Upaniṣad, namely the *Bṛhadāraṇyaka*, was composed. Its author or authors asserted that the realization of the Supreme Spirit was the supreme goal of man, which, when attained, enabled the spirit of man to live in a transformed, real world in which the apparent goods and evils of the outer world creased to appear.

It is difficult to demarcate historically these stages in the growth of Indian religion. It was not a matter of one faith substituted for another, but of a gradual growth through about one thousand years of experience, reflection and self-analysis. However, out of a religion of sacrifices and other ritualistic observances there evolved a meditative reflection, a religion of inwardness. If we treat the early Aryan religion of sacrifices as the second stage – the first being the Mohenjo-daro religion – we may treat the meditative philosophical religion as the third. But the religion of sacrifices has not been given up, it continues to live by being interpreted as a symbolic act of giving up the outward for the sake of the inward reality. For instance, the *Bṛhadāraṇyaka Upaniṣad* asks the sacrificer to think of the horse he is about to sacrifice in the following way:

> The head of the horse is the dawn. Its eye is the sun. Its breath is the vital principle. His open mouth is the fire. His body is the year; his back the sky; his belly the atmosphere; the underpart of the belly the earth; his flanks the quarters; his ribs the intermediate parts; his limbs the seasons; his joints the months and half-months; his feet days and nights; . . . his fore-part the orient; his hind-part the occident.[3]

When the horse is sacrificed, all that it signifies is sacrificed and so the whole external world is given up. Yet the sacrifice is performed. But culturally, this combination of the outward religion of sacrifices and the inward religion of meditation created a balance of outwardness and inwardness in the life of man.

But when the sacrifices by themselves were not considered to be important, it was felt that the shedding of the blood of animals for nothing was not only unnecessary but also sinful. We know that the world contains evil; to experience evil is painful, and so to be made miserable; the aim of man's life is to transcend this world of evil by realizing through meditation the essential truth of his being. To live a life of outwardness is to be active; action leads to consequences and the necessity of enjoying its fruit; this necessity brings back our souls to the world containing evil; and so action also has to be transcended. In the sixth century BC Jainism and Buddhism, therefore, rose in protest against the religion of sacrifices and much that it implied. And Indian religion became one-sidedly inward.

But one-sided inwardness had unfavourable effects on the political, economic and social life of the people, who were therefore dissatisfied with these two religions, which were regarded as unorthodox, since they rejected the authoritativeness of the traditionally accepted sacred

[3] *Bṛhadāraṇyaka Upaniṣad* I, i, 1–2.

scriptures, namely, the Vedas. The two religions attracted the best fighters, thinkers, and leaders of men, and society therefore became weak and disorganized. Foreign invaders found India an easy prey. This was the time for the orthodox religions to reassert themselves, and they did so by incorporating much that Jainism and Buddhism contained, and by pointing out that the essential truths these two religions taught were already included in their own teaching. The revolt was staged by Kumārila following the religion of sacrifices and by Śaṅkara following that of meditation, both from the orthodox point of view. But there was no bloodshed and no persecution. It was only a retransformation of world-outlook and ways of life. Kumārila and Śaṅkara belonged to the eighth century, Kumārila being an older contemporary of Śaṅkara. If we treat the rise of Jainism and Buddhism as the fourth stage in the development of Indian religion, then the revolt against them and their assimilation by Kumārila and Śaṅkara, respectively, constitute the fifth stage.

It is usual to think of Jainism and Buddhism as religions distinct from Hinduism, which may lead to some misunderstanding. There was no religion called Hinduism, just as there are no Indians belonging to the same race or nationality regardless of their being inhabitants of America, the East Indies, West Indies, or India. The words Hindu, Hind and India came into existence due to the mistake of some foreigners and have come to stay. Hind and Hindu were the corrupted forms of the word Sindhu, which is the original name of the River Indus. The people living there were called Hindus, which was further corrupted into Indians. But the Aryans themselves called their religion the Aryan Way of Life (Āryadharma). The orthodox people called it the Vedic Way of Life (*Vaidika-dharma*) also. Buddha, the founder of Buddhism, taught the Aryan Truths, and Mahāvīra, the founder of Jainism, said that an Aryan was one who followed his teachings. The founders of both these heterodox schools had no objection to the term 'the Aryan Way of Life', but would not accept 'the Vedic Way of Life', which included sacrifices. So if we prefer using the word Hinduism for all religions of India, then Jainism and Buddhism also are branches of Hinduism. And this view is philosophically correct.

Now in spite of the reassertion of the orthodox way of life in the eighth century AD, Buddhism lingered on throughout India up to about the fifteenth century AD and Jainism continues to live in the western part of India and in Mysore through some reconciliation with the orthodox way. But the fourteen centuries from the time of Buddha and Mahāvīra to the time of Kumārila were long enought to leave their emaciating effects on Indian society, and India could not withstand the onslaught of the zealous Muslim invaders. The first Muslim invasions occurred in the eighth century, but had very little effect. The important invasions began from the eleventh century and Islam spread by force. The spread of Islam and its influence on the indigenous religions may be regarded as the sixth stage.

Islam contributed very little to the reflective side of religion and philosophy of India. Its chief characteristics which some Indian religious sects noticed and adopted were the lack of caste system, giving up idol worship, and conversion by force. One sect of Śaivism adopted all three. The Sthānikavāsi Sect of Jainism gave up idol-worship, and Sikhism founded by Nanak (1469–1538), adopted the first two and wanted to be a reconciliation of orthodox Hinduism and Islam. But Islam did not tolerate Sikhism, and so the latter became a part of what is called Hinduism or is at least affiliated to it. Hinduism also had some influence on Muslims like Kabir, who started some minor religious sects and adopted Hindu mysticism.

Then came the advent of the British in the seventeenth century and along with them spread Christianity, criticizing caste system, the position of women in both the Hindu and Muslim societies, and the practice of untouchability. But along with the advent of the British came science, new types of philosophy, a new understanding of man and new political ideas. The Indians felt that reflectively Christianity was not superior to their own religion, but wanted to assimilate all that was new and good. So a number of reform and revivalist movements were started, which aimed at changing the structure of society, in the name of progress or of going back to the original pure ways of the Aryans. The Brahmasamaj of Raja Ram Mohan Roy (1771–1833) and the Aryasamaj of Dayananda Sarasvati (1824–83) are two of the best examples. But in practice, both were blends of reformism and revivalism. The advent of Christianity may therefore be regarded as the seventh important stage in the development of Indian religion. It is possible to regard the stages as more or less in number, but the above stages can give us a clue to the understanding of how Indian religion, as a Way of Life oriented towards the sustaining foundation of our being, evolved up to the present.

The stages of the growth of Indian religion may be given thus:

The religion of the Mohenjo-daro civilization (from about 4000 or 3000 BC).
The Aryan religion of sacrifices (from about 2000 or 1500 BC).
The religion of contemplation (from about 900 BC).
The rise of Jainism and Buddhism (sixth century BC).
The orthodox revolt by Kumārila and Śaṅkara (eighth century AD).
The advent of Islam (eighth century AD).
The advent of Christianity and the starting of reformist movements (seventeenth century AD).

GROWTH OF INDIAN PHILOSOPHY

Since the core of Indian religion has all along been reflective, Indian philosophy also grew along with it. Even in the other countries, neither religion nor philosophy, and for that matter, not even science was pure and logical in the beginning. Early religion was a spiritual quest, but was mixed up with a good deal of mythology. The reflections of early philosophers were carried out not in terms of pure and abstract concepts, but through mythological ideas and concepts of concrete external entities. Science also had similar beginnings. The early religion of the Aryans in India was one of sacrifices, in which the sacrificer offered his best to the gods, promised them to lead an ethical and good life, and expected as reward a happy life here and hereafter. It had no ideas of salvation, of eternal life hereafter. Man thought only of action, action in the form of performing sacrifices and action within family and society. Early religion was therefore a religion of action and of active life. And philosophy was obliged to supply later a philosophy of action and of active life. Such a philosophy is the philosophy of the Mīmāmsā school, and it is based upon the first two parts of the Vedas.

We speak generally of the Veda in the singular and also of the Vedas in the plural. The word Veda means knowledge, and the Indian Aryans believed that the sacred compositions that were handed down from generation to generation and went on increasing in volume contained the essence of knowledge about man and the universe. So they called the composition Veda. But in course of time a classification was introduced and the Veda was divided into four. Their nature and content will be discussed in the next chapter. Each Veda contains the same four parts.

The latter two parts of a Veda contain reflections on the inward and spiritual experiences of the Aryans. They were obviously later than the first two parts. They attempt to reveal the inner spiritual reality dwelling within man and the universe, which can be realized through prayer and meditation. The philosophy of spirit based upon these two parts is called the Vedānta.

But there were people who doubted the value of sacrifices, the reality of gods to whom they were offered, the reality of soul, spirit, and God, and therefore the truth of objective ethical laws. Of such people, the most important was Cārvāka, who founded the school of the Cārvākas, which is thoroughly materialistic and hedonistic, and taught that pleasure here and now is the ultimate aim of life.

But there were others like Buddha and Mahāvīra, who accepted the truth of some ultimate reality lying beyond the world of senses and the truth of the validity of ethical laws, although these two thinkers also denied the value of sacrifices and the authoritativeness of the Vedas. They also laid the foundations of their philosophies. Since the followers of Buddha and Mahāvīra did not accept the Vedas as the scriptural authority, their doctrines were developed independently through a rational examination of experience. We may call them independent thinkers untrammelled by any scripture, although what Buddha and Mahāvīra themselves said, when compiled together by their followers, became their scriptures later.

There were other independent thinkers like the founders of the Nyāya, the Vaiśeṣika, the Sāṅkhya, and the Yoga schools, who did not deny the authoritativeness of the Vedas, but pursued an independent line of approach to the problems of philosophy and life. These schools are called orthodox, and their followers are called 'believers', because they accepted the sacredness of the Vedas, although they made very little use of them. The schools that depended directly on the Vedas were the Mīmāmsā and the Vedānta, although they did not agree with each other in interpreting the Vedas. They developed their philosophies by interpreting the Vedas through commentaries and commentaries upon commentaries, and by introducing new doctrines and developing them.

Since the Vedas are the main sources of Indian philosophy and influenced either positively directly or positively indirectly or negatively all the other schools, we may classify the Indian schools as follows:

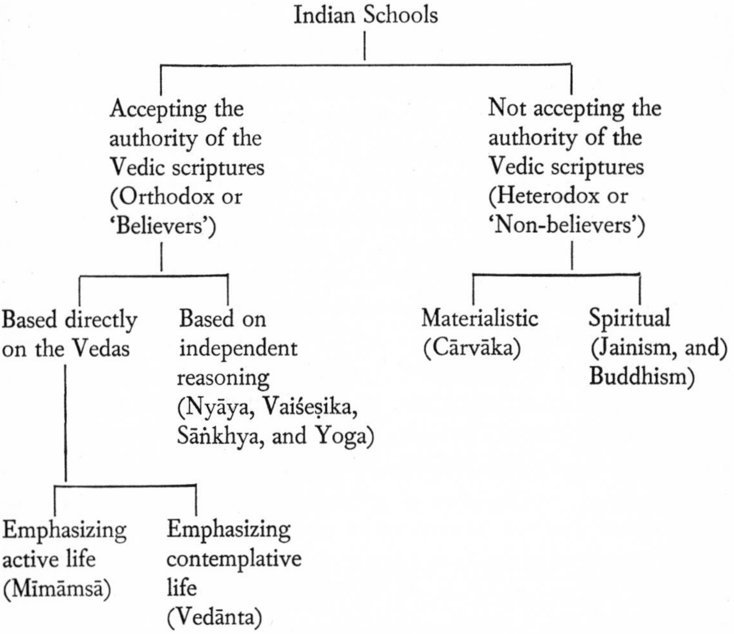

The first stage in the development of the philosophical ideas in India may be regarded as the composition of the first two parts of the Veda, and the second stage as that of the latter two parts, since the first two gave rise to one kind of philosophy and the other two to another. But all the four parts were regarded as sacred and authoritative and so it was felt necessary to interpret them, reconciling conflicting statements wherever found. These interpretations are the first attempts at systematic thinking and systematic philosophies. The other schools also, which did not have their basis in the established scriptures, had to present their ideas systematically, as otherwise they would be rejected as false and self-contradictory. These first attempts at systematization were presented in the form of aphorisms (*sūtras*), which are pithy and often incomplete sentences, easy to remember at a time when writing was not in vogue and knowledge was transmitted orally from father to son and from teacher to pupil. The composition of the aphorisms by the various schools may have started in about the fourth century BC[4] and vigorously continued up to about the fourth century AD. Some aphoristic literature appeared even later. The period of aphoristic compositions, which is also the period of system-building, constitutes the third stage of philosophical development.

But the aphorisms, being pithy and incomplete, themselves required explanation. And this was furnished in the form of commentaries, in which different commentators introduced their own ideas and doctrines to supply missing links in thought, giving rise to systems within systems of thought. The period of commentaries thus forms the fourth stage and may have begun from about the fourth century AD. This period lasted up to the fifteenth century AD.

But the commentaries were very bulky and the central doctrines could not easily be understood by reading them. The need was felt for presenting the ideas of the schools in a connected way in the form of structures of thought. Such work started after the commentaries and may be regarded as the fifth stage. Its period, although certainly later, overlaps that of the commentaries, for even on these independent treatises commentaries and commentaries upon commentaries were written. Generally the expansion and development of a system, and the development of different systems within systems was made possible through commentaries.

From about the fifteenth century up to the advent of the British, that is, the seventeenth century, there was little or no philosophical development in India, because the Muslim rulers in India did not care for any philosophy, to say nothing of Indian philosophy. This is the sixth stage, which is practically a blank period. Along with the British came Christian religious thought, the free humanistic and rationalistic philosophies of the West, and science. Then came the discovery of Sanskrit as the original or at least the oldest language of the Aryans and researches were started into Sanskrit literature, philosophy and religion, particularly after the founding of the Asiatic Society of Bengal in 1784. A new philosophical ferment started in India, which at first took the form of reinterpreting the classical philosophies in

[4] Some Western scholars assign the *sūtra* period to a later date. Dating in ancient Indian philosophy is difficult, as the authors do not give their dates and a number of interpolations were made later. On the whole, I follow S. Radhakrishnan and S. N. Dasgupia.

terms of the new ideas and doctrines of the West. Then arose new developments. The nineteenth century is the beginning of the Indian Renaissance, which led to a new awakening to the past glories of India's culture, to a new enlightenment achieved through a discovery of the truths of ancient philosophies and by relating them to those newly brought in by the West, and to a new creative effort to combine the truths of science, humanism and spiritual life. The stimulus for the study of comparative religion came through the discovery of the Indian religion, and comparative philosophy is still the strongest in India, due to the work of S. Radhakrishnan. This period of philosophical ferment and creativity may be regarded as the seventh stage, at which the Indian mind is open to all the thought currents of the world.

Depending upon the available philosophical literature, the stages of philosophical development may be shown as follows:

The first two parts of the Veda (from 2000 BC).
The next two parts of the Veda (from 1000 BC).
The aphoristic period (from 400 BC).
The period of commentaries (from AD 400).
The period of independent treatises (from AD 600).
The blank period (1500–1800).
The modern period of philosophical ferment and creativity (1800 onwards).

It should be borne in mind that the periods or stages cannot be chronologically fixed. The earlier overlaps quite a number of the later stages. Quite a number of the Upaniṣads, which form the fourth part of the Vedas, were composed after the aphorisms began to be written. And it was not the practice of the authors of works and composers of the Upaniṣads to give their dates, or even their names, which are inferred and roughly fixed by orientalists whenever possible. And in some cases the difference of opinion concerns only a few centuries.

It is, therefore, more meaningful to speak of the development of Indian philosophy than of its history. Even then, the development is a development of each of the schools, particularly from the time of the aphorisms, the first attempt at systematization. In Western philosophy, one school or system generally develops out of another, and each philosopher brands his thought with a new name. In India, on the contrary, every philosopher considers it an honour to belong to one or the other school, whatever differences he may have from his predecessors in the same school, and considers himself as an interpreter and elaborator of his teacher's thoughts. Even when the differences are very marked, he would still treat himself as belonging to that tradition of thought. This tendency keeps the historical process in the background and even conceals it. But the advantage is that it keeps philosophy as a reflection on life, by life, and for the sake of life. No truth, if it is truth, is irrelevant to life; but its relevance to life has to be brought to light. The interest of the Indian thinker is to discover the relevance of every progress made in thought to the life of spirit. And as this interest dominates almost all the great philosophical schools of India from the very beginning, Indian philosophy apparently looks as though it has not been making any progress, and baffles the historian. But the progress it is making is assimilation of all types of new knowledge to its spiritual quest, and is therefore self-development.

So far as the classical philosophies of India are concerned, there is no difference between school and system. We speak equally, for instance, of the Nyāya school and the Nyāya system. Usually, the word school means a number of philosophers belonging to a particular trend of thinking, adopting a particular standpoint. Each of such philosophers may have a system of his own. They are not unanimous on every point and doctrine. For instance, in the West we speak of the idealistic school, the realistic school, the empirical school, etc. But there is not only one idealistic system or realistic system or empirical system; there are many. But in India, as mentioned above, since the development of a particular line of thinking was carried out through commentaries, although some of the commentators differed from one another, they did not claim starting different systems, but elaborating the system of the original founder himself. So the words, school, tradition, and system, have come to be indifferently used in interpreting Indian philosophies. Of course, this usage is not always right, because there are different systems within a particular tradition or school, and in some cases like the Vedānta, there are systems within the sub-schools of the main school of thought or tradition. But this peculiarity should not confuse the student, when it is known as a peculiarity.

Chapter II

THE VEDAS AND OTHER SOURCES

THE VEDAS

Reference has already been made to the Vedas, which, so far as the philosophical literature of India goes, contain the earliest expressions of Indian reflective thinking. Historical researches show that the earliest parts of the Vedas were not composed in India, but somewhere in the original home of the Aryan race, which is likely to have been in or near Arctic Siberia, as one Indian scholar, B. G. Tilak,[1] pointed out. This view is not accepted by Western scholars, for whom the Aryan race is Caucasian. However, Max Müller regarded the Veda as the first book ever written by the Aryans. The Vedas contain the names of gods, which are related to those in Greek mythology. For instance, the name Dyaus, of a Vedic god, is from the same linguistic root as the name Zeus, of the Greek god. Max Müller's studies in comparative mythology[2] show many such names common to the Vedic mythologies and to the Iranian and European mythologies. Although some of the deities having related names perform different functions in India, Iran, and Europe, they show that the Aryans belonged to the same race and for some reason left their original home and spread out in different directions. Some of them came down to India. And when they came, they brought with them their religious practices and traditions, which of course were not written down, since no books existed at that time, but were handed down orally from father to son and teacher to pupil.

Whatever was brought into India as sacred by the religious leaders and as worthy of being preserved, was called the Veda or Knowledge

[1] B. G. Tilak, *The Arctic Home in the Vedas* (Tilak Bros., Poona, 1956).

[2] See Max Müller, *Origin and growth of Religion* (C. Scribner's Sons, New York, 1879); and *Science of Language* (Scribner's, 1887). This is not accepted by Western scholars.

itself because it was supposed to contain the secrets of the universe, by knowing which and acting accordingly man could obtain from the presiding deities what he wanted. If the Aryans entered India, as is supposed, about 2000 BC,[3] the beginnings of the Veda may be much earlier; perhaps they belong to the time when the Aryans lived in the Arctic or Caucasian regions. However, as the knowledge of the Indian Aryans grew, the written Veda also grew, and finally, for various reasons, was divided into four Vedas, each having four parts.

These four Vedas are: Ṛgveda, Yajurveda, Sāmaveda, and Atharvaveda. Each of these Vedas contains four parts: Hymns (*Samhitās*), Ritual Texts (*Brāhmaṇas*), Forest Treatises (*Araṇyakas*), and Upaniṣads. The Hymns were sung in praise of those deities who were worshipped and to whom sacrifices were addressed. The Ritual Texts also were recited, and their directives observed. The Forest Treatises contain the reflections of people retiring to the forests, and the Upaniṣads are those treatises which contain the teachings of sages about the nature of the soul, the spirit, the world, and the Supreme Being. The total number of the Upaniṣads belonging to the four Vedas was very large. But usually about twelve of them are considered to be the principal Upaniṣads. But there is no unanimity of opinion on how many and which are primary.

Philosophically, for those who think that active life is the ultimate aim of man and that it alone accords with reality, the first two parts of the Veda, and of these two especially the second, or Ritual Texts (*Brāhmaṇas*), are important, and the other two parts are secondary. But for those who accept contemplative life as the highest aim of man, the other two parts, and of them especially the Upaniṣads, are of primary importance. And the conflict between a philosophy of active life and that of a contemplative life, and the various attempts at reconciliation are an interesting feature of the philosophical development of India.

THE FORMATION OF THE CASTES AND OF THE DIVISIONS OF LIFE-CAREER

The Aryans themselves, it seems, had originally no caste system. But when they came to India and conquered brown peoples, now known

[3] It is difficult to give exact dates. Some scholars speak of it as the fifteenth century. Many give a much earlier date.

as 'Dravidians' and established themselves as rulers of the land, they did not like to mingle with the brown races and tried to assert their superiority. They did not wish to exterminate the original inhabitants, but to live in peaceful relations with them. For the purpose, they found the idea of the caste system very convenient. We do not know how they got this idea. Some scholars think that the original inhabitants themselves had a caste system and that the Aryans adopted and expanded it. In any case, the caste system enabled the Aryans to accomplish many things: (1) they could preserve their superiority culturally, politically and socially; and (2) they could live peacefully with the non-Aryans in the same social fold. Now, those were the days when religion governed practically every aspect of social life and the priests were religious leaders. So the Aryans kept priesthood to themselves. The pre-Aryans, as the Mohenjo-daro excavations reveal, were good in defensive warfare, but the Aryans were good at the offensive also. As they did not want the non-Aryans to learn their art of fighting, the Aryans kept their art of warfare to themselves. The non-Aryans were adept in trade and commerce. But the Aryans did not like it that wealth should remain entirely in the hands of the non-Aryans; so they took over also trade and commerce, though they could not deprive the non-Aryans entirely of this art. So some non-Aryans were admitted to this caste, leaving the others to work in the fields, to prepare food, and to perform domestic service. But there still remained some wild tribes, who did not take to a settled life and were living a sordid life, stealing from, and pillaging, settled communities. Some of these tribes began to live near settled communities and were given the work of the disposing of carcasses, etc. and so were treated as untouchables. It is likely that even the pre-Aryans treated these as untouchables. The other four castes were touchables.

The priests are called *Brāhmaṇas* or *Brahmins*. This word Brāhmaṇa is different in meaning from the word Brāhmaṇa, which refers to the second part of the Veda. Although the word is the same, one should understand its meaning according to the context. The warrior caste was known as the *Kṣatriya* caste, to which the kings and the soldiers usually belonged. The traders belonged to the *Vaiṣya* caste. In some parts of India, particularly in the south, some members of this caste seem to belong to the non-Aryan race. However, these three castes were allowed to read the Vedas, perform sacrifices, etc. But only the

Brāhmaṇas were allowed to officiate at sacrifices and be priests. The fourth caste was called the *Śūdras*.

It should be noted that the castes formed themselves, in the historical process which brought different races with different colours of skin together, to found a common society. The caste system was not theoretically preconceived and then applied. It was only later, after the formation of the castes, that theories were invented and religiously sanctioned to support an established fact. But historical factors again contributed to the mixing up of blood and colour of skin. First, there was illegal mixing up of races. Secondly, some of the new invading Aryan tribes refused to accept the Vedic religion and enter the established Aryan fold, and were treated as Śūdras. This brought about mixed blood even among the Śūdras.

There also arose the division of man's life into four stages: the life of the student, that of the householder, that of the forest-dweller, and that of the monk, called respectively *brahmacarya*, *gārhastya*, *vānaprastya*, and *sannyāsa*. During the first stage one spends his time studying at the teacher's house. During the second, man marries, has children, and pays back the so-called three debts: the debt to the forefathers which is paid back by having children, particularly male children, and maintaining the family line; the debt to the gods, givers of prosperity and comforts, which is paid back by offering sacrifices; and the debt to the teachers, which is paid back by transmitting the knowledge obtained to the next generation, that is, by teaching as oneself has been taught. During the third stage, man hands over the family duties and burdens to his son, retires with his wife to the forest and reflects on the values of life in this world. When he is convinced that he has nothing more that is of value to him in this world and does not feel attracted to any, he sends back his wife to his son's care, renounces this world and becomes a monk, living continually until death a life of contemplation of the Supreme Spirit. It is the reflections of the third stage that created the *Forest Treatises*. Although life is planned according to the four stages, not every man follows the last two. Almost all live through only the first two stages. But generally it is during the last two stages of life that man is capable of reaching metaphysical and spiritual depths, and achieves the concentration of mind needed for thinking and meditation.

Although it was believed by the orthodox tradition of the time that the three debts above referred to had to be discharged and that therefore every man should pass through the life of the householder, it was asserted, after the rise of Buddhism and Jainism and due to their influence, that man could renounce the world without going through the stages of the householder and the forest-dweller. Therefore the practice of going through the four stages in succession could not be strictly enforced even by the orthodox tradition, although it strongly objected to the leap from the student's stage to that of the monk. Though some of the men who became monks immediately after their student's life made valuable contributions to the development of the philosophies of their respective traditions, it should not be thought that householders did not make such contributions. They were and had to be teachers and some of the greatest philosophical teachers were householders like Vaśiṣṭha and even kings like Janaka.

ACCESSORIES TO THE STUDY OF THE VEDAS

The Vedas were very difficult to understand. There were difficulties of language, because they contained very archaic words; difficulties of pronunciation, of understanding the exact time when sacrifices had to be performed, and so on. Hence, for the study of the Vedas six 'subsidiary studies' (*aṅgas*) were prescribed. (1) *Śikṣā* or phonetics, helped exact pronunciation and intonation; (2) *Kalpa*, or ceremonial, helped to understand when and which act of sacrifice had to be performed; (3) *Vyākaraṇa*, or grammar, taught how declensions and conjugations were done and how sentences were constructed; (4) *Nirukta*, or lexicon, contained the meanings of obscure words; (5) *Chanda*, or prosody, taught the structure of metres; and (6) *Jyotiṣa*, or astronomy, taught how to determine the time of the different constellations appearing in the sky and fix the time of sacrifice.

Then there were also four 'secondary subsidiaries' (*upāṅgas*). (1) *Purāṇas*, or epics, depicted the careers of great men and dynasties. They were generally world histories, in which the Vedic, or the Aryan way of life was exemplified and extolled; (2) *Nyāya*, or logic, (not the Nyāya school of philosophy) which taught how to argue and think coherently; (3) *Mīmāmsā*,[4] or textual discussion, (not the Mīmāmsā school of philosophy) interpreting the texts and reconciling apparently conflicting statements of the Vedas; and (4) *Dharmaśāstras*,

[4] Not the same as the Mīmāmsā school of thought.

or ethical codes, prescribing the different duties of castes, sub-castes, and stages of life.

These 'subsidiary studies' are outlined and 'secondary subsidiaries' are mentioned here because it was the practice of the people to develop a philosophy on the basis of each one of them, although many of them are not widely known and studied. These philosophies created controversies and even criticisms of the main traditions of the time. For instance, the grammarians and the lexiconists developed philosophies, which not only controverted each other but also the other schools. But a philosophy based entirely on word and sentence construction may not entirely correspond to the structure of reality; nor has man developed a usable language that corresponds exactly to the structure of reality. Such philosophies could not become important, although very interesting. Then again, astronomy became astrology also and developed the idea that the planets control the destinies of men. The epics, as we shall see, show by illustration how the Vedic philosophies of life could be adopted to life. Logic became a rigorous system of philosophy; textual discussions helped to build up the Mīmāmsā and the Vedānta systems; and the ethical codes propounded, though not systematically, a philosophy of active life. There was practically no line of thinking, no kind of philosophical activity that was untouched by India, although not all were equally well developed.

NON-VEDIC RELIGIOUS INFLUENCES

Although the Aryans brought into India their mythological conceptions, gods and religion from outside, they could not retain them in the form in which they brought them. They got blended with the indigenous ideas and practices. The Aryans might have at first shown hostility to the local practices, but when they observed them more closely and understood them, they found some truth in some of them and incorporated whatever they thought was true and useful. But on the whole, their tendency was to regard man as responsible for his own future and destiny. Whether he wanted salvation and an eternal life of peace or an unending active life, the choice was left to him and he was taught – so far as the Aryans understood – how to achieve what he wanted. The Aryans as adventurers fighting their way into a foreign, unknown land, thought of man as the maker of his destiny, and thought that even salvation had to be worked out each by himself, and that no god would come down to help him in spite of himself. This attitude of the Aryans forms the dominant trend of thought in the Vedas. Gods were offered sacrifices and prayers, but the relation of sacrifice and prayer to their fruit was understood almost as a causal relation.

Such a burden of responsibility on man seemed too heavy and men craved for the grace, mercy and the parental love of God, who would help them in spite of their weaknesses and failures. So a new kind of theism was introduced. And what is called the Āgama literature came into existence. The word *āgama* means 'coming down', and the literature is that of traditions, which are mixtures of the Vedic with some non-Vedic ones, which were later assimilated to the Vedic. There was much assimilation of this kind in the case of some of the gods, such as Śiva. These Āgamas seem to have come into existence by about the first century BC or AD and are of three kinds: the Āgamas treating Śiva as the Supreme Spirit, those treating Viṣṇu as such, and those treating the Energy (*Śakti*) of the Supreme Deity as more important for the purposes of man than the deity himself. This Energy was conceived as the Mother of the universe.

These Āgamas belong to the three religious sects: Śaivism (of Śiva), Vaiṣṇavism (of Viṣṇu), and Śāktism (of Śakti). The Āgamas contain their own philosophies and practices meant for realizing the Supreme Spirit. They are mostly theistic, accept the idea of God's grace, and preach love of God as the main way for salvation. They were composed mostly by the Aryans themselves.

Now the followers of these Āgamas also attempted to interpret the Vedic texts and read their own philosophies into them, thus giving rise to different Vedāntic schools. Thus the Āgamas formed one of the sources of Indian thought as well as of Indian devotion (*bhakti*).

THE APHORISTIC SOURCES

We have referred to the Age of Aphorisms, which were really the first attempts to present systematic philosophies, and which characterized the philosophical work of the period from about the fourth century BC to the fourth century AD. Most of the Aphorisms are pithy, incomplete sentences like telegraphic language. What the Buddhists composed and called Aphorisms are not pithy, but compositions of complete sentences and even discussions. So we should not try to be very exact in definining what an aphorism (*sūtra*) is.

Gautama, the founder of the Nyāya school, composed his *Nyāya Aphorisms* (*Nyāyasūtras*); Kaṇāda, the founder of the Vaiśeṣika school, the *Vaiśeṣika Aphorisms* (*Vaiśeṣikasūtras*); Jaimini, the founder of the Mīmāmsā school, the *Mīmāmsā Aphorisms* (*Mīmāmsāsūtras*); Bādarāyaṇa, the founder of the Vedānta school, the *Vedānta Aphorisms* (*Vedāntasūtras*, also called *Brahmasūtras*); and Patañjali, the founder of the Yoga school, the *Yoga Aphorisms* (*Yogasūtras*). Cārvāka, whose name is also given as Bṛhaspati and who was the founder of the Cārvāka school, composed his *Bṛhaspati Aphorisms* (*Bṛhaspatisūtras*), but they have been entirely lost. Some of them are referred to by the rival philosophers and hence we know of their existence. Kapila, the founder of the Sāṅkhya schoool, composed the *Sāṅkhya Aphorisms* (*Sāṅkhyasūtras*), but they have also been lost. But in the fifteenth century, one of the great Sāṅkhya philosophers by name Vijñānabhikṣu, composed the *Sāṅkhya Aphorisms*, which may or may not exactly be the same as the original *Sāṅkhya Aphorisms*. Mahāvīra, the founder of Jainism, did not compose any Aphorisms. But one of the later Jaina scholars called Umāsvāti of the third century AD composed his *Aphorisms for Understanding the Nature of Reality* (*Tattvārthādhigamasūtras*). Buddha also did not compose any Aphorisms. But his followers a hundred years later composed them and called them 'Baskets' (*Piṭhakas*). But still later the Buddhists called some of their works the *Prajñāpāramitāsūtras* (which may be freely translated as the *Aphorisms of the Apex of Wisdom*). These belong to the Mahāyāna branch of Buddhism, which was formed about six hundred years after Buddha. The earlier forms of Buddhism, called Hīnayāna, also had their aphorisms like the *Vaibhāṣika Aphorisms* (*Vaibhāṣikasūtras*) and *Sautrāntika Aphorisms* (*Sautrāntikasūtras*). The words Vaibhāṣika and Sautrāntika are the names of two branches of Hīnayāna Buddhism. Buddhism had many branches, many more than Jainism, and we shall treat of some of them later, when we discuss Buddhist philosophies.

MINOR SCHOOLS

It should not be thought that the Indian philosophical schools were limited to those that are usually included in the books written in the Western languages. The *Sarvadarśanaśaṅgraha* (*A Compendium of all*

Philosophies) written by Mādhavācārya of about the fourteenth century discusses the doctrines of sixteen schools. The Buddhist works refer to rival schools of thought, with which Buddha and his followers had to enter into controversy, and which were either absorbed or became so small and unimportant that later they have been ignored. But some of them like the school of *Pāśupatas* had their own Aphorisms called the *Pāśupata Aphorisms* (*Pāśupatasūtras*), composed much later than the birth of this school, which is not exactly that of Śaivism, but formed one of the basic texts of Śaivism; for Paśupati, after whom the Aphorisms are named, is another name for Śiva. It is said that Pyrrho, the great sceptic philosopher of Greece, accompanied Alexander the Great to the East and came across the oriental sceptics. Perhaps some of them were Indian. There were sceptics in India who held similar views. Sañjaya, one of those sceptics, is said to have taught that no ethical law was either right or not-right or both or neither, and he would not say Yes to any question, even to the question whether he made a denial. This No to all questions was developed later into the principle of four-cornered negation[5] (S is neither P, nor not-P, nor both P and not-P, nor neither P nor not-P) by the Buddhists and the Vedāntins and absorbed into their logic and metaphysics. The literature of this school has not yet been discovered, and the existence of the school is known only through references by others. But the thought of all such schools contributed to the development of Indian philosophy.

All these schools were either avowedly or practically independent of the Vedic scriptures. But all of them were concerned with the questions, What am I?, What is the nature of the universe?, What is the meaning of life?, and What should man do in order to realize the aim of life?. Since philosophy has always been a philosophy of life, whether the school was Vedic or non-Vedic, orthodox or heterodox, materialistic or spiritual, theistic or atheistic, all the schools contributed to the growth of each other through mutual criticism. Such philosophies were religious for the Indians. For them philosophy was without exception the theoretical presentation of a way of life. So when one speaks of the religions of India or of Hinduism, they should not be understood just as Christianity or Islam is understood. They are philosophies and ways of life combined. Hence the students of Indian

[5] See the author's 'Principle of Four-cornered Negation', *The Review of Metaphysics*, June 1954.

philosophy should understand what religion means particularly to the thinking people of India. For it was in such religious groups, groups that wanted to discover the right way of life, that Indian Philosophy originated, because to discover the right way of life implies to know the nature of the reality in which men live.

THE EPICS AS SOURCES

We have already referred to the epics as one of the sources when we discussed the accessories to the study of the Vedas. But we have to say something more about them, because of the importance given them by some Vedāntic philosophers. The epics are regarded as one of the accessories for the study of the Vedas. They are not methods of explanation, but stories, histories, etc. interspersed with philosophies and doctrines presented in simple, popular language, and their aim is to teach the doctrines of the Vedas in an easily understandable way. The epics reflect the philosophy of the Vedas, but there are many of them. And which of them can be accepted as true representations of the Vedas? Of all the epics, the *Mahābhārata*, which is one of the biggest, is often called the fifth Veda, not only because it teaches what the Vedas teach but also because it is as authoritative a scripture as the Vedas themselves. The well-known *Bhagavadgītā* (*The Lord's Song*), a small part of the *Mahābhārata*, has been uniformly accepted as one of the basic scriptures for the construction of the Vedāntic systems. But why can we not use the other epics and their teachings also as basic for the same construction of the Vedic philosophies? Most of the Vedāntic philosophers like Rāmānuja and Madhva, whom we shall discuss, use, each of course in his own way, several epics along with their respective Āgamas in developing their systems of the *Vedānta Aphorisms*. Others, like Śaṅkara, object to such use of the epics and Āgamas, although they make an exception in Śaṅkara the case of the *Bhagavadgītā*. But they interpret the *Bhagavadgītā* also in their own way. However, what we have to note is that the epics also became sources for the development of the Vedāntic systems. Since we are not concerned with textual interpretations, but only with the conceptual structures of the important systems and the central ideas of the schools, the following chapters will present only the philosophies without the textual criticisms.

Chapter III

THE CENTRAL IDEAS OF THE UPANIṢADS

NATURE OF THE UPANIṢADS

The Upaniṣads, as pointed out already, form the fourth part of the Veda. Some belong to one Veda, some to another, and so forth. Each Veda contains some Upaniṣads. It is accepted by the general Indian tradition that all the Vedas have the same teaching, and so all the Upaniṣads also teach the same philosophy. That philosophy is called the Vedānta. The word Vedānta means the end of the Veda, because the Upaniṣads form its last part, and it also means the final teaching of the Vedas. The Vedas are supposed to teach different philosophies to different men with different levels of maturity, and the Vedānta is meant, it is said, for those men whose minds are the most mature. But this view is not accepted by the other philosophies, each of which contends that its doctrines are meant for the most mature and that the doctrines of the Vedānta are not true enough. But since each philosophy makes this contention, it is advantageous to study each separately, because each attempts to be a self-consistent system.

The Upaniṣads contain the teaching of seers who realized the reality inwardly and called it the Ātman and the Brahman. The word Brahman always means the Supreme Spirit, and literally means the 'ever-growing', the 'ever-expanding'. It corresponds to the Western concept of the Absolute. The word Ātman means 'spirit', and is translated also as 'self'. But it may mean also what the word Brahman means.

The Upaniṣads are many and, like the Vedas, were not composed at the same time or place or by the same person. And sometimes their teachings appear to be conflicting. They had, therefore to be interpreted as teaching the same doctrine. Although Bādarāyaṇa wrote the *Aphorisms of the Brahman* for interpreting the Upaniṣads and for removing apparent conflicts, his *Aphorisms* themselves needed explanations, and the commentaries written for the purpose introduced different systems of philosophy. Thus the Upaniṣads became the basis for different philosophies, each of which was again called Vedānta, and became a kind of school or tradition.

The Upaniṣads often speak of the Ātman as the highest reality and also as the same as the Brahman. Both are spirits, although the latter is the Supreme Spirit. But how can the finite spirit be the same as the Supreme Spirit? In explaining the nature of the identity between the two, the commentators differed, some maintaining that the identity is absolute in a sense of its own, some saying that it means only similarity, and others holding some middle positions. So the word Ātman in the Upaniṣads and the Vedānta literature sometimes means the Brahman itself, but other times the finite individual self. And we have to understand the meaning of the word according to the context, when we read this literature.

Because the word self does not convey the exact meaning of the word Ātman, it is perhaps better to use the word spirit. But the word spirit also may be misleading, since it has other meanings in English. It is therefore better to use the word Ātman itself, provided it is understood that it has something to do with the word 'I' or self, and is something that appears as the 'I' in our experience. But the 'I' does not express the whole nature of that entity, and the Upaniṣads, therefore, attempt to explain its nature. However, for the word Brahman, one may safely use the word Absolute.

PRE-UPANIṢADIC PHILOSOPHICAL IDEAS

Although the ideas of the Ātman and the Brahman are the most important in the Upaniṣads, they occur in the earlier parts of the Veda also, but in different senses. The change in the meaning of the words signifies that, as the Aryans became more and more reflective, they saw deeper and deeper significance in the same words, and their conceptions of man and the universe changed. The word Ātman in the *Brāhmaṇas* meant the 'I' or self, but it did not mean anything metaphysical. Very likely, it meant breath originally, and was akin to the German word *atmen* – similarly the word 'spirit' originally meant breath – but by stages it changed its meaning. The word Brahman meant generally in the *Brāhmaṇas*, prayer, then the power of prayer, then the creative power behind the universe; and also sacrifice and its power. In the *Taittirīya Brāhmaṇa* we begin to meet the idea that the Ātman and the Brahman are identical.

Another idea of importance is that of *ṛta*, which has the same root as the English word 'right', and meant straight, correct, true, and rite, which also was considered to be right. But the truth here meant was practical or ethical truth, or rather the correspondence of an action to the Vedic injunctions including rites. The god Varuṇa was said to be the custodian of *ṛta*; he was the god encompassing the whole universe and rewarding those who followed *ṛta*. But he was later dethroned from the throne of the highest god and made the god of the oceans. The Greek word Ouranos, meaning the god of the heaven and the Sanskrit word Varuṇa are derived from the same root.

For a time the concept of *ṛta* as moral law given by Varuṇa remained important, but later, when the Aryans became more metaphysical and interpreted the gods as principles of the cosmos, the word *ṛta* yielded to the word *dharma*, which originally meant 'abstract law'. *Dharma* became not only the law of the universe, but also moral law, thus governing both the conduct of man and the behaviour of the universe. In the Mīmāmsā philosophy, which was based on the first two parts of the Veda, *Dharma* became the central concept, just as the Brahman became the central concept of the Vedānta philosophy, which was based upon the other two parts of the Veda.

In the *Brāhmaṇas* themselves one finds the doctrine of the five elements: earth, water, fire, air, and ether. These elements form the components of the world. They correspond to the qualities perceived by the five senses: smell, taste, colour, touch, and sound. Just as in Greek philosophy there were speculations about the origin of the universe, and one comes across doctrines that each of these elements was such a source, in the Upaniṣads also there are such speculations and doctrines. It is difficult to know the names of philosophers who held those views. But ultimately, the doctrine that the world is made up of all the five together was accepted.

The elements were not conceived in the beginning as material particles or atoms, but as gods or deities, who controlled the different senses and their activities on the one side and the corresponding objects perceived, on the other. And when the gods were turned into cosmic principles, they became co-ordinating principles of the senses and their objects.[1]

[1] See the *Aitareya Upaniṣad*.

This idea led to the ideas of microcosm and macrocosm. Man with all his senses, organs, mind and *ātman* is a representative centre of the whole cosmos. The cosmos is the macrocosmos and man, its representative, is the microcosmos, i.e. the tiny cosmos. For everything in the universe, one can find a corresponding representation in man. The senses, for instance, are the representations, philosophically, of the five cosmic elements, and theologically of the five gods. But who is the macrocosmic god that corresponds to the *ātman* in man? The *Brāhmaṇas* say that it is Prajāpati, the monotheistic god, who became the *ātman* (self) and entered man. But later this Prajāpati became the monistic Brahman.

We find also the ideas that the world was created through the power of prayer and that of sacrifice. These two forms, prayer and performance of sacrifice, develop the power of the will; and the world was created, it was thought, through intense willing by the Supreme God. But when sacrifice came to be associated with self-denial and penance, it was also thought that the world was created by the Supreme God through penance. Prayer, sacrifice, and penance were the ways, it was thought, for intensifying creative will. If man wants anything, even heaven, he should intensify and strengthen his creative will for it, which automatically produces what he wants. And this creative will is deep down in man himself, although he does not generally know its existence. To strengthen it and make it work in the direction he wants, he has to resort to prayer, sacrifice, and penance: this is how the Aryans of the *Brāhmaṇa* period and even of later times thought. *Karma*, or action, strengthens the creative will. If it is good action, the creative will produces good things in this life or in the next; if it is evil action, it produces bad things. And action includes all good and bad actions; prayer, sacrifice, and penance are good actions. All the duties prescribed by the Veda for man in the different castes and the stages of life were good actions; and the prohibited actions were evil actions. The Vedas alone were the final guide in differentiating good actions from the bad.

This idea of action producing the world through an inner creative will was developed into the doctrine of *Karma*. But we should note that this doctrine of the creative will was not clearly conceived by the *Brāhmaṇas* and even the Upaniṣads. It was developed much later in the Mīmāmsā concept of *apūrva* (unseen force). But it was thought that every action must have its fruit, and the fruit have to be enjoyed in this life or the next. The next life is not necessarily that of eternal heaven or hell, but also that of rebirth in this world. If a man performs actions, some of which produce heaven, some hell, some good things in this world, and some others bad things, and does not enjoy the fruit in that life itself in which the actions were performed, then he should go to heaven, then to hell, and then take on one life to enjoy the good things and another life to enjoy the bad things. So he should be able to take on many lives. Thus the doctrine of reincarnation came into existence. The essence of the doctrine of *Karma*, as philosophically developed later by the Mīmāmsā, is that Action, in the form of an inner, ever-creative will of the universe, rules it. And the roots of the doctrine are found in the *Brāhmaṇas* themselves. Man makes this will of the Universe favourable or unfavourable through good or evil actions. An ever-creative will is activity itself.

Even the Hymns are not devoid of philosophical enquiries. The first most important philosophical hymn ever composed, according to Max Müller, by the Aryan race is the *Nāsadīya Hymn* of the Ṛgveda. It raises questions about the origin of the universe in the abstract terms of Being and Non-Being. It reads:

> There was no Non-being, nor was there Being
> What were its contacts, but where?
> In whose protection did it exist?
> Was there water, deep and unfathomable?
> There was neither death nor immortality then.
> There was not the guidance of night and day.
> That One breathed by its own power, without air.
> Other than that there was nothing.
> Darkness was concealed by darkness then.
> All was water indistinguishable.
> That which was coming into Being was covered by void.
> That One was born through the power of penance.
> Desire was in the beginning,
> That was the first seed of mind.
> The wise discovered in their hearts
> The bond of Being to Non-being.

This is a philosophical questioning about what there can be beyond Being and Non-Being, with which we are acquainted in this world.

And the composer himself of this *Nāasdīya Hymn* ends:

> Whence is this creation?
> Is it founded or not?
> The presiding Deity in the skies knows it,
> Or perhaps He does not.

THE MAIN DOCTRINES OF THE UPANIṢADS

Philosophically, the ideas of the Upaniṣads are more important than those of the earlier parts of the Veda, because the ideas of the Upaniṣads obtained the form in which the Vedānta philosophies took them up for developing their systems of thought.

In the *Bṛhadāraṇyaka Upaniṣad*, which is considered to be the earliest, we find several important doctrines. This Upaniṣad has a special importance, because it is both a *Forest Treatise* (*Araṇyaka*) and also an Upaniṣad, and belongs evidently to the period of transition from the former to the latter. It is the largest of the Upaniṣads, and contains several speculations, all leading to the same result, namely, the reality of the Ātman (Spirit).

The first doctrine that strikes any reader is that the original reality was the Ātman. In some passages it is also called the Brahman. And out of the Ātman[2] or the Brahman[3] everything, the material elements, the various species of animal life, and the natural and ethical laws (*dharmas*) originated. Before they came out of the Brahman, they were in an unmanifest, indeterminate (*avyākṛta*) state; then they assumed the manifest, determinate forms.

This Upaniṣad says in clear, definite terms that the Ātman is the Brahman, and that its nature is consciousness (*prajñāna*) and bliss (*ānanda*). It also indicates that the light of the sun and the light of the Ātman are one and the same. But how can we locate and identify the light of the Ātman? The answer is given in a dialogue between King Janaka and his teacher Yājñavalkya.[4] Janaka asks his teacher what light guides man. The answer is the light of the sun, because we see things with the help of the sun's light. But when it is absent, what can be that guiding light? One may say: the light of the moon and the stars. But when that also is absent? The light of fire. But when fire

[2] *Bṛhadāraṇyaka Upaniṣad*, I, iv, 1.
[3] *Ibid.*, I, iv, 10.
[4] *Ibid.*, IV, ii.

also is absent? The light of speech, for the words of some one can tell us what and where things are. But when that also is absent, as in dreaming? The light of the Ātman. In dreams we see objects, but what is the light in which we see them? It is the light of the Ātman.

Everything in the world has three factors:[5] name, form, and activity. The manifestation of the unmanifest takes on these three aspects. This Upaniṣad describes various approaches to discover the Ātman, which is also called Person (*Puruṣa*).

The *Īśāvāsya Upaniṣad* describes the Ātman as the lord of the Universe and says that it moves and does not move, that it is near and far, and that it is inside everything and yet outside it. By using these contradictory predicates, it shows that an earlier view that the Ātman is pure activity or movement is only a one-sided description, and that in fact no definite descriptions can express its nature.

The *Kena Upaniṣad* raises the question about who it is that makes the mind, senses, speech, etc. active. It is the Ātman. None of these can know their activator, but he knows them. If anyone says that he knows the Ātman, verily he does not know it; but it is known even by those who think that they do not know it. The senses and organs cannot work without the activation of the Ātman.

The *Kaṭha Upaniṣad* describes the famous story of Naciketas, the son of Vājaśravasa, who at a particular ceremony gave away in charities all that he had. Then the lad asked his father: 'To whom will you then give me?' The father got angry and said: 'To Death.' The boy then went to the house of the god of death. But Death, who was away, could not take notice of him. Then Death heard a warning, saying that if a Brahmin guest came to a house and was not received properly, the host would lose everything including the merit he had earned. So Death told the boy that, since he had stayed in his house for three nights without eating, he would give him three boons, and he could choose anything. The boy asked as his first boon that, when he returned to his father from the abode of Death, his father should receive him without anger, tears and regret. The second boon was to explain the nature of the sacrificial fire, called also Naciketas, which led the sacrificer to heaven. But the third wish is of interest to us. The boy wanted to learn what happens to man after death. 'Some say that he exists, but others say that he does not exist; I want to be instructed by you.' But Death wanted to dissuade the boy from

[5] *Bṛhadāraṇyaka Upaniṣad*, I, vi, 1.

pressing for an answer by offering him instead all the wealth, greatness, comfort, and sovereignty over the earth. But the boy would not yield, and Death had already promised to grant whatever the boy wanted. So he had to give out the secret of the universe, and explain the nature of the Ātman present in every man.

The Ātman is the ultimate truth. But it is smaller than the smallest and yet greater than the greatest.[6] It is imperishable, it has no birth and death. In truth, there is no death for the 'I'. Only the body is destroyed at death.

But how can we find the Ātman? The objects are higher (deeper) than the senses,[7] for with reference to the objects we measure our reality. Mind (*manas*) is deeper than the object, reason (*buddhi*) is deeper than mind, the Logos (*Mahān Ātmā*, Cosmic Reason) deeper than reason, the Unmanifest (*Avyakta*) deeper than the Logos, and the Ātman (*Puruṣa*) deeper than the Unmanifest. There we find the Ātman, deeper than which there is nothing. It is not an object towards which the senses, mind and speech can be directed. Yet it is not Non-existence or Non-being, but Existence or Being itself.

The *Muṇḍaka Upaniṣad* distinguishes between two kinds of knowledge,[8] the higher and the lower. By having the higher knowledge, we know everything. This is the knowledge of the Ātman. For out of the Ātman originates everything and has its existence only in the Ātman. Just as the spider[9] creates the world out of itself, lives in it, and then takes it back again into itself, the Ātman creates the world out of itself and even withdraws it again into itself. The other kind of knowledge is that of the arts and the sciences.

This Upaniṣad speaks of two birds,[10] inseparable and friendly, living in the same tree. One of them eats the sweet fruit of the tree, but the other only looks on without eating any. Similarly, the *ātman* lives in the body and enjoys the pains and pleasures of the world, and unable to get over the bonds that tie it to the world, finds itself powerless and miserable. But when it sees the higher Ātman, the bird that is not eating but is only looking on, realizes his greatness, his sorrow leaves, and he becomes like the other. That is, by realizing the higher Ātman, the lower becomes great like it. But these two Ātmans are not separable at all, and exist always together.

[6] *Katha Upaniṣad*, I, ii, 20.
[7] *Ibid.*, I, iii, 10–11.
[8] *Muṇḍaka Upaniṣad*, I, i, 4.
[9] *Ibid.*, I, i, 7.
[10] *Ibid.*, III, i, 1.

The *Māṇḍūkya Upaniṣad*, although the smallest of the important Upaniṣads, is considered by some philosophers to be the most important. It explains how the same *ātman* passes through the three states: dream, waking state, and deep sleep. It can be realized in its original nature only in a state beyond deep sleep. So there are really four states: the state of the pure *ātman*, waking state, dream and deep sleep.

In the waking state, the *ātman* has a gross body, and knows only objects external to itself. It has nineteen limbs. They are the five senses (sight, hearing, touch, taste and smell), the five organs of action (speech, hands, feet, the generative organ and the excretive organ), the five vital principles (*prāṇa*, *apāna*, *samāna*, *udāna*, and *vyāna*) and sensorium (*manas*), reason (*buddhi*), ego (*ahaṁkāra*), and apperception (*citta*).

The four – sensorium, reason, ego and apperception – are the psychological divisions within our inner being. The conception of *Prāṇa* is peculiar to Indian philosophy, psychology and medicine. *Prāṇa* means originally air, but later it has come to obtain the specific meaning of life, or life-principle or vital principle. *Prāṇa* is responsible for the involuntary, organic processes of our body and is divided into five kinds. The first kind also is called *Prāṇa*. It resides in the heart and is responsible for respiration. *Apāna* resides in the anus and controls the excretory functions. *Samāna* has its abode in the navel and governs the digestive functions and the temperature of the body. *Udāna* is in the throat and is responsible for speech and the other functions of the upper part of the body. And *Vyāna* pervades the whole body and co-ordinates the functions of the various parts.

In the waking state, the *ātman*, or the 'I', identifies itself with the physical body, and its consciousness is directed outwards. Its nature is therefore that of consciousness directed outwards. But in dream also we see objects, and so the *ātman* has the same number of limbs, or parts in dream. We see colours, hear sounds, take foods, etc.; we perceive men, trees, animals and other objects, and think also of some as good and of the others as harmful. This experience shows that all our limbs, although in their subtle forms, are active. But the consciousness we have in dream is inner consciousness. The objects we see in dreams are not impressions of the objects of the waking state, but can be caused by those impressions. And for the dreaming 'I', they are as real as the objects of the material word are for the waking

'I'; otherwise, the dreaming 'I' would not be frightened by the dream tiger. The mere impression of a remembered tiger does not frighten us.

The *ātman* in the waking state is called *Vaiśvānara* (the worldly person), and in the dreaming state *Taijasa* (the person of the psychic force). The word *Tejas* means force, fire, and light also. The consciousness in which the dream objects are seen is not only the light in which they are seen, but also the force that creates them.

Now in deep sleep, man sees nothing, knows nothing, and desires nothing. In it the different senses, organs of action, mind and the other parts of our inner being are not distinct from one another. Everything becomes one undifferentiated, solid, massive consciousness, which is covered up by complete unconsciousness. When I wake up and come out of deep sleep, I say: 'I did not know anything then, I did not know even myself, I remember that I did not know anything'. This experience shows that the 'I' was present then, but did not know anything. If the 'I' knows anything, then the state cannot be deep sleep. This state of complete unity of man's being is a blissful state, a state of complete rest, in which man finds complete satisfaction, the effects of which are known only when he wakes up. Good deep sleep has always only good effects. The *ātman* in this state is called *Prajñā* (Intensely Conscious Being or Conscious Intensity), because the person in this state is not divided into the various limbs.

This unconscious state is the Lord of the above two states, it knows everything that happens in them and preserves every experience. In order to preserve those experiences, it must be present in each state. The states of dream and waking originate out of it and merge in it. It is similar to what the psychologists call the Unconscious; but they study its nature only in abnormal cases, whereas Indian thought discovered its presence and significance even in the normal cases.

The original nature of the *ātman* is discoverable in a state beyond the three states. It is consciousness, but not directed either inwards or outwards. It is beyond thought, speech, and the senses, because it is their source, not their object. And the *ātman* is the same as the Brahman itself.

In the *Taittirīya Upaniṣad* is given a summary of five ways of explaining the world, which were current at the time.[11] The explanations, at that time of the development of man's mind, were mixed up with mythology. The Upaniṣad does not give them as doctrines of

[11] *Taittirīya Upaniṣad*, I, iii.

explanation, but as the secret meanings. But to these five correspond the five forms of explaining world-processes.

The first is explanation in terms of physical entities (*adhilokam*). The world may be regarded as one of physical things connected with one another through some relations. The second is explanation in terms of luminaries or gods (*adhijyotiṣam*), for gods were regarded as so many luminaries. The world is due to the activities of gods. The third is explanation in terms of the creative powers (*adhividyam*) obtained through secret knowledge gained through prayers, sacrifices, and initiations by teachers. It was thought that the gods could create the worlds through such powers. The fourth is explanation through the creativity of sexes (*adhiprajam*). The world is the result, it was believed also, of the interaction of cosmic sexes. The fifth is the explanation given in terms of the Ātman, and this explanation was regarded as the truest and the final. The world originates out of the Ātman.

This Upaniṣad definitely states[12] what the *Bṛhadāraṇyaka* indicates, namely, that that which is in man and that which is in the sun are one and the same.

According to this Upaniṣad, out of the Ātman was born ether,[13] out of ether air, out of air fire, out of fire water, out of water earth, out of earth plants, out of plants food, and out of food man, who speaks of himself as 'I'. This is the Ātman. But what is this 'I'?

If a child's name is John, and we ask it: 'Who is John?', it points to its body. So the 'I' or *ātman* is first regarded as the body. But is it really the body? When a man dies, the body is there, but it does not speak of itself as the 'I'. It does not breathe, and so we say the life-principle has escaped, and identify the life-principle with the *ātman*. But is the life-principle then the *ātman*? When a man is fast asleep, his body is alive but does not call itself 'I'; so we may say that his mind is not there. But the mind also is not the *ātman*, because a mad man may say that he was dead long ago and refuse to eat and drink, because dead bodies do not eat and drink. What is lacking in him is reason. We may therefore say that reason is the *ātman*. But we say, 'I have reason, it works rightly'. But what is this 'I' that *has* reason. That is the *ātman* and is the fullest bliss.

This Upaniṣad speaks of every lower stage as the body of the higher and of every higher stage as the *ātman* of the lower. The

[12] *Taittirīya Upaniṣad*, III, x, 4.

[13] *Ibid.*, III.

physical body is not the *ātman* of anything else. We have, therefore, to be careful in understanding the meaning of the word *ātman*, which means many things, and which has to be understood according to the context.

This doctrine of the body-*ātman* relationship taught by the *Taittirīya Upaniṣad* shows how the idea of the 'I' or the *ātman* slowly evolved in the minds of the Indian Aryans until it became metaphysical and was even identified by some philosophers with the Universal Spirit itself.

The *Aitareya Upaniṣad* gives an interesting story of creation,[14] which, although clothed in mythological terms, has philosophical importance. The Ātman existed alone in the beginning. He wanted to create the world. Then he created the waters surrounding the universe, the worlds of light, those of death, and the waters underneath those worlds. Then he wanted to create the rulers of the worlds, i.e. the gods. Then he drew forth a person from the waters and gave him a form. Next he concentrated his mind on that person. The person's mouth burst open, out of the mouth came speech, and out of speech the god of Fire. His nostrils separated, from the nostrils came breath, and out of breath the Wind-god. His eyes opened, out of the eyes issued sight, and from sight the Sun-god. And soon from his different limbs came the different gods.

The gods then found themselves thrown into this vast world and were overtaken by hunger and thirst. They then begged the Ātman to give them an abode. The Ātman gave them first a cow and then a horse. But each time they said that it was not enough. Then the Ātman gave them man and they were contented.

Then the god of Fire became speech and entered the mouth of man; the Wind-god became air and entered the nostrils; the Sun-god became sight and entered the eyes, and so on. But man cannot work without the Ātman or the 'I'. He always says: 'I eat, I hear', and so on. If the 'I' is not there, the ear cannot hear, the eye cannot see, the skin cannot touch, and the tongue cannot taste. So the Ātman entered man through the parting at the top of the head and became the 'I'.

This account of the creation of man and the gods by the Ātman, although apparently mythological, is full of philosophical significance. The person drawn out of the waters is the cosmic person or merely the cosmos in its undifferentiated state. The gods or the rulers of the

[14] *Aitareya Upaniṣad*, I, i–iii.

worlds issue out of this cosmic person, and are therefore the objective fields corresponding to the different parts of that person. When they come out they become independent. That they have no abode means that they want an instrument through which they can become active; and man is such an instrument. They are the rulers of the world, because whatever exists, acts in accordance with them as the formative and constitutive principles such as the principle of sight, of hearing, touching, thinking, etc. The gods, whatever be their functions at the beginnings of the Vedic religion, gradually became the deities of the different parts of man and still later the principles co-ordinating the subjective (senses, mind, etc.) and the objective poles of our experience. Nothing that is not controlled by these forces can be there in the world. All the gods were unified under the Ātman by the time of the Upaniṣad, just as the different parts of man are unified under the principle of the 'I'. And the 'I' in man corresponds to the Universal Ātman. A relation of microcosm and macrocosm was thus established between man and the universe and the tendency towards a spiritual absolutism and idealism became very strong.

The *Chāndogya Upaniṣad* enunciates: 'Verily everything is the Brahman.'[15] It issues out of the Brahman. This statement does not mean that everything, as we see it, is the Supreme Spirit itself, but that without the Supreme Spirit nothing, not even the worst, can have existence. The Supreme Spirit is the whole universe and much more besides. But this identity had to be asserted by the Upaniṣads, because people of the earlier times were thinking that God had to be realized somewhere outside man and outside the universe. But he resides in our very hearts, deep down in the depths of our being and watches everything just as the Unconscious, according to the psychologists, watches everything and retains every experience, and yet we are one with our Unconscious. And we are identical with the Supreme Spirit, just as our mind and the senses are identical with us. Just as the mind cannot act without the 'I', the 'I' also cannot act without the Supreme Spirit. So this identification of the world and the Brahman should not be understood as an equation.

The *Chāndogya Upaniṣad* says emphatically that originally there was Being and that the world came out of Being, but not out of Non-being.[16] This world consists of Being, and how can it come out of Non-being? This Upaniṣad therefore dismisses the idea that the world

[15] *Chāndogya Upaniṣad*, III, xiv, 1.

[16] *Ibid.*, VI, ii, 2.

came out of Non-being. The *Śvetāśvatara Upaniṣad* enumerates a number of doctrines prevalent at that time.[17] One held that Time was the source of the universe; another that it was Nature herself; another that it was the nature of things to be as they are and that we need think of no further cause; another that it was Fate; another held to the doctrine of elements; and still another to that of the Ātman. There must have been several philosophies at that time, but unfortunately we do not know the names of the founders or the protagonists of all these schools. And all the others were superseded by the philosophy of the Ātman.

This Upaniṣad declares that the world is due to Māyā. But Māyā is not illusion, but a peculiar power of God for creating the world. He is the possessor of that power. It is only some centuries later that the word Māyā was given different meanings, one of which was illusion. In the Upaniṣads one finds the idea of the Ātman almost everywhere; but the world is not regarded as false or illusory. The man who thinks that there is nothing besides the world is regarded as holding a false view and as being deluded and suffering from ignorance.

The word Māyā has led to many misunderstandings. At first it meant the original, inexplicable power, or energy of the Supreme Spirit, which in an equally mysterious way becomes the world. It is the mysteriousness or inexplicability that was emphasized by the word. It did not mean the unreality of the world or that the world is merely Non-being. The Upaniṣads ask: How can Being (meaning this world) come out of Non-being?, and say that Being can come only out of Being. If the world were considered to be Non-being, the Upaniṣads would have asked: How can Non-being come out of Non-being or how can Non-being come out of Being? In the popular language later, the power of the juggler and the mesmerist to make non-existent things appear was called Māyā; and as the power of the Supreme Spirit also was mysterious like that of the juggler, some people took the world of God's Māyā to be unreal. And we should also note that for all the Vedāntic philosophies, the word Māyā does not mean the same thing.

Another word often misunderstood is Avidyā, which has synonyms like Ajñāna and Avijñapti. Literally translated, they mean Un-conscious, No-cognition, No-knowledge, etc. But usually they are translated as Ignorance and Nescience. But Ignorance is not-knowing, and it has only a negative meaning. In the Vedānta and Buddhist

[17] *Śvetāśvatara Upaniṣad*, I, i, 2.

philosophies, Avidyā and Māyā are generally equated. But if Avidyā means ignorance, or not-knowing, how can a negative entity produce the world? This translation ignores the aspect of creative energy in the meaning of the word. The best available word to translate Avidyā and its synonyms is Unconscious, because, as it is used, it retains the meaning not only of being unconscious of something but also that of being a creative force. But we should remember that the Unconscious, according to the Indian philosophers, is not abnormal. Its meaning of the abnormal was not known to them. It belongs to the absolutely normal people. And we should remember also that words like Māyā and Avidyā are used in ordinary language in their popular and even vulgar meanings, and the common folk generally mix them up with philosophical meanings.

A more difficult word to understand is *manas*. It is in the popular language and sometimes in the philosophical literature also used in the very wide sense in which the English word mind is used. All inner functions are attributed to it. But in that wide sense, the technical term used is 'inner instrument' (*antahkaraṇa*), meaning thereby that inner to all the five senses, which are instruments for knowing the external world, there is another instrument common to all of them for cognizing the objects as unities, having colours, sounds and so on; and its function is also the cognizing of pains and pleasures.

But we should know also the narrow technical meanings of the word *manas* and the words associated in meaning with it. We have used some of the words when explaining the *Kaṭha Upaniṣad*.

Now *manas* in its narrower meaning has the function of combining and separating, or synthesis and analysis. When I see an orange and say: 'That is an orange', I combine the yellow colour, and sour taste, the round shape, and the cool touch into a unity, calling the unity 'orange' and distinguish this unity from a similar unity, the table, on which the orange lies. That which thus synthesizes and analyses is called *manas*. This is assigned also the function of knowing pains and pleasures.

The ego (*ahaṁkāra*) is that which says: 'I see an orange.' The ego appropriates the experience to itself in such statements as 'I see an orange', 'I pluck the rose', and 'I am six feet tall'. The ego is not the same as the 'I' or the Ātman; but we may say that it is the first step leading into the deeper significance of the 'I' or the Ātman.

Then comes the word *buddhi*. It has many synonyms, of which the important ones in philosophy are *vijñāna* and *prajñā*. To translate it as 'understanding' does not convey the right meaning of the term. Its function is described as resolve, determination, decision.

But strangely enough, not all the Indian philosophers use the word *buddhi* in the same sense. For some it means only cognition, knowledge or even mere consciousness. We have therefore to be careful about the contexts. The word *Vijñāna* also means in some contexts something different. The Buddhists often use the words *vijñāna*, *manas*, and *citta* in the same sense, as we shall observe, and they mean something like consciousness, but with additional creative and existential significance.[18]

Now the word *citta* has a narrow technical meaning in the Vedānta philosophies, although it is often identified with *buddhi*. *Buddhi* is reason, but *citta* is a higher kind of reason. It means literally 'what collects together'. This function of collecting together all the assertions and building them up into an interconnected system is that of *citta*, which may be translated as apperception, because the result is a rational apperceptive mass of asserted experience. Now *manas*, ego, *buddhi*, and *citta* are together called 'inner instrument'.

We should here explain the word *jñāna*, which has become another stumbling block in understanding Indian thought. We have referred to some usages, in which *buddhi* means cognition, knowledge, and mere consciousness. The word *jñāna* is used in these meanings also, so that *buddhi* and *jñāna* mean the same for some philosophers. But *jñāna* is used in some other meaning also. The nature of the 'I' itself is consciousness, and it reveals its own existence to itself. It is not merely a knowledge obtained through the activity of *manas*. The consciousness or rather self-consciousness of the 'I' also is called *jñāna* by most of the Indian thinkers. Thus consciousness, knowledge and cognition in all their forms, and also when there is an object and when there is none, are called *jñāna*, and all are regarded as various classifications of *jñāna*. When we express this idea in English, we should say that all are various forms which consciousness assumes. But again, we should be careful in attributing this classification of consciousness to all the Indian philosophers, because some of them, as we shall see, do not think that the 'I' is by nature consciousness at all, and some do not even draw the distinction between the ego and the I-consciousness.

[18] See the author's article, 'Religion and Spiritual Values in Indian Thought', footnotes on pp. 282–3, in *Philosophy and Culture: East and West*, ed. by C. A. Moore (University of Hawaii Press, Honolulu, 1962).

Here we should explain the word *jīva* also. Except in the philosophy of Jainism, the two words, *jīva* and *ātman* do not mean the same. If *ātman* is spirit, then *jīva* is soul. It is the ethical personality that includes the senses, mind, ego, reason, and the individual Unconscious (*Avidyā*). It is rooted in the *ātman*, but is not the same as the *ātman*. By its very nature, the *ātman* transcends, or goes beyond the *jīva*, and so it transcends our ethical personality. The jīva enjoys the fruits of its ethical actions; but the *ātman* is free from all such bonds. Yet it may falsely identify itself with the *jīva* and think that it is enjoying the fruits of actions. The Jainas do not like to make a sharp distinction between the *ātman* and *jīva*. They say that the *jīva* is the same as the *ātman* in its pure original state, and the *ātman* is the *jīva* in the state of ignorance of its original nature. These are, however, important distinctions. But the *ātman* is also variously conceived by the different schools, and we shall know their views when we study those schools.

Chapter IV

THE ACTIVIST TRADITION AND THE MĪMĀMSĀ SCHOOL

INTRODUCTION: ACTIVISM AND CONTEMPLATION

The Vedas were interpreted as teaching two basic philosophies, the philosophy of a life of unceasing activity and that of contemplative life, although in the tradition of philosophical ideas created by the Vedas, a number of other interpretations sprang up, some of which became strong while the others were either absorbed in the stronger currents or discarded as false.

Activism is the name or all philosophies that teach that activity, process, movement, energy or force is the ultimate reality and all that we see and experience in this world consists of the forms which such a reality takes. But the Indian philosophers who have propounded such a doctrine have each his own conception of what activity is; and so there are different types of activism. The first type belongs to the school of the Nairuktas or Lexiconists. *Nirukta* is the name of the first Sanskrit lexicon, explaining mainly some difficult Vedic words, and this school of thought derived its name from that book. The Nairuktas maintained, as did some of the Vedāntins, that the Ātman is the sole reality and everything else is only its form. But they differed from the Vedāntins, and said that the nature of the Ātman was pure activity, a continual, uninterrupted process. They maintained also that the Vedic language was the only language that exactly corresponded to the nature of reality, and further that any language, in order to be true, must exactly correspond to the nature of reality. Therefore since the Ātman alone is real, and since the Ātman is pure activity, the verb, which expresses activity in any sentence, is the primary part of the sentence. And just as everything else in the universe is only a mode of the Ātman, which is activity itself, all the other parts of the sentence – the subject, the object, etc. – are only modes of the verb. So in interpreting the Vedas, the Nairuktas say, we should take the words denoting activity as primary and the rest as secondary, and give importance to sentences asking us to act, and treat the other sentences as subsidiary to them. The aim of such teaching is two-fold: first, it confers on activity (*Karma*) the role of the creator and the controller of the universe; and secondly, it exhorts man to lead a life of endless activity, if he is to realize his true nature, which is the Ātman.

The second type of activism is that of the Mīmāmsakas. They did not go the whole way with the Nairuktas in equating the Ātman with activity. They retained the idea of Activity as the controller of the universe, but not as its creator. Activity can modify only what already exists, but cannot create it. And what exists need not necessarily be process, but may also be the substance to which the process belongs. Yet since the Vedas teach only a life of action, only those sentences meaning action are primary, and the rest have only subsidiary importance. The *ātmans* also are many, because they are the agents of action, and each performs action with its own motives and has, therefore, to enjoy the fruit of its own actions. The *ātman* is not activity itself, but the initiator or agent of activity. We have to accept the existence of a single universal Activity[1] as the controller of the universe, which co-ordinates the activities of the various *ātmans* and enables the actions to produce their fruit without conflict.

Now the texts are not interpreted merely to get their verbal meaning, but to expound a system of philosophy. The conditions of a true philosophy are that it should be self-consistent and that it should be in accord with reality. Thus every school of philosophy discusses the sources of knowledge including logic, metaphysics, and certain rules for the guidance of life towards approved goals.

The *Mīmāmsā* as a school of critical inquiry or discussion divided itself into two schools of thought: that Mīmāmsā which interpreted the first two parts of the Veda is called *Pūrva Mīmāmsā* or Prior Mīmāmsā, and that which interpreted the other two parts the *Uttara Mīmāmsā* or Posterior Mīmāmsā. But when the word *Mīmāmsā* is used without any adjective, it means only the Prior Mīmāmsā, that teaches a philosophy of the life of action. Posterior Mīmāmsā is generally called the Vedānta.

The founder of the Mīmāmsā School was called Jaimini, who composed the *Mīmāmsā Aphorisms* (*Mīmāmsā- sūtras*) about 400 BC. His

[1] See the author's article, 'Activism in Indian Thought', *Annals of the Bhandarkar Oriental Research Institute*, Poona, Vol. XXXIX, 1958, Parts III–IV.

aphorisms were first commented upon by Śabara about AD 400. The aphorisms and their commentary form the basic literature. Then Śabara's commentary was explained by Kumārila Bhaṭṭa (or simply Bhaṭṭa) and Prabhākara (also called Guru), both of about the same period, early eighth century. Each differed from the other on many points,and founded two sub-schools. There were others also, but not considered to be equally important. Of the two, Kumārila and Prabhākara, Kumārila is the more popular. Part of what Prabhākara wrote has been lost, and part is still unpublished. We shall point out the interesting differences of these two thinkers at their proper places.

THEORY OF KNOWLEDGE

Sources of Knowledge

There are six sources of knowledge according to the Mīmāmsā: Perception, inference, comparison, verbal testimony, postulation, and non-cognition. On the number of these sources Kumārila and Prabhākara differ from each other, because Prabhākara does not admit that non-cognition or absence of cognition can be a source of knowledge at all.

Knowledge (*buddhi*) belongs to the *ātman* and is obtained when mind (*manas*) comes into contact with it. The *ātman* by itself does not have any knowledge without contact with mind (*manas*), and it is not even conscious of itself. Kumārila says that the *ātman*, although not by itself conscious, has, even without contact with mind, the potency or power to become conscious and know objects; but Prabhākara does not accept this view.

The Mīmāmsakas maintain that knowledge has three factors – the object known, the knowing subject, and knowledge. This doctrine is called the three-factor theory (*tripuṭī-vāda*). Kumārila maintains that the subject, or the knower, is directly known as the object of the I-consciousness; but Prabhākara maintains that the knower can never be made an object of cognition like chairs and tables, and is therefore known only as the subject of cognition. Regarding the object of knowledge, Kumārila says that its presence is not known directly but through an inference. Cognition, according to Kumārila, confers on the object congized the attribute of cognized-ness or known-ness. Through this attribute we infer that the object is present, or that there is an object. But then knowledge also is not directly known. But having a known object implies that there must have been knowledge. So knowledge is inferred, but is not directly known or self-revealing. Prabhākara also accepts that knowledge has three factors, but he does not accept that the presence of the object and knowledge are to be inferred. The subject, object and knowledge are directly revealed in the very act of knowing the object.

According to Prabhākara, mind (*manas*) is atomic in size, and unless it is atomic it cannot instantaneously run from sense to sense in order to combine their informations into a unity. For instance, when I perceive an orange, my eye sees the colour and shape, my nose its smell, my touch its coolness, and then my mind unites all these sensations into one idea, the idea of the orange. But the cognition of all these sensations is instantaneous. So the mind must have collected them instantaneously. It can do so only if it has no size, i.e. if it is an atom. For every object that has size takes time for movement. Kumārila does not favour this view, because according to him, mind is all-pervading and so it can receive the sensations simultaneously.

a. Perception. Perceptual knowledge[2] (*pratyakṣa*) is knowledge obtained through the senses. It has two stages: indeterminate (*nirvikalpa*) knowledge and determinate (*savikalpa*) knowledge. Supposing there is an orange in front of me, when my senses come into contact with it, I have a vague knowledge of the form, 'There is some object'. That is indeterminate knowledge. Then my mind brings together the different qualities like colour, smell, and taste, and I say: 'That is an orange.' Here my perception is complete with regard to that object, and the object is not vague, but definite, or determinate.

b. Inference. Inferential knowledge (*anumāna*) is knowledge derived from some other knowledge. But it has come to mean in Indian epistemology knowledge obtained through syllogistic reasoning. The view of the Mīmāmsakas on inference is practically the same as that of the followers of the Nyāya school, or Naiyāyikas. So its details will be given, when the Nyāya is discussed. In fact, it is the Nyāya school that first gave an elaborate theory of inference.

c. Comparison. Comparison (*upamāna*), according to the Mīmāmsā, is the way by which we know similarity, which is a distinct kind of object and is also a category according to this school. If we see first an American bison, and then an Indian Buffalo, we perceive the similarity

[2] For the epistemology of the Mīmāmsā, see G. N. Jha, *The Pūrva Mīmāmsā in its Sources* (Benares Hindu University, Benares, 1942).

between the two. When we see the buffalo, we at once perceive that it is like the bison. This likeness or similarity is known through comparison, which is a spontaneous, unique process. Similarity is not an object of perception. What we have before us is only the buffalo, and our senses do not come into contact with similarity, but with the buffalo. So similarity cannot be an object of perception. It is also not an object of inference, because even without an inference, we often cognize similarity between objects. There must, therefore, be a particular way of knowing similarity, and that is comparison, which is a spontaneous cognitive process like the process of perception.

One should not understand the word comparison as a voluntary process that has before it two objects, the bison and the buffalo, and then sets out to find out similarities by examining the qualities. It is a spontaneous and unique process of cognition that has for its object similarity, which is discovered there, but not invented. The Mīmāmsakas defend this way of knowing as one distinct from the others. Some of the other schools do not accept this view.

The Nyāya, unlike the Mīmāmsā, maintains that comparison is the identification of the buffalo by the American through knowledge of similarity between the two animals, which he obtained from his friend who had seen both. But the Mīmāmsā says that this is not cognition of similarity, but the perceptual recognition of similarity verbally cognized from the friend's words at first.

d. Verbal Testimony. Verval testimony (*śabdapramāṇa*) is accepted by all the orthodox schools of philosophy with varying emphasis. It is knowledge obtained through words as sounds. When we hear a sentence orally uttered, it is not merely the sounds that we know, but the meaning of the sentence. If it is merely the sounds we know when the sentence is uttered, then the knowledge is merely a sense-perception of sounds. But these sounds produce a knowledge of the meaning, in which we are more interested than in the sounds themselves. This ability of the words to produce a meaning in our minds is called by the Indian philosophers the power, or potency (*śakti*) of the words. And the knowledge we get through words is also a distinct kind of knowledge, which is neither perception nor inference, but is reliable.

In defending the validity of this way of knowing, the Mīmāmsaka's main interest was to defend the authoritativeness of the Veda. The Veda in the beginning was not written on paper or stone, but was orally handed down from generation to generation. It consisted therefore of sounds. And so this way of knowing was called verbal testimony, as distinct from the testimony of the senses and of inference.

The Naiyāyikas accepted that God was the composer of the Vedas, and that they were, therefore, absolutely true. But the Mīmāmsakas did not accept the reality of God at all, and had, therefore, to defend the validity of the Vedic utterances in a different way. They said that the Vedas were not composed by anyone, they existed in the world without a beginning and would exist without an end. The world also had no beginning and will have no end. The Vedic sound is eternal. In fact, according to this school, all words are eternal. If I utter the word 'chair' ten times, am I uttering ten different words or am I uttering the same word ten times? The Mīmāmsakas say that, if the word is not the same, then it cannot have the same meaning. Always in every significant language, the word must have the same meaning. The Mīmāmsakas did not accept that the Vedic language was conventional, but that it was the natural language with natural meanings, and that, therefore, it must have existed forever and had been transmitted from time without beginning. This view, is, of course, fallacious and may be called the fallacy of 'the idolatry of sounds and language'. The doctrine of this eternity is called the doctrine of the eternity of sound, because words are sounds.

In spite of some fallacious elements in the above doctrine, it contains the seeds of another interesting doctrine. Since the words are eternal and since knowledge is associated with, and communicated through words, word and knowledge came to mean the same, and the doctrine of the Word as the doctrine of the Logos or Cosmic Reason grew out of this identification. This philosophy was called the philosophy of the Word-Brahman (*Śabda-brahman*), which was, however, not accepted by the Mīmāmsakas, who did not accept the reality of God and did not want to personify the knowledge of the Vedas. Much later, about the thirteenth century, however, when the Mīmāmsakas became theistic, they showed some inclinations towards the theory of the Logos. But such thinkers were not pure Mīmāmsakas.

The above argument, we can easily see, is fallacious. But it shows that the Mīmāmsakas expected a rigorous ethical life, every bit of which was controlled by the Veda, from the people. They demanded complete obedience to the words of the Veda. The question was indeed raised: Is an action good for man, because it is commanded by the Veda? Or does the Veda command men to perform the action, because it is good for them? Here again Prabhākara and Kumārila gave different answers. Prabhākara maintained the former position and, like the Jewish prophets, demanded unquestioning obedience to the words of the Veda, saying that actions were good, because they were commanded by the Veda. Kumārila also maintained unquestioning obedience to the Veda, but said that the Veda commanded the actions because they were good.

Now, the Veda consists of both informative sentences and also commands. We have mentioned that the primary aim of the Vedas, according to the Mīmāmsakas, was to ask people to act, and that, therefore, the sentences commanding action were primary. Out of this doctrine grew another that not only in the Veda, but also in ordinary language, sentences of command, i.e. in the imperative mood, only have meaning and the other sentences have their meaning only as associated with them. For instance, an informative sentence like, 'Your father is doing well', does not have its meaning, unless it also implies, 'Send a letter of congratulations to him', i.e. unless the former sentence has reference to an action. So no word has meaning without reference to action. This doctrine was called *anvita-abhidhāna-vāda*, or the doctrine that sentences have meaning only when the words are associated with action. This is the activistic (behaviouristic) theory of meaning, propounded by Prabhākara. Although Kumārila also says that the primary sentences of the Veda are those meaning action, yet sentences that are not directed towards action also have their meaning. Some of them in the ordinary language do not refer to action. We may later, when necessary, associate informative sentences with action. This doctrine is called *abhihita-anvaya-vāda*, or the doctrine that words and sentences have independent meaning, which may later on be associated with one another and with action. Prabhākara's view has much in common with the pragmatic theory of education. He says we teach the child the meaning of a word like 'cow' by asking the child, 'Bring the cow', but not by telling it, 'That is a cow.'

e. Postulation. Postulation (*arthāpatti*) is the postulating of a fact or principle. It is the acceptance by us of something in order to explain apparently conflicting experiences. The Mīmāmsakas and some other philosophers treat it as distinct from inference, equating inference to syllogistic reasoning. And this spontaneous postulating of something to remove an apparent conflict between two experiences is a distinct source of knowledge.

f. Non-cognition. Through non-cognition (*anupalabdhi*) is known absence or negation. There is no pencil on the table. Now, how is this absence of the pencil cognized. If the pencil were there, I would cognize it. But I do not cognize it. That is, there is non-cognition of the pencil. So what this non-cognition reveals is the absence of the pencil.

Kumārila accepts, like the Naiyāyikas, the reality of negation (*abhāva*). But unlike the Naiyāyikas, he accepts a distinct way of knowing negation and calls it non-cognition. The Naiyāyikas explain it as a variety of perception combined with anticipation of the object not seen.

Like the Naiyāyikas, Prabhākara also does not accept Kumārila's view, but for a different reason. Prabhākara does not accept the reality of negation or absence at all. If negation is a reality at all, it must be positive. There are no negative facts. When I say, 'I see the absence of the pencil on the table', what I actually cognize is the table and some other objects if they are there, but not the absence of the pencil. What we call the negation of the pencil is only a concept, framed by our mind with the help of the kind of anticipation which the Naiyāyikas have explained.

Error and Illusion

In Indian philosophy the problem of error and illusion is as important as the problem of truth. There can be an error in all the ways of knowing. Non-cognition will err if it perceives the absence of the object where the object exists. This may be either due to lack of light, or due to a defect in the eye or mind, or due to the object being hidden by some other object. In that case, we try to remove the obstacles of perception. And this source of knowledge does not give rise to a serious epistemological problem. Postulation and inference are processes of thinking and their results are only objects of thought. When there are errors in these two processes, we say we have committed fallacies and try to correct our thinking. Comparison can commit the error of taking superficial similarities for significant similarities. This error can be corrected by knowing the purpose for which the cognized similarity can be used. And there can be no special epistemological problems here. In the case of verbal knowledge, error can enter either because the source of knowledge, i.e. the person or scripture imparting knowledge is defective or the listener cannot understand what is said.

Of course, the Vedas are not regarded by the Mīmāmsakas as defective at all. Our understanding only can be at fault. The persons who tell us something may be ignorant or may be telling falsehoods. But the Veda was not composed by any person and is above such defect. We have only to wrestle grammatically and etymologically with the words of the Veda to obtain their true meaning. So verbal testimony had no epistemological problem for all those philosophers who accepted the authoritativeness of the Veda. But the greatest attention was paid to perceptual error by all the Indian philosophers, because perceptual error presents not merely a defect and confusion by subjective factors and functions that operate in perception, but also a distinct object that is later denied as being really there. And if an object given in perception, which is the basis of all our thinking and experience, can be false, then how are we to build up our knowledge? In erroneous non-cognition we do not see an object that is there, but in erroneous perception we see an object that is not there. That is, only erroneous perception is called illusion. And the nature of illusion and the status of the illusory object became important problems in Indian epistemology.

Now, the Mīmāmsakas believed (1) that all knowledge and every cognition are valid in themselves. If we do not trust our own knowledge, then there is no way of knowing the truth of anything at all. They believed also (2) that the very conditions of knowledge generate the truth of knowledge. If so, why do we see illusory objects at all? Why does perception commit errors? The Mīmāmsaka view is that perception does not really commit any error. The illustory object is only due to incomplete perception or non-perception of some of the factors in the object. This view is upheld by Prabhākara in its decisive form.

The most common example of perceptual illusion in Indian epistemology is that of mistaking a piece of rope for a snake. This perception may occur in the dusk or when a man is walking through thick grass and bushes. What exists is really the rope, but one sees instead a snake. So long as the illusion lasts, we see the illusory object as existing in front of us. Now, we could not have mistaken the rope for a snake, unless we already know what a snake is, i.e. unless we have seen the snake already. Prabhākara says that, when we see the illusory snake, we have the rope in view and remember the snake already seen; but we do not cognize the difference between the two, and we, therefore, take the object to be a snake. So illusion is only this non-cognition (*agraha*, *akhyāti*) of the difference between the object seen and the object remembered. The illusory object is not a non-entity; there is no positive error in illusion, and perception – in fact all knowledge – is always true. Our consciousness cannot commit mistakes.

But Kumārila does not accept this view. He says indeed that knowledge cannot commit mistakes by itself. Yet mere non-cognition or non-apprehension of the difference between the rope in front and the remembered snake cannot explain the positive perception of the snake in front. Our perception of the object in front is of the form, 'That is a snake', but not of the form 'That and snake'. It is not merely the non-cognition of the difference between the rope and the snake, but an identification of the That and the snake that makes the perception an illusion. In fact, until later we do not know the rope at all. So there is no question at all of the difference between the rope and the snake being cognized or not cognized. What we have is the That – the demonstrative pointing to the rope – and the snake. So we have mistaken the rope for another object, namely, snake. Here the object in front is identified by us with an object remembered. This doctrine is called the doctrine of the cognition of a different object (*viparīta-khyāti*), because the serpent is a different object from the rope.

Both Kumārila and Prabhākara are realists even with regard to the illusory object. We generally think that the snake is false, it is only an idea. But the Mīmāmsakas say that it is real, because it is a remembered snake. If, after realizing that the object in front is a rope, we ask ourselves why we saw a snake instead, we shall find that it is a remembered snake and, if we try, we can trace it back to some past perception of a snake. So the That is real, the rope is real, and the snake also is real.

Validity of Knowledge

The doctrine of the validity of knowledge (*prāmāṇyavāda*) is another characteristic of Indian epistemology, not generally found in the western. This doctrine should not be equated to the western doctrine of truth, although the two are related. The doctrine of truth deals primarily with logical truth and fallacies and with the doctrines of correspondence, coherence, etc. But the doctrine of the validity of knowledge deals primarily with the question of the nature of truth in its relation to knowledge.

I have knowledge of many things. I cognize the illusory snake, the real rope, the pen, the wall, the mountain, and many other things.

Each cognition brings me knowledge of its object. Now, what is meant by truth? We say that some knowledge or cognition is true when it comprehends the object as it is. Then, truth is a quality of cognition or knowledge. We speak of true objects and false objects also, but only because the knowledge of those objects is true or false. If truth is an attribute of knowledge, is it an adventitious attribute or an inherent attribute? If it is an adventitious attribute, then knowledge by itself must be neither true nor false, but is made true or false by something else. If it is not an adventitious attribute, but is inherent in all knowledge, then knowledge can be made false only by something other than knowledge. Besides, there is another important question. If truth is an attribute of knowledge, when knowledge itself is known, its attribute truth also must be known. That is, the same process that makes knowledge known must also reveal its own truth. Then, knowledge, when it reveals itself, must reveal its own truth. These two aspects of the problem are combined, and philosophers expressed different views on them.

The Mīmāmsakas maintained that knowledge is inherently true, and that it reveals its own truth when it is known. It does not matter how it is known, be it directly or through inference. If knowledge is not inherently true, we have to know whether it is true or not again through knowledge. So we have to rely upon knowledge itself for knowing its truth. I perceive the pen in front of me. To make sure whether it is a pen or not, I may again look at it, or touch it, or write with it and perceive that it is writing. But all these are different acts of knowing or involve such acts, and I have to trust knowledge in any case. Then why should I trust the last act and not the first? What the Mīmāmsakas, therefore, mean is that, upon ultimate analysis, every cognition, when revealing the objects, reveals its own truth. It never reveals its own falsity. If cognition is in some instances false, then its falsity is revealed by another cognition or by some other fact.

The above view contains two factors: (1) that knowledge or cognition is inherently true and only adventitiously false; and (2) that every knowledge or cognition reveals its own truth and can reveal the falsity only of other cognitions. No cognition can reveal its own falsity, it has to be revealed by some other cognition or by some other fact. And the truth of a cognition is not revealed by any other cognition, it is revealed by itself. Others may confirm it, but they do not reveal its truth, not revealed by itself.

Doctrine of Truth

So far as logical truth goes, the Mīmāmsakas accept the test of consistency as do the Naiyāyikas. But so far as perceptual truth goes, the Mīmāmsakas are more or less pragmatists. But this pragmatic test, they would say, only confirms the truth of a cognition that has already revealed its truth. Now, a cognition, according to the Mīmāmsakas does not merely claim truth, it contains it and reveals it. But we may like to have confirmation also, which can be obtained through action. If I perceive the rope as a rope, then if I use the rope in action, e.g. for tying a cow, then the truth of my perception is confirmed. But if I see it as a snake, whatever action I take against that snake does not confirm, but contradicts the truth of the cognition. Then the cognition is rendered false.

We have seen that Prabhākara insists that the meaning of every word and sentence is associated primarily with action. He would therefore say that action is the test for confirming the truth of any perception. Other tests like correspondence are secondary. For instance, I look at the object and say: 'That is a rope.' If there is any doubt, I again look at it and say: 'That is a rope.' Here my two perceptions correspond with each other. According to the Mīmāmsakas, there is no difficulty in knowing this kind of correspondence, because they say that our mind sees the objects directly through the senses, although Kumārila's view of the inferability of the presence of knowledge does not agree with direct presentation in perception. However, Kumārila, although giving a high place for action as an epistemological test, does not emphasize it so strongly as Prabhākara, because Kumārila accepts that words and informative sentences have also their independent meaning apart from action.

METAPHYSICS

Dharma

The Mīmāmsā philosophy is a philosophy of *dharma*. The word *dharma* is usually translated as duty. Although the translation is not wrong, it does not give the full significance of the term. The word is defined by Jaimini, the founder of the Mīmāmsā school, as 'that the characteristic of which is a command'. And that of which command – the Vedic command is meant here – is a characteristic is, as Kumārila explains, action. So *dharma*, as Kumārila explains, is action (*Karma*) as enjoined by the Veda. The actions we perform are of two kinds: (1) actions like daily prayers, taking daily baths, family and social duties, etc. which were all considered to be rituals; and (2) actions done for a purpose like having riches in this world and happiness in the next. If the former are performed, we shall be doing our duties, the non-performance of which brings evil, but the performance of which brings no particular reward. They are performed without any particular desire. But it is not a duty to perform the actions meant for a purpose. For instance, one may like to become an emperor or a multi-millionaire and so he performs a particular kind of sacrifice. Or one may want to have heavenly happiness, then one will perform another kind of sacrifice. The Veda orders what one has to do in every case. But to desire wealth, sovereignty, or heaven is not a duty. So not to desire these objects and not to perform the corresponding sacrifices is not unethical.

When a man violates his duties and commits evil acts, the evil that visits him may not visit him in this life, but in the next. Similarly, the man who performs a sacrifice for having heavenly pleasures can have them only after death. In each case, the actions are the causes for the corresponding results. But there is a lapse of time between the cause and the effect. How can the effect be produced when the cause has ended and is dead? In order to overcome this difficulty, the Mīmāṃsakas maintained that action does not die, but assumes a potential form and resides in the *ātman* of the agent. And when the proper time comes, it produces its results. The potential state in which action remains till fructification is called the extraordinary state (*apūrva*) by Kumārila.

Although the stages into which a course of action is divided are the same for Kumārila and Prabhākara, the latter maintains that the *apūrva* (the extraordinary state) is not action itself, but what is produced by action. And that is *dharma*. Of course, evil actions will produce its opposite, *adharma*. We may translate *dharma* and *adharma* then as merit and demerit. But we should not understand them as qualities or attributes but as potencies, which will later produce good and evil results. Prabhākara says, therefore, that the Veda asks men to produce this or that kind of potency, but not directly to perform this or that kind of action. Certainly, the potency cannot be produced without the corresponding action. The difference between Kumārila and Prabhākara on this point is scholastic.

We include *dharma* in metaphysics, because, although the Mīmāmsakas do not treat action as a substance, they give it a high metaphysical significance. It is action that controls the universe and its forms, either as potent and latent activity as Kumārila says, or as the potency created by activity as Prabhākara says. And the tendency is strong among the Mīmāmsakas to treat all activity as One, and the different activities of the agents as its various forms and manifestations.

After the eighth century AD the Mīmāmsā philosophers became more and more theistic. But they maintained, unlike some of the theistic Vedāntins later, that action either in its potential form or as merit and demerit resides in the *ātman* of the agent, but not in God, who apportions the fruits of the respective actions to the agent.

The World

The world, according to the Mīmāmsā, had no beginning and will have no end. The conception of God as the creator of the world is unnecessary. The existence of God cannot be proved. If God created the world, he has to be an evil being who has created so much evil. Both the good and the evil in the world are the results of man's ethical and unethical actions. The various gods also, with whom the Hymns and popular imagination people the universe, are only mental creations. Even heaven is not an abode with beautiful gardens, women and wine. It is a peculiar, undiluted happy state of mind, which popular imagination interprets in its own way.

The Ātman

Reference has already been made incidentally to the Mīmāmsā conception of the *ātman*. It is merely the I-consciousness. However, no distinction is drawn between the ego and the I-consciousness, as some Vedāntins like Rāmānuja later did. According to Kumārila, the *ātman* is the object of this I-consciousness. But according to Prabhākara, it is the subject; it is always the agent of action and the knower in knowledge, and is capable of inner self-transformation. But it knows itself only when acting and when knowing an object. Knowledge or consciousness is its adventitious attribute and the *ātman* is not by nature conscious even of itself. As mentioned already, Kumārila says that it has the power or the potency to know, but does not know even itself when left to itself; but Prabhākara does not allow even this potency. According to both, knowledge arises and *ātman* obtains consciousness when mind (*manas*) comes into contact with the *ātman* bringing some information of the external world. Mind is a different entity from the *ātman*. There is, indeed, a difficulty in Kumārila's position, because, as he says, the existence of knowledge is to be inferred and not directly known; the existence of the object, even if it is the *ātman*, which knowledge reveals, has also to be inferred and cannot be directly known. And if the existence of the inferential knowledge also is to be known through another inference, we land in an infinite regress and the *ātman* becomes completely unknowable. We have already mentioned the difficulty in Prabhākara's position also. To know the 'I', it is not necessary to know an object, and furthermore, if the mind (*manas*) is an atom, as Prabhākara maintains, it cannot reveal the 'I' which is not atomic in size.

The *ātman* is eternal and has no beginning and end. In it reside all the actions in their potential state or, as Prabhākara contends, their potencies as merit and demerit. And they produce the consequences even without the knowledge of the *ātman*. They constitute the unconscious will of the *ātman*, an unconscious force residing in it, producing for it, according to their nature, the favourable and unfavourable conditions of existence and the objective world here and hereafter.

The Categories

The Mīmāmsakas, it has been said already, are realists and pluralists. The world is not one thing, but consists of many things. And each kind belongs to a category. The following is the table of categories according to Kumārila:

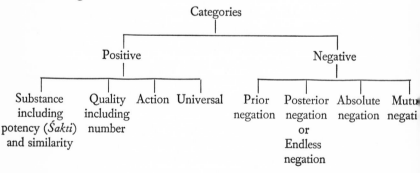

- Categories
  - Positive
    - Substance including potency (*Śakti*) and similarity
    - Quality including number
    - Action
    - Universal
  - Negative
    - Prior negation
    - Posterior negation or Endless negation
    - Absolute negation
    - Mutu negati

The table of categories according to Prbahākara is as follows:

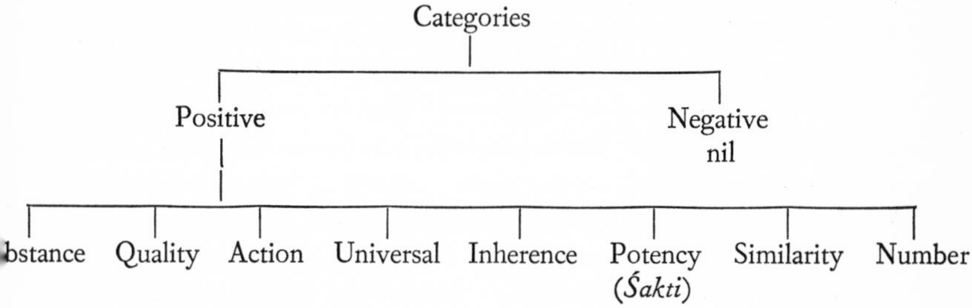

We shall see that there is a similarity between the Mīmāmsakas and the Naiyāyikas in their categorization of reality. But there are important differences also. The list of Kumārila's categories is nearer to that of the Nyāya. Prabhākara does not accept any negatives at all, because, according to him, negation is not real. Negation is of four kinds. Prior negation is the negation of an object before it comes into existence. Before the pot comes into existence, there is negation of the pot. But Prabhākara says that there is nothing called negation existing in the world. Whatever exists is positive only. Before the pot comes into existence, we do not have negation of the pot, but the existence of clay, with which the pot is later made. Posterior negation is the negation of the pot after it is broken up. Prabhākara says that then what is called posterior negation is really the existence of pieces of pot or of mere clay. Endless negation is, for instance, the absence of my pen on my table. This pen is present in my pocket, but absent in every other place and these places are infinite. It is therefore called endless (*atyanta*) negation and also absolute negation. But what I see, when I am said to see the negation of my pen on the table, says Prabhākara, is really the existing table. Mutual negation is the negation of two objects by each other. It is difference. For instance, the pen and the pencil are different from each other and so negate each other: The pen is not a pencil and the pencil is not a pen. But this negation, says Prabhākara, is only the existence of two objects, and it is nothing more than the reality of a plurality.

In the classification of the positive categories also, we find differences of opinion between Kumārila and Prabhākara. According to Kumārila, potency (*śakti*) and similarity (*sādṛśya*) are kinds of substance; and number is one of the qualities. But Prabhākara does not think that they are substances, but separate categories. Again, according to Prabhākara, there are nine kinds of substance – earth, water, fire, air, ether, *ātman*, mind (*manas*), time, and space. But Kumārila adds darkness (*tamas*) and sound (*śabda*, word) to the list. Prabhākara says that darkness is only absence of light, and is not a positive entity. Word (*śabda*) is only sound, and sound is only a quality. But Kumārila distinguishes between mere noise (*dhvani*), which is a quality, and sound (word, *śabda*), which is meaningful, and treats the latter as a substance.

Although Prabhākara accepts inherence (*samavāya*) as a distinct category, he means by it something different from what the Naiyāyikas mean. The Naiyāyikas define it as an eternal inseparable relation between two entities. The relation between a particular horse and the universal horse-ness is inherence. But Prabhākara points out that this relation need not be eternal, it may be transient. When the horse dies, the relation vanishes; if it is eternal, the horse will never die. Prabhākara defines inherence as only dependence (*paratantratā*). The horse is dependent on the universal, horse-ness, for its being a horse, and the horse-ness depends on the horse for its existence. Similarly, a quality depends for its existence on its own substance. Kumārila does not accept inherence as a distinct category. He says that it is nothing more than the relation of identity-and-difference (*bhedābheda*, identity in difference). The universal is both identical with the particular and also different from it. So also is quality identical with, and different from substance.

Prabhākara accepts, as do the Naiyāyikas, the reality of atoms. Earth, water, fire, and air – the four elements only – have atoms. But Kumārila does not accept the reality of any imperceptible matter. So the ultimate parts of these elements are only the smallest perceptible particles.

HUMAN LIFE: ITS NATURE AND AIMS

The Nature of Human Life

The philosophy of life as expounded by the Mīmāmsā school has already been indicated. It is a life of unending activity. The Mīmāmsakas say that the *ātman* is not the same as pure activity, but is distinct from it. Yet action has no abode except the *ātman* and, when completed, becomes a part of unconscious, creative will, producing the conditions and kind of life for the *ātman's* embodiment. The creative and controlling function is performed by action (*karma*), but the agent and abode of the action is the *ātman* itself.

Man has to live a life of constant activity. Without action, he cannot have any conditions of life, and any life, good or evil. He cannot, therefore, have either pleasures or pains. Every man desires pleasures and a happy life, here and hereafter. He has, therefore, to know what actions to perform and what to avoid. A conscious happy life, enjoying all the values which the universe can offer, is the ideal for the Mīmāmsakas. To live means to be active. The Mīmāmsakas had contempt for the life of the monk and also for the life of life-long celibacy. They would not allow any of the sacrifices and ceremonies to be performed in the presence of a monk. And they ridiculed life-long celibacy as a cloak for hiding impotence.

Since the world had no beginning and will have no end according to the Mīmāmsakas, they think that life is meant for eternal activity. Man performs actions and enjoys their fruit in this life and the next. He comes down to this world again, performs more actions and enjoys their fruit. For this process of performing actions and enjoying their fruit, there is no end.

There is a tendency among the Mīmāmsakas to place man higher than the gods even, because it was thought that man was the master of his destiny, but not gods. Gods cannot perform sacrifices for building up their future, because they do not have the physical body. Their present status is the result of their good actions, when they were men. Now they can only enjoy their lives and can do only what they are predetermined to do. But man is free to choose what he likes to do and can build up his destiny.

But in course of time, the Mīmāmsakas regarded the gods to whom even the sacrifices were addressed as mental creations of the agent of the sacrifice. Yet we have to address our sacrifices to those mental creations, because it is only thus that we can strengthen our unconscious creative will for good or evil. Merit and demerit, and action that has become a potency in the *ātman* have to be understood as the potency of the creative will in us, which belongs deep down in the unconscious. We do not see it and are not conscious of it; yet it belongs to us and is creative. And only by acting can we strengthen our will.

We should note here that the extreme activistic attitude of the early Mīmāmsā was largely modified when the school became theistic. In fact, all the other schools were obliged to give some place to the life of action in their world-outlook, and to a greater or lesser extent accepted the original Mīmāmsā teachings of *Karma* and *Dharma*, but subordinating them to their own. One has to recognize that, so far as life in this world is concerned, the followers of all the orthodox schools accept the Mīmāmsā teaching. In the re-interpretations and incorporations by the other schools, and through controversies with them, the original Mīmāmsā became as if unwillingly theistic, introducing the concept of God as an after-thought.

The Aim of Life

The aim of life is to live and, because life is activity, to be constantly active. But to live does not mean to vegetate, but to enjoy. The greatest and perfect enjoyment is found in heaven, and so it is the aim of human life to attain heaven. This heaven is a state of mind, and without mind there can be no pleasure, not even pain. And pleasure can be had if one performs the actions, including sacrifices, necessary for producing heaven.

In the beginning the Mīmāmsakas did not believe even in the possibility of salvation. Salvation is the obtaining of eternal quietude and so freedom from a life bound down to the laws of action, and so liberation from birth and death. But the early Mīmāmsakas did not believe in an existence free from such laws. But later on, the idea of salvation entered their school and it was left to man to choose salvation or a life of action. Now, pleasure or pain is had when mind comes into contact with the *ātman*. A pleasure or pain that is not known is no pleasure or pain. The *ātman* by itself is absolutely unconscious and knows nothing, not even itself. So contact with mind is necessary, if the *ātman* is to enjoy the heavenly pleasure, which is not possible without performing good actions.

The state of salvation is not a state of bliss, because bliss is a pleasant state of mind, but in salvation no mind can exist. If it exists, as it is its nature to be always active, the *ātman* cannot have any quietude (*nirvāṇa*). And if it does not exist, the *ātman* cannot have any consciousness, and therefore the state of salvation is one without pleasure or pain, and without any consciousness. The Mīmāmsakas do not recommend such an unconscious existence as that of a stone to any person. So they gave to salvation only a lower place than to a dutiful life of action. Salvation is meant for only those people, who are tired of action and retire forever from the world of action. There is no credit in longing for salvation and in obtaining it. That is why the life of the monk was not respected by the Mīmāmsakas.

But gradually the followers of this school began accepting that the ideal of salvation was higher than that of dutiful action, and that man should rise higher than the world of action. But they maintained that, so long as man lived in this world, he should lead a life of action. But if action produces its fruit, should he not be born again to enjoy the fruit? Then man should avoid all prohibited actions and also those actions done with an objective like obtaining heaven (*kāmya karmas*). He should perform only those ac ions that are daily duties. And finally whatever actions he performs should be surrendered to God. Then since no action in its latent form or in the form of merit or demerit remains in his *ātman*, he will obtain liberation from the laws of the world of action. But this view was the result of accepting by some of the later Mīmāmsakas the Vedāntic conception of the *ātman*. It was due to the incorporation of the Mīmāmsā by the Vedānta.

Chapter V

THE MATERIALISTIC TRADITION OF THE CĀRVĀKAS

INTRODUCTION

The first, strongest and the extremist reaction against the Mīmāmsā school was expressed by Cārvāka, who belonged to the later Vedic (*Brāhmaṇa*, about 600 BC) times. He seems to have been called Lokāyata and Bṛhaspati also. Lokāyata literally means 'one who goes the worldly way'. We do not know how exactly the word Cārvāka was derived. It is perhaps a combination of *cāru* (sweet) and *vāk* (speech) and so meant the 'sweet-tongued', because he taught what all human beings generally want, viz. that pleasure is the ultimate aim of life. Perhaps the two names, Lokāyata and Cārvāka, were his titles, and Bṛhaspati his original name. The *Aphorisms* (*sūtras*) he composed also go by the name of *Bṛhaspati-sūtras*. But Bṛhaspati was the name also of the priest of gods. And so tradition tells that this priest of gods propounded a rankly materialistic philosophy in order to mislead the enemies of gods, namely, the demons. However, the *Bṛhaspati Aphorisms* and also a commentary on them seem to have been irrecoverably lost. We find references to them in works of the rival schools up to the fourteenth century. The literature of this school is very scanty. We find only one systematic work on it, Jayarāśi's *Tattvopaplavasimha* (*The Lion that Devours all Categories*)[1] of the seventh century AD, which shows that no category (*tattva*) can be proved to be real, that nothing can be real except what we see with our senses, and that therefore everything that man does is justified. Thus the philosophy of Cārvāka was turned into a philosophy supporting any immoral policy and action. However, we have no evidence to show that Cārvāka himself went so far.

As a reaction against the whole of the Mīmāmsā teaching and claim, the Cārvāka philosophy attacked almost every doctrine of the

[1] Published by the Oriental Institute, Baroda, 1940.

Mīmāmsakas – their epistemology, metaphysics, and way of life. It constituted a strong check on the excesses of speculation and practice of the followers of the Mīmāmsā.

EPISTEMOLOGY

Of the three important sources of knowledge accepted in common by all the orthodox schools (perception, inference, and verbal testimony), the Cārvākas accepted only perception as the valid source of knowledge and rejected both inference and verbal testimony. Whatever we know through perception is true and real.

The Cārvākas at first seem not to have been aware of the difficulties in accepting perception as a valid source of knowledge, which were pointed out later by the Buddhist and Vedānta dialecticians. The later Cārvākas showed that they knew of the difficulties, but they did not discuss the implications of this question and maintained on the whole a realistic position.

It is interesting to note that, in their examination of inference, the Cārvākas anticipated the European sceptics. They said that inference was not a valid source of knowledge, because the major premise of an inference cannot be proved. For example:

> Wherever there is smoke, there is fire (*Major premise*);
> This mountain has smoke (*Minor premise*);
> There is fire in the mountain (*Conclusion*).

This is the classical example of inference in Indian epistemology. The Cārvākas ask: (1) How can we formulate the major premise unless we have seen all the instances of smoke? If we have not seen all the instances, how can we logically be justified in using the word 'wherever'? If we have seen all the instances, we must have seen the present case, viz. the mountain also. (2) Then what is the use of making an inference when we have already perceived that there is fire in the mountains? So the Cārvākas say that inference is either impossible or unnecessary. Inference cannot yield truth.

But are not causal statements like 'Fire causes the bodies to expand' true? And they are universal propositions like the major premise. The Cārvākas say that these causal laws also cannot be true. If we are able to apply causal laws and find them to be true, it is only an accident. In fact, there are no causal laws. Every event is a chance. Everything comes into existence and passes out of it according to its own nature. Even this nature is not a universal law; it too may change.

On verbal testimony the Cārvākas make a strong attack. Verbal knowledge is only knowledge of words and their meanings based upon inference. My friend says: 'The orange is red.' Now, through the established meanings of the four words, I infer that the object before the mind of my friend is an orange and that it is red. But it has already been pointed out that inference is a risky source of knowledge. And how can I be sure of the reliability of my friend? For either reason, verbal testimony is not a reliable source of knowledge.

But are not the Vedas reliable? Whereas the Mīmāmsakas were greatly concerned to defend the reliability and authoritativeness of the Vedas, the Cārvākas make their strongest attack on them. The Vedas are not reliable at all, because they are self-contradictory. 'At one place they enjoin on us not to commit any injury; but at another place they ask us to sacrifice animals to gods.' How can one believe that the killing of animals in sacrifices brings one merit?

The Mīmāmsakas say that sound is eternal, that is, the words of the Vedas and their meanings are eternally existing. But how can we believe that the word-sounds are eternal? There is no sound, when no one utters it. And it stays only when produced by the vocal organs. If it is said that its eternity can be proved by inference, we have already shown that inference is not reliable. And perception does not show that the word-sound can be eternal.

We must admit that the Cārvāka theory of knowledge is not exactly scepticism or agnosticism, but a fairly thoroughgoing positivism. They accept the reality of whatever we can perceive with our senses and deny the reality of whatever we cannot so perceive. We should note also that they did not deny the formal validity of inference, because they used the very laws of inference to show that we could not obtain material truths about the world through inference. They questioned only how we could obtain the major premise, but they did not say that, even if we had the major premise, inference was wrong. They did not criticize the structure of the syllogism, but only wanted to show that it was utterly useless for obtaining any new truth about the world. In fact, they used the law of contradiction in refuting the doctrines of their rivals.

METAPHYSICS

The Mīmāmsakas maintain that the *ātman* is eternal and that it is not the same as the body. But the Cārvākas say that there is no such thing as the *ātman*. We do not and cannot perceive the *ātman*, and we cannot prove its existence with the help of inference, because inference is not a valid source of knowledge. The Cārvākas say that consciousness is not due to the *ātman*. When a man dies consciousness disappears and we cannot prove that it goes away and exists somewhere else. Being conscious is a peculiar quality of the living human body. It can retain the consciousness so long as the physical parts are healthy and stay together in a certain form. Consciousness therefore is an emergent quality of the physical parts coming together in certain proportion. For instance, when yeast is mixed with certain juices, they become wine. The property of being wine is a new quality which yeast and juices obtain when mixed. Life also is only a new configuration of matter. Nothing but matter is real.

Therefore the *ātman* or self-awareness is only the physical body with a new emergent quality. But do we not say, 'I *have* a handsome body, a tall body' and so on? If the 'I' is not different from the body, how can it say: 'I *have* such and such a body'? To this the Cārvākas answer by saying that the use of 'have' in these expressions is only conventional, created by the false notion that the 'I' is different from the body.

The Cārvākas speak of mind (*manas*), which, acccording to the Mīmāmsā, is different from the *ātman*. But the Cārvākas seem to think of mind as the consciousness in its knowing function, which of course is not separate from the body. The body along with its consciousness is the *ātman* and consciousness in its experiencing function is the mind. Mind knows the external world through the senses.

The world is the material world only. According to the Cārvākas, it does not consist of five elements, as the Mīmāmsā believes. Earth, water, fire, air, and ether are the usual five elements corresponding to the qualities smell, taste, colour, touch, and sound, and also corresponding to the five sense organs, nose, tongue, eye, touch, and ear. The first four elements are perceivable, but not ether. So the Cārvākas deny the reality of ether. It was thought that the cause of sound in the ear was the all-pervading ether. But the Cārvākas say that sound is caused by air touching the ear. It is due to the movement of air, not of ether.

The other four elements constitute the world. They consist of tiny particles, which are not, however, the invisible atoms of the Naiyāyikas. The particles accepted by the Cārvākas are visible particles; they could not accept the reality of anything that could not be perceived with the senses.

There is no external cause for the four elements coming together and obtaining the qualities of life and consciousness. It is their nature to come together and to have those qualities. But we cannot generalize on this process and establish a law that, whenever these four elements come together in certain ratio, life and consciousness will emerge. The elements may change their nature any time. We cannot, therefore, say that Nature contains some eternal laws. Every event is a chance, and if it develops into something, then it develops according to its own particular nature. One may conclude that, according to the Cārvākas, the existence of everything is a chance, and that there are no laws of nature, but every object has its own nature.

WAY OF LIFE

The concept of *dharma*, as we have seen, is the central concept of the Mīmāmsā philosophy. But the Cārvākas denied its validity. Action when completed, the Cārvākas would say, ends there. *Apūrva* or the latent potential form, which action takes, or merit and demerit cannot be perceived at all by anyone. They are therefore not real. It is foolish to think that past actions become a kind of unseen force (*adṛṣṭa*) and determine our future births. In fact, there is no rebirth. We have only one birth and that is the present one. If there is rebirth, we ought to remember it. No one remembers his previous births.

Accepting only perception as the valid source of knowledge, the Cārvākas rejected the reality of God. No one has ever seen God and no one can see him. The minor gods also do not exist. They and the Vedas belong to the imagination of crafty priests, who invented them to make a living out of them by officiating at sacrifices, and to awe people into obedience by saying that God would punish them, if they did not follow the Vedas. There is no heaven, no hell, no God, and there are no objective ethical laws. The only laws binding on man are the laws of the state, obedience to which brings rewards and disobedience of which brings punishment. And the science (*śāstra*) of the laws of state is the only science worth studying.

What is meant by heaven is the pleasure we have in eating, drinking, singing and in the company and embrace of women. And hell is the pain we experience in this world itself. There is no point in trying to obtain salvation and a life of eternal quietude; there is an end to life at death and all will be quietude then. The differences between castes and their distinctive duties are falsely laid down by interested persons. There are no objective ethical laws, so one can do what one likes, provided he is careful that his actions do not bring pain as a consequence.

The religion of sacrifices is false and is propagated only by interested priests. The life of the monk belongs only to impotent persons. If the animal offered in sacrifice goes to heaven, why should not man offer his parents in sacrifice instead and send them to heaven? Really, the priests do not believe in what they preach. They tell us that the offerings made in this world on death anniversaries of the ancestors satisfy their hunger and thirst in the other world. If so, an extinguished flame in one lamp should burn, when oil is poured in another. To the people gone it is useless to make food offerings; one may as well offer food in his house to a person that has already left the house for another village. There is no soul that leaves the body after death and goes to the other world; otherwise, because of its attachment to its family and friends, it ought to come back to this very body. Life belongs only to this world and ends in this world. There is no other world. Man should try to make the best of this life, without believing in all that the Brahmanic religion teaches. The teachings of the Veda are those of fools, rogues, or demons. The priests tell us not to injure life, but because they are fond of flesh like the demons – *niśācaras* or night-wanderers, whom the Aryans found to be eating dirty, raw flesh and called them demons – they find an exception for themselves when eating the flesh of the animal burnt in sacrifice. These priests should not be trusted and man should do whatever is possible to enhance his pleasure and avoid pain. And any action done for the sake of pleasure is justified.

The Cārvākas do not seem to have recommended pleasures of the moment, because pleasures of the moment and over-indulgance may result in pain and pain has to be avoided. It is also said that, because pleasure is associated with fine arts like music, they encouraged them and contributed much for their development. And because they were averse to killing animals, some of the Cārvākas are believed to be vegetarians.

But the peculiar contribution which this philosophy seems to have made to the philosophy of life, was the philosophical justification it tried to supply to any kind of action for the sake of pleasure. Of course, pleasure is not possible without wealth (*artha*). By spending money we can obtain pleasure (*kāma*). The value of *dharma* (duty) and the value of salvation (*mokṣa*) were rejected by this school. But how can we obtain wealth for the pleasures we want? Does what we do for obtaining wealth have to follow any objective ethical laws? Nothing is recognized by this school as a duty. A man can do anything – beg, borrow, steal or murder – in order to have more wealth and more pleasure. But the state laws prevent a man from doing whatever he likes and punishes him when he disobeys them. If he is clever enough to circumvent them, then his action is justified. Otherwise, he should follow them to avoid the pain of punishment. Kings, who have the power over the state's laws, themselves can do whatever they like and do anything for increasing their wealth, power, pleasure and dominion. Thus the Cārvāka philosophy was later made to support what in Europe was called Machiavellian policies of princes. Jayarāśi calls his exposition of the Cārvāka philosophy 'the supporter of the value, wealth.' Wealth (*artha*) is one of the four values of life recognized by Indian philosophers – wealth (*artha*), pleasure (*kāma*), duty (*dharma*), and salvation (*mokṣa*).

Chapter VI

THE HETERODOX TRADITION OF JAINISM

INTRODUCTION

By heterodox tradition is meant the tradition that does not accept the testimony of the Vedas. The words heterodoxy and orthodoxy should not be identified with what they mean in Christianity. The heterodox is that which does not accept the Vedas, and the orthodox is that which accepts them. The two main heterodox traditions – Jainism and Buddhism – are atheistic in the sense that they do not accept the reality of God. But they are not heterodox for that reason, but for the reason that they rejected the Vedas. Yet they are spiritual philosophies and are not materialistic. The Cārvāka philosophy also is heterodox, since it also rejected the Vedas. But since Bṛhaspati, the founder of the school, was a great Vedic scholar and the holy priest of the gods, the Cārvāka system, although rejected by the orthodox school, is not regarded by tradition with as great concern as Jainism and Buddhism. The orthodox call the Cārvākas, Jainism, and Buddhism *nāstikas* (non-existence-theorists), that is, those who say, 'It is non-existence'. But the 'it' may refer to an eternal sacred scripture, or the *ātman*, or the Brahman. The Cārvākas and early Buddhism too denied all the three, Jainism denied the first and the last. The Cārvākas denied all objective ethical laws, but the Jainas and the Buddhists affirmed their reality. They accepted the Mīmāmsā position that this world is a world of action; but while the Mīmāmsakas regarded the life of action as the only kind of life worth having, the Jainas and the Buddhists maintained that the life of realization of one's true nature is higher and the highest. Both believed in the doctrine of *Karma* (action), reincarnation, and the Vedic gods, But they rejected the value of sacrifices, and taught how to transcend the world of action and obtain salvation.

The roots of Jainism go back to very early Vedic times; but the founder of this school, Vardhamāna, who obtained the title Jina (Conqueror, viz. of all passions) and Mahāvīra (the Great Hero) was an older contemporary of Buddha. The leaders of this philosophy are called Tīrthaṅkaras and the Jainas count twenty-four of them, the first being Ṛṣabha, a name mentioned in the Vedas, and the last Vardhamāna himself. Ṛṣabha must have lived some centuries before Vardhamāna and is regarded as the original founder of this school. But it was strengthened and propagated by Vardhamāna.

Although the Jainas have a vast amount of literature, it is believed that they were people who originally had no books, but after Vardhamāna's teachings and propagation of the philosophy, the teachings began to be compiled. Even then the first attempt to compile them seems to have been made about two hundred years after Vardhamāna's death. Yet the first systematic presentation was made by Umāsvāti (about AD 300) in his *Tattvārtha-adhigamasūtras*[1] (*Aphorisms for Understanding the Nature of the Categories*). Later appeared several systematic works on the different branches of philosophy.

THEORY OF KNOWLEDGE

One finds in Jaina epistemology the usual three sources of knowledge: perception, inference, and verbal testimony. But the Jaina approach to the problem has its own peculiarity. To know an object is to be conscious of it. How can consciousness then grasp the object? Unlike the Mīmāmsakas, the Jainas maintain that consciousness is the essence of the *ātman*; and since the *ātman* is all-pervading, it is by nature all-knowing. Consequently, it should be able to know all objects at once. But by the activity particles (*karma* dust) entering it, its knowing power is limited and it has to use its senses and mind for cognizing objects. Knowledge is only a transformation or modification of the consciousness of the *ātman*, when directed mediately or immediately towards objects. The Jainas are pluralists and realists and believe in the independent existence of the material world. We should remember here that the Jainas use both the words *ātman* and soul (*jīva*), saying that they are the same except that the *jīva* is the *ātman* in its impure state.

The nature of consciousness is to reveal itself and the objects in all acts of cognition. But it has the original power to reveal the objects

[1] Published by the Government Branch Press, Mysore, 1945.

directly without the help of mind and the senses. So there are two distinct kinds of knowledge, immediate knowledge and mediate knowledge. The Jainas do not regard even perception as immediate knowledge, because it is mediated by mind and senses. There is always the possibility of mistakes in the case of mediated knowledge, because mind and senses may go wrong. Immediate knowledge is obtained directly by the consciousness of the *ātman* itself. One who has perfect immediate knowledge can know anything in the world, however distant that object may be. But the *ātman* has lost its power of omniscience through the impurities accumulated by action (*karma*) which enters it. That is, the all-pervading consciousness of the *ātman* becomes veiled and limited by them. In order to regain the original omniscience, therefore, man must get rid of action, which, according to the Jainas, is a substance consisting of small particles like dust. When man succeeds in getting rid of all action and its impurities from his *ātman*, he becomes a *Kevalin* (the Alone) and his knowledge is called *Kevala-jñāna* (knowledge of the Alone).[2] It should not be thought that, according to the Jainas, there is only one *ātman*. There is an infinite number of them, and each is perfect, omniscient, and infinite.

The knowledge of the *Kevalin* (the Alone, the Absolute) is the highest and can have no error. But two other lower stages of this immediate knowledge are recognized, and they correspond to the degree of purity one attains. The next lower stage is called *manah-paryāya* (entering another mind).[3] When a man gets rid of hatred, jealousy, etc., he rises to this stage, and entering the minds of others, can know all they contain. This idea implies that, were it not for the impurities of our minds, every *ātman* could know the others. The next lower immediate knowledge is called *avadhi* (limited) knowledge. One can attain this stage, when one partly succeeds in destroying the impurities of action (*karma*). This knowledge is limited in scope, because it can know only objects with forms, although distant and small.

Mediate knowledge is divided into two main varieties – *mati*, or what is inferential, or that in which mind is active, and *śruti*, or what is heard or known through spoken words. *Mati* is, again, divided into perception, remembering (*smṛti*), recognition (*sanjñā* or *pratyabhijñā*),

[2] Because such knowledge is obtained without the mediation of instruments of knowledge like mind and senses.

[3] Such knowledge is obtained by mind alone without the help of senses.

cognition of modal relation (*tarka*, or *curita*),[4] and syllogistic inference (*anumāna*, or *abhinibodha*). This is a five-fold division. There is a three-fold division also into perception (*upalabdhi*), memory (*bhāvana*), and application (*upayoga*, i.e. inference). In this division, recognition is regarded as a combination of perception and memory, and *cognition of modal relation* (this can also be a modal negative inference of the form of the counter factual conditional like: 'Had x been not y, it would not have been z; but x is z; therefore x is y') as a kind of inference. *Śruti* knowledge is simply verbal knowledge. It may be the verbal knowledge obtained from scriptures (of course, the Jainas mean only Jaina scriptures) or from the statements of reliable persons. It has three main stages. The first stage is obtaining the words of an assertion and their association or relationships. The second stage is the reflection on the words and attending to them. The words must be kept together in mind, i.e. have to be retained and attended to in their togetherness. The third stage is application of these words in their togetherness for obtaining the object meant. That is why the last form of *mati* knowledge and the last stage of *śruti* knowledge are called 'application' (*upayoga*). After all, inference, too, is an application of past knowledge in order to obtain new knowledge.

Perceptual process is divided into two states: The first is called simple apprehension (*darśana*), and the second knowledge (*jñāna*.) But even simple apprehension involves several stages: first, I perceive only the stimulus on my sense organs; at the second stage, my consciousness is excited and I know that there is an object; in the third stage, I become inquisitive or questioning and want to know what exactly the object is; in the fourth stage, I look more attentively and get some details of the object, my memory also is excited so that the object can be classified under its genus and then its species, and finally cognized as a particular object. This stage is called that of the removal of doubt, and in the fifth stage, what is cognized without doubt is retained in memory.

[4] *Tarka* in Jainism is not the same as that of the Naiyāyikas, for whom it is counter-factual, positive or negative, but generally negative. The Jainas include in it even the universal proposition (major premise of the syllogism), which is at the basis of all counter-factual conditionals and may be affirmative or negative. It is a modal, necessary relation between two terms and is called *ūha*. See Yaṣovijaya, *Jainatarkabhāśā*, pp. 10 ff. This is the best introductory work on Jaina epistemology and is published by Sanchalaka Singhi Jaina Granthamala, Ahmedabad, 1938.

When all the stages of apprehension (*darśana*) are completed, we obtain knowledge (*jñāna*). In the case of the two highest forms of immediate knowledge, the forms of apprehension and of the complete knowledge arise together. Such knowledge is real intuition. We may, therefore, say that intuition constitutes the two highest forms of immediate knowledge, in which the instrumentality of the mind and the senses for the rise of the consciousness of the *ātman* is not needed at all, and in which there is no possibility of error.

All knowledge for which there is no contradiction is valid; otherwise, invalid. But since the world is one of action, the test of practical efficiency confirms its truth. This is a kind of pragmatism, but it does not mean that all that is useful is true, but that all that is true is useful. But, again, usefulness means only practical efficacy. Of course, no tests are needed in the case of the two highest forms of immediate knowledge. Error is the presentation of objects as they are not, and truth the presentation of objects as they are.

The Jaina doctrine of modes (*nayas*)[5] corresponds to the Greek doctrine of tropes, modes, moods, conditions, or stand-points. The Jaina epistemology elaborated this doctrine in order to show that several judgments or propositions may be true about the same object, but from different points of view. 'John is a father' is true from the point of view of his son. 'John is not a father' is true from the point of view of his own father. Then 'John is a father and not a father' is true from a combined point of view. We can think of many other types of instances to show that even contradictory judgments can be true of the same thing, provided we acknowledge that there can be different viewpoints. According to the philosophical doctrines of the time, the Jainas recognized seven kinds of tropes, and they are applicable only to two forms of knowledge, apprehension and verbal knowledge, because it is only in these two cases that stand-points influence our judgments. In the other cases, we have knowledge of things as they are, although in the case of clairvoyance (*avadhi*, cognizing remote objects) there may be errors.

These tropes are applicable not only to judgments, but also to different systems of philosophy. The Jainas want to show that every school and system is true, but from a particular standpoint, and false from another. Of course, the rival schools asked why the Jainas did not apply this principle to their own philosophy. But the Jainas would say that their

[5] *Jainatarkabhāṣā*, Chapter II.

philosophy was the teaching of Mahāvīra, who became a *Kevalin* (the Alone, the Pure) and his knowledge was absolutely true.

The classification of the tropes given by the different Jaina thinkers is not always the same, and some of them define the same words differently. So the main simple ones will be given here. These tropes become fallacies (*nayābhāsās*) when their relativity is forgotten.

1. *The trope of the final cause* is judging a thing in terms of purpose. A man brings together water, firewood, utensils and rice. You ask him: 'What are you doing?' He will say: 'I am cooking food.' But is he cooking food or is he collecting water, fire, etc.? From the stand-point of what he is actually doing, he is not cooking food, but from the stand-point of the purpose of his activity, he is cooking food.

2. *The trope of the class or collection* takes only the common feature as real and the rest as false. The common feature may be the highest class characteristic or a lower class characteristic. Some philosophers may say that the most common feature of all beings, viz. Being, alone is real and the rest false; some others may say that the particular beings alone are real, and Being is not real; still others may say that both Being and beings are equally and absolutely real. But the Jainas say that such distinctions have only relative truth, i.e. each is true from a particular point of view.

3. *The trope of convention* takes the conventional meanings only as true and does not take the deeper nature of the object into consideration. The Jainas would not dismiss such meanings outright, but try to find out under what conditions they can be true. For there is some relative truth in every view and meaning.

4. *The trope of the straight cord* takes only what is apparent as true, without taking the trouble of looking deeper. The Buddhists, for instance, see that everything is changing, and straight away conclude that all existence is momentary. But they are jumping to an inductive conclusion from what is only apparent. There is continuity also in the world behind this momentariness. According to the Jainas, static Being and momentariness are not absolute realities, they are true only with reference to each other, and so relatively.

5. *The trope of the word* is based upon the supposed unchanging relation between a word and its meaning. The Jainas do not accept the Mīmāmsā view that this relation is eternal. Different words may have the same meaning and the same word may have different meanings and may also change its meaning. The relation between the word and meaning is only relative to the time, place, and context.

6. *The trope of etymology* understands the nature of an object by taking the etymological root of its name into consideration.

7. *The trope of 'it is so'* takes the root meaning of a word, in cases where it is legitimate to do so, but refuses to take the other meaning, which may also be true of the objects. Every object has many qualities, and its original name may refer etymologically to one of them. But there may be another name referring to another of its qualities, and one may say that the first name only is the correct one. But each word is correct relatively to the quality of the object it refers to. For instance, one may call spirit by the name *ātman* (spirit) or *jīva* (the living one) according to the attribute of the object one has in mind.

Out of the doctrine of tropes arises the doctrine of *the seven-fold conditioned predication.*[6] The seven forms of judgment given under conditioned predication do not correspond, one to one, to the seven tropes given above. Under each trope a seven-fold predication may be made. Once it is accepted that truth is conditioned by a trope or point of view, then seven kinds of judgment can be made, every one of which is true relatively. These seven forms may be called modal assertions (*naya* means a mode), but they should not be confused with the judgments of modality in Western logic.[7] The seven forms are the following:

[6] See Mallisena, *Syādvādamañjarī*, ed. by A. B. Dhruva (Bombay Sanskrit Series, Bombay, 1933).

[7] They may be called conditioned truths about an object rather than 'conditional truth.'

If N, then S is P

is a conditional judgment. But

Because of N, S is P

is a conditioned judgment. In the former judgment, we do not know whether N actually exists or not and therefore we do not know also for certain that S is actually *P* or not. But in the latter, we know that N exists, and so we accept

(1) Somehow, S is P.
(2) Somehow, S is not P.
(3) Somehow, S is both P and not-P.
(4) Somehow, S is indescribable.
(5) Somehow, S is P and indescribable.
(6) Then we may combine (2) and (4) and get
    Somehow, S is not-P and indescribable.
(7) And finally we may combine (3) and (4) and obtain
    Somehow, S is P and not-P and indescribable.

'S is indescribable' means that we reject P, not-P, and both P and not-P, and therefore

S is neither P, nor not-P, nor both.

It means that we cannot describe S by any of the opposite predicates.

Now, this seven-fold prediction can be applied to existential propositions also like 'S exists'. The Jainas would say that from the point of view of microscopic perception, germs exist; and that they do not exist from the point of view of ordinary perception. Accordingly, we again have seven propositions:

(1) S exists.
(2) S does not exist.
(3) S exists and does not exist.
(4) S is indescribable.
(5) S exists and is indescribable.
(6) S does not exist and is indescribable.
(7) S exists and does not exist and is indescribable.

This doctrine of seven-fold predication is called *syādvāda* (the doctrine of 'let it be so') or the doctrine of conditioned predication.

METAPHYSICS

The Jaina philosophy, it has already been said, is realistic and pluralistic. There is a plurality of objects and *jīvas* (*ātmans*) and all of them are

that S is P and that SP exists. It is the latter that the Jainas mean. But they would not mention the antecedent, 'because of N,' but say only: 'Somehow, let it be, because some of the conditions may be unknown, or we can allow it.'

real, and the objects of our knowledge also are real, but are not mere ideas. But the Jaina metaphysics is a metaphysics of substance. Everything, including action, is a substance. One may find the idea of action being a substance to be very strange, but it is found in the modern theory that the stuff of the universe is only process. The Jainas conceive any existence as a substance. Action exists and is, therefore, a substance.

The following is the table of categories given by the Jainas:

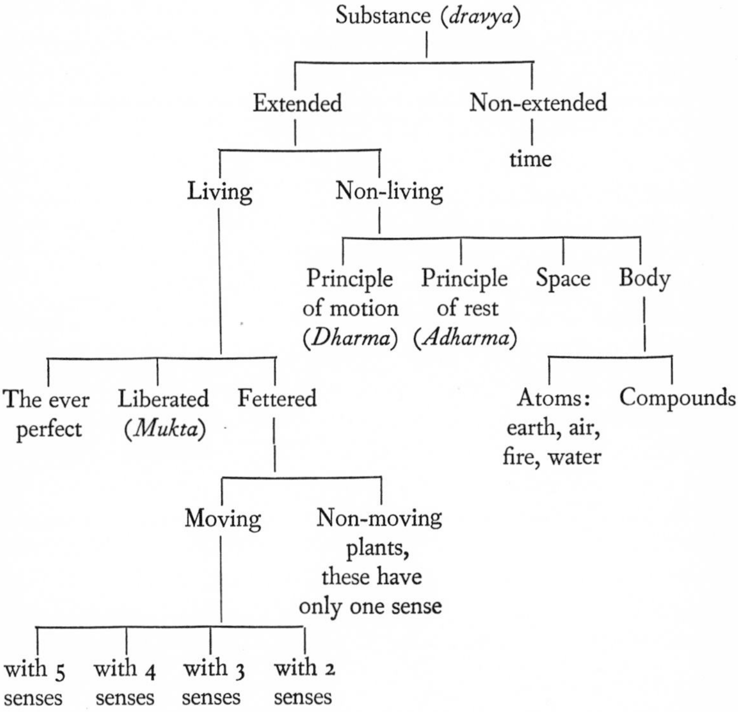

The main division which the Jainas adopt is that between living or animated substances and the non-living or inanimate substances. Time (*Kāla*) is included in the inanimate substances. But since it is not extended like space, it is given as a category by itself in the above chart. There are really five inanimate substances – Time, Motion, Rest, Space, and physical bodies, of which only the bodies have parts, which can be divided and divided till we reach atoms. Only the four elements – earth, water, fire, and air – have atoms.

Without time, we cannot cognize continuity, change, movement, novelty, and age of substances. Therefore time is real. But it cannot be seen, it can only be inferred. If a substance continues to exist, it does so for some time. Now it may be hot, then cold. This change takes place in time. Similarly, movement can be cognized only against time. Our observation, 'This is new', implies time. So also oldness implies time.

Now, time, according to the Jainas, is not extended in space or even like space. It is one and indivisible, it is simple duration. Bergson, a French philosopher, held a similar view. Now, if time is unextended and indivisible, how can we speak of two hours, two days, two years and so on? To this question, the Jainas reply that there are two kinds of time, the real time and the conventional time or the time of usage. The real time is one, without beginning and without end, it is simple passage, duration. But usage-time is the time artificially divided into parts according to some changes assumed to be regular and constant. But such a division is only artificial and does not affect the real time.

Although the jainas use the word *ākāśa*, they do not mean by it ether – which, according to the Nyāya and the Vaiśeṣika, is the cause and propagator of sound – but simply space. The Jainas say that sound in the ear is caused by the movement of air particles.

Everything exists in space, which is not the same as extension, but the principle that makes the extension of objects possible. We may perceive the extension of objects, but we cannot perceive space, its existence is only inferred. For extended objects to exist, there must be place. And this place is space (*ākāśa*). Descartes in Western philosophy rejected this theory, but Hobbes held a similar view.

Space is infinite and is divided into world-space (*lokākāśa*) and non-world-space (*alokākāśa*). The former is the space that is occupied by the substances. The latter extends beyond the former and is empty.

Although the Jainas could think of empty space, some of them could not think of empty time extending beyond the time belonging to the filled space. So some Jainas thought that time was not a separate substance, but only a mode of the other substances.

Motion and Rest are also substances for the Jainas. The two do not mean what we observe as motion and rest, but the principles that make motion and rest possible. For instance, changes in a substance are made possible by time; and their extension is made possible by space.

Similarly, the motion and rest of substances are made possible by these two principles.

The principles of motion and rest (*dharma* and *adharma*) are each one and occupy the whole of the world-space, although we see different movements and different resting substances limited to particular parts of space. These principles cannot be perceived, and being passive like time and space, they cannot be causes of anything.

The material substance consists of four elements: earth, water, fire, and air. Each of the four consists of atoms, which possess their qualities. But according to the Jainas, all substances are capable of undergoing change. Accordingly, the atoms do not inherently possess specific qualities; only when they interact, some get the qualities of earth, some of water, and so on. The material world is produced by the combination of the atoms. All material objects are capable of transformation, and every object possesses an infinite number of qualities, not all of which are known. They possess some unchanging, essential characters (*guṇas*) and changing modes (*paryāyas*). Every object is born, stays for some time, and then perishes.

Mind (*manas*), according to the Jainas, is, like speech and breath, a product of matter. But the Jainas distinguish between two kinds of mind, the substantial, or material mind and the psychological, or ideal mind. In fact, they make such a differentiation between material senses and psychological senses also. The former belong to the physical body, and the latter correspond to them.

The Jainas call mind the inner instrument, but say that it is not a sense. The psychological senses and the psychological mind work through the physical counterparts, when we observe material objects.

The Jīva or Ātman

It is in Jaina philosophy that one can use the words soul (*jīva*) and spirit (*ātman*) freely and in the same sense, because, as mentioned already, the *jīva* is the *ātman* in bondage, and the *ātman* is the *jīva* pure and out of bondage. Bondage is limitation of the unlimited, determination of the indeterminate. The *jīva* is by nature infinite, has infinite knowledge, and infinite power; but its original nature is obscured by the impurities of action (*karma*). Knowledge or consciousness is its essential nature, not an adventitious quality, which it gets when mind (*manas*) comes into contact with it and gives it some information.

Even without mind (*manas*), the *jīva* can know everything. The presence of mind works only to limit the *jīva's* knowledge, and is necessary for the *jīva* in bondage, when the *jīva* cannot know the objects without mind and sense organs.

The *jīva* is not merely the knower (*jñātā*) but also the enjoyer (*bhoktā*). The Jainas do not accept the view of the Advaita philosophers that, while the *jīva* is the knower and the enjoyer, the *ātman* is neither the knower nor the enjoyer. The existence of the *ātman* itself is to be proved as that of the knower and the enjoyer. The Jainas, like the orthodox schools, attempt to prove, as against the Cārvākas, the existence of the *ātman*. First, the knower of objects is not the physical body, but something else. The physical body is inorganic and cannot know anything. The mind and the senses cannot be the knower, because the knower is the knower of the mind and the senses also and the knower cannot be the known. Secondly, there is a director and controller of the actions of the mind and the senses and also of the physical body. And the director and the controller is the *ātman*. Thirdly, the *ātman* as the controller must, therefore, be active and it is not a mere on-looker of action. If it is not the agent of actions, then it will not suffer from the demerits of evil actions. And if it does not suffer, there is no need of ethical laws and struggle for salvation. In the fourth place, because the *ātman* itself suffers from the demerits of evil actions and enjoys the fruit of the merits of good actions, it is the enjoyer (*bhoktā*).

The first and the second arguments are directed against the Cārvāka view that the *ātman* is only the physical body. The Jainas accept that the *ātman* cannot be perceived by the senses, and say that the reason is that it is not an external object. But it is directly known as the subject of knowing and enjoying and its very nature is consciousness. To remove doubts, the Jainas advance more arguments. First, material particles cannot produce the *ātman*, because their activity has to be guided by some intelligent agency. And that agency is the conscious *ātman*. Secondly, we cannot prove that consciousness can be produced by matter. There is no instance at all in which mere matter produces consciousness, and on the basis of which we can affirm that matter produces consciousness. The Cārvākas say that we should believe only what perception reveals, but perception does not give a single instance of matter producing consciousness. And actually here the Cārvākas are making an inference, which they themselves regard as useless. In the third place, if consciousness is a peculiar characteristic which the physical body obtains when its parts enter a particular configuration, then there must be consciousness always so long as our body is alive. But in sleep and swoon there is no consciousness. In the fourth place, therefore, we have to explain such statements as 'I am lean', 'I am tall', etc. as only figurative, due to the habit of the *ātman* identifying itself with the body.

We should note here that these arguments are advanced by all the orthodox schools also against the Cārvākas. The followers of the Advaita Vedānta, as we shall see later, maintain that the *ātman* by nature is neither the knower nor the enjoyer. But almost all the other orthodox schools including the Mīmāmsā believe that it is the knower and the enjoyer also. As against the Advaita Vedāntins, they advance, along with the Jainas, the third and the fourth arguments given earlier to show that the *ātman* is both the knower and the enjoyer.

The *ātman* or *jīva*, according to the Jainas, is not spatial by itself, but it can occupy space. The light of the lamp, for instance, can occupy any kind of space. If the room is round, it occupies round space; if it is rectangular, it occupies rectangular space. If the room is small, it occupies a small space, and if big, a large space. Similarly, the *ātman* can occupy the space of the body with which it is connected. In a mosquito, the *ātman* is as small as the mosquito; but in an elephant, it is as big. It is the nature of the *ātman* to become small or big until it becomes as large as the universe itself. Yet by nature it has no shape, but takes on the shape of the object with which it identifies itself.

Karma

The Jaina doctrine of action (*karma*), so far as its ethical results go, is the same as that of the Mīmāmsā. Except the Cārvākas, all the schools of Indian philosophy, both orthodox and heterodox, accepted its ethical importance and regarded the world as a world of action. But while the Mīmāmsā school developed the idea of action into a metaphysics of potency (*apūrva*, *adṛṣṭa*), the Jainas developed it into a metaphysics of substance. But curiously enough, it does not find a separate place among the categories given in the chart. It seems that it is associated somehow with the principle of Motion (*Dharma*), and is perhaps one of its forms. But one cannot be too sure, because the

Jainas say that action (*karma*) consists of particles, but *Dharma* (motion) does not consist of particles. It is one and undivided.

Action (*karma*) is like dust, and the *ātman* is like a clean wet cloth, into which passions and emotions enter. It is the nature of dust to stick to a wet cloth and make it impure. When the *ātman* is stained by *karma*, it loses its purity, becomes bound to it, and determined by the laws of *karma*. It then becomes finite, and the goal of the *ātman*, therefore, is to get rid of *karma*. The Jainas emphasize the importance of getting rid of *karma* as stongly as the Advaita Vedāntins and the Buddhists emphasize the importance of getting rid of Māyā or Avidyā (Ignorance, the Unconscious).

NATURE AND AIM OF LIFE

Every *ātman*, according to Jainism, was originally pure; but the action-particles or *karma* dust manage to enter it and it becomes impure. Then it begins to think that it lacks this or that, desires it, and acts for obtaining it. This activity further adds to the impure *karma* dust in the *ātman*, which then becomes, a member of the world of the law of action. It forgets its superiority to the world of action and is bound to it. That is, it enters bondage and is fettered by the laws of the world of action. Bondage, in Indian philosophy, is to be understood as bondage to the laws of action of the world, and the world is to be understood not merely as the material world in which causation rules, but also as that world in which motivation rules so far as the motive is the motive of the finitized *ātman* and is for finite ends. Such a motive becomes a factor of the creative forces of the world.

How a motive or intention becomes a cause, according to Indian thinking in general, can be explained thus. In Indian philosophy the distinction between motive and intention is not clearly drawn, and we shall therefore overlook it. Now, I want a wealthy life and I perform certain charities. These charities, i.e. my charitable actions, will fructify either in this life or in the next. These actions enter my *ātman* in the form of potencies – as *karma* dust in Jainism – and contribute to the creation of conditions in which I become wealthy. The Jainas say that my actions, when completed, become like subtle dust particles and enter my *ātman*; Kumārila, one of the Mīmāmsakas, says that my actions become potencies and reside in my *ātman*, and Prabhākara, another Mīmāmsaka, maintains that they produce the creative potencies.

But in all cases, we find that our actions become or produce some subtle forms and reside in our *ātmans* and from there begin to act upon the world. We may say that the Jaina conception of action as a kind of substance, although dust, is a somewhat cruder conception than that of the Mīmāmsā. And the general tendency of all the schools, except the Cārvāka, is to think that actions become subtle causal forces determining the conditions in which the finite *jīva* finds itself in this and the future lives.

Now, no action is done without a purpose, without a desire to attain something. This purpose is the motive of our actions, which in turn become creative potencies in the immediate and the distant future, until they exhaust themselves. Further, if I am a philanthropist and continue doing philanthropic actions (works), my will to do such actions also is intensified. Similarly, the repeated criminal actions of a criminal strengthen his criminal tendencies, i.e. his will to commit criminal acts becomes stronger and stronger; and he commits them both consciously and unconsciously. Now, the Indian philosophers thought that providence is so nice and yielding that, in our next birth, it will create for us a life in which we can enjoy performing such actions all the more. That is, the unconscious will in us is capable of producing such conditions for us. For instance, if a man indulges in cruel acts in this life and finds that unfortunately for him the conditions of life do not permit him to continue in his life of cruelty, he will be born in his next life as a tiger, which can continue its killings in the forest without any question of compunction. Extravagant and fantastic applications of this idea were made in popular literature. But the philosophically important part of this doctrine is that not only our will but also our character is to a very large degree fashioned by the actions we perform. It is difficult to prove or disprove that our actions determine the conditions of our future life also. Neither can we prove or disprove the doctrine of rebirth. But if all actions must have their fruit, which we have to enjoy, some doctrine like that of rebirth seems to be the most satisfactory, provided the inner freedom of man to shake off his present nature and to rise above the present conditions is also given full consideration.

Thus there are three kinds of existence for all the spiritual philosophies of India. Firstly, there is the world of matter, which is absolutely governed by the determinate laws of cause and effect. Secondly, there is the ethical world, which covers not only the world of human beings with its social laws, but also a part of the world beyond. This part is that of the unconscious deeper layers of our personality, subject to the laws of ethics, but yet creative even without our knowledge, and in spite of our conscious will. The deep inner layer in each one of us has its roots still deeper down in the unconscious creative, but spiritual force of the universe. This may not be accepted as a person either by the Mīmāmsakas or the Jainas, but is accepted in different forms by each school. In the third place, there is the existence of the pure souls, or spirits, existing all by themselves. The first two forms of existence are governed by laws, the laws of matter and the laws of the unconscious inner force, both of which are unconscious. Now, the *ātmans*, which are originally pure, somehow get entangled in the network of these two kinds of laws. But there is no hopelessness. The *ātmans* are by nature pure, and free from the bondage of these laws. They often show their freedom even when working within the network of these two kinds of laws. And in order to be completely free from bondage to the laws, the *ātmans* have to realize their original nature.

The Jainas say that, when action (*karma*) enters the *ātman*, it assumes eight forms, all of which together constitute what is called the 'body of action' (*kārmaṇaśarīra*). First, the action (*karma*) obscures right knowledge (*jñānāvaraṇīya*), and produces different degrees of knowledge. Second, it obscures the right type of direct contacts with objects (*darśanāvaraṇīya*). Third, it obscures the original happy nature of the *ātman* and produces transient pleasures and pains (*vedanīya*). Fourth, it produces infatuation, weakens our rational life, stirs up passions and emotions, disturbs our fatih in truth, and ruins our conduct (*mohanīya*). Fifth, it determines the length of our life (*āyuṣka*). Sixth, it determines the form of the individual's existence – his physical body, its form, health and so on (*nāma*). Seventh, it determines the family, community, nationality, and race of the individual (*jāti*). And in the eighth place it produces obstacles for the soul in attempting to rise above bondage, and prevents doing good even when there is a desire to do it (*antarāya*). It acts as a downward pull for the soul, even when it wants to rise.

The Jainas give a set of categories showing the process how the individual comes into existence and how he can liberate himself. A classification of categories from the standpoint of substance has already been given. The Jainas give another classification of concepts from the standpoint of a philosophy of life.[8] They are seven: (1) the soul (*jīva*),

[8] Mādhavāchārya, *Sarvadarśanasaṅgraha* (Anandasrama Press, Poona, 1928) pp. 29 f.

(2) the non-soul (*ajīva* or inanimate substance), (3) inflow (*āśrava*), (4) bondage (*bandha*), (5) damming (*samvara*), (6) exhaustion (*nirjara*), and (7) liberation (*mokṣa*). The connecting link between the soul and non-soul (matter) is activity (*karma*). Soul and non-soul have already been explained. Inflow is the flowing in of the dust of activity (*karma*) into the pure *ātman*. Then the first thing one has to do is to dam or obstruct this inflow. This is called damming. But some action-dust has already flowed in and that has also to be destroyed. It can be destroyed by allowing it to exhaust itself or exhaust its creative activity. This is called exhaustion or wearing out. The word implies that it works itself out or becomes old and unproductive. Then when all the impurity of action dies out, one attains liberation (*mokṣa*). Of course, both good and evil actions must be allowed to wear out.

The inflow of the action-particles is called *yoga* also, and this should not be confused with the *yoga*, which means the physical and psychological practices meant for obtaining salvation. The *ātman* becomes like a wet cloth due to passions, desires, etc., and the actions it performs enter it like particles and pollute it further. The readiness of the *ātman* to absorb these particles is due to the four impurities – anger, pride, delusion, and greed. The inflow may be of good actions or evil actions. When once the actions get into the *ātman*, they become a kind of vibrations or movements within the *ātman*.

After the inflow of the *karma* particles, the *ātman* becomes bound by the laws of the ethical and the material world. It then begins to hold wrong beliefs about itself and the world (*mithyādarśana*), becomes attached to physical matter and continues to be so attached (*avirati*), and becomes unmindful of the essential truth (*pramāda*). The above impurities and these tendencies strengthen its bonds to the material world and it remains in bondage (*bandha*). And this bondage assumes the form of the action-body (*kārmaṇaśarīra*), the eightfold form of which has been described above.

The ideal of intelligent human life, therefore, is to get rid of all action. It should be noted that the performance of action, the form it takes when it enters the *ātman*, and the form with which it becomes a part of the bound *ātman* are all called by the same name *karma*. So when the Jainas say that the *ātman* should get rid of *karma* (action), we should take the third meaning. The determining characteristic that makes the *ātman* finite is *karma* in the third sense. And when this is got rid of, the *ātman* becomes infinite again.

But action (*karma*) cannot be got rid of easily and by force. So the first thing one has to do is to dam the new inflow, i.e. practice damming (*samvara*). But one cannot stop all activity, one has at least to take care of his body. So five kinds of practice are prescribed. (1) One should control one's movements of hands, feet, etc., in such a way as not to injure or destroy any life. (2) Then man should control his speech, speaking only when it is necessary, telling only the truth, and without hurting anyone. (3) He should eat the food obtained by begging at several places, a little from everyone, so that he will not put anyone to inconvenience. And he should not accept a complete meal from any single house. (4) In going to accept gifts, one should carefully avoid injury and give away whatever is obtained. And (5) one should deposit all excretions from the body at a place where no animal life exists.

After stopping the new inflow, one should try to purify what has already got in. This aim is achieved through penance (*tapas*). One should suffer the fruits of his past evil deeds, but should give away the fruits of his past good deeds. Thus when all action (*karma*) is got rid of, man obtains liberation.

The ethics necessary for obtaining salvation and freedom from action (*karma*) is worked out slightly differently by the different Jaina writers; but the main principles are the same and the differences come under the seven main categories. All virtues and modes of self-discipline and self-control come under the heads, damming (*samvara*) and exhaustion (*nirjara*). First, bondage is due to the ignorance of one's original, infinite nature. This ignorance is not exactly the same as the Avidyā (the Unconscious) of the Advaita Vedānta, although some similarities can be picked up through criticism, because it is the main cause of bondage and no one can say how the pure *ātman* suddenly gets infected by this principle. But the Jainas are averse to raising it to the status of a metaphysical principle, and treat *karma* (action) as the evil cause for the fall of the *ātman* from its exalted position. However, this ignorance of the original state has to be removed, and it can be removed naturally by knowing the ultimate truth about the *ātman*. Hence every attempt to obtain right knowledge is a virtue. But secondly, right knowledge (*samyagjñāna*) is not possible without right attention (*samyag-darśana*) to truths. This involves the readiness to accept what one rationally thinks is true. One should not doubt simply for doubt's sake. Eternal doubt is due to evil actions (*karmas*) polluting our being.

Therefore, in the third place, one should try to purify oneself of all action, both good and bad. Even good actions cause emotions; and even one's goodness, by affecting one's emotions, may prevent one from seeing truth as such. However, one should overcome evil actions through good actions, and then be free from good actions (*karmas*) also. For this purpose one should practice right conduct (*samyakcarita*). These three virtues – right faith, right knowledge, and right conduct – are called the three gems (*triratna*) by the Jainas.

Right faith is respectful attention to truth. When it comes to the question of what ultimately truth is, the Jainas will say that it is as taught by Mahāvīra, because he was a *Kevalin* (the Alone, the Pure) whose knowledge was absolutely direct and could not be mistaken. Right knowledge is one's own detailed, discrimitative knowledge of the *ātman* and the non-*ātman*. Right conduct consists of seven parts: (1) the five great vows (*pañcamahāvratas*), (2) the five forms of self-control (*samiti*), (3) self-restraint (*gupti*), (4) bodily and mental purifications (*dharmas*), (5) meditation on the truths, (6) conquest of pain and hungar, and (7) absolute equanimity.

The five great vows are: (1) not to injure any life, (2) to speak only truth, (3) not to steal, (4) to remain celibate, and (5) to abstain from receiving objects of pleasure. The forms of self-control are, as described already, obedience to the injunctions about walking, speech, begging, receiving of gifts, and the disposal of excretions. The *guptis* also are forms of self-restraint, they are forms of reserve in thought, speech, and movements. The *dharmas*, which are bodily and mental virtues, are forgiveness, humility, truthfulness, straightforwardness, cleanliness, self-restraint, austerity, charitableness, celibacy, and non-attachment. It should be noted that the word *dharma* here means something different from the category *dharma*, meaning the principle of motion. The sixth form of conduct is meant to train man to be absolutely indifferent to his bodily needs like hunger and pain. The seventh, equanimity, is the state of the *ātman* itself, which is pure, without desire, and perfect. So one should practice equanimity in order to be like the original *ātman*, not disturbed and made impure by the *karma* dust.

The Jainas practice the most severe kind of austerities in order to develop utter disregard of the physical body. Some of them go to the extent of giving up all clothing and treat space itself as the covering cloth. They are called Digāmbaras, the space-clad. But the others do not consider it right to go naked and so use an ordinary white cloth. They are called Śvetāmbaras, or the white-clad. But there are no philosophical differences between the two sects. In fact, Jainism has not allowed any change in the development of its metaphysics. The Jainas observe the principle of non-injury in its extremest forms, and all of them are vegetarians. And in order to prevent unseen, small, animal life from entering the mouth, the Jaina monks wear a piece of white cloth, through which such life cannot pass. And they go to the extent of doubting what to do when a tiger attacks a man, whether to allow the tiger to kill the man and eat him up or kill the tiger and save the man, because in either case destruction of life becomes unavoidable. Some sub-sects were formed, one holding the one view and the other the other view. And because, according to Jainism, even atoms have some kind of souls, even destruction of matter became a problem for the Jainas. Jainism allows fasting unto death after twelve years of austerities. It is only after such death can man observe absolute non-injury of both seen and unseen life, for then the *ātman* becomes absolutely inactive. So long as there is movement, even in breathing, there is always the likelihood of microscopic life being destroyed. However, the vegetarianism of many Indians who are not Jainas, is due to the influence of Jaina teachings.

The Jainas do not believe in a personal god, or even in a universal spiritual principle, but build temples for their ancient religious leaders (*tīrthaṅkaras*) and worship them. One sub-sect of the white-clad Jainas, called Sthānikavāsis, gave up idol-worship, i.e. they do not worship the idols of their religious leaders. Although Jainism is treated as a non-Vedic religion, the Jainas are very tolerant and respect all other religions and saints. As followers of the principle of non-injury, they do not generally take to the life of the soldier, but of the tradesman. And as merchants and businessmen they got mixed up with the third caste. And some of them have even accepted the Vaiṣṇava religion of the Vedic tradition. The Jaina community as a whole is not a very distinct community from the Hindu, but has many kinds of affiliation through marriages, forms of worship, even employing Brahmin priests at marriage ceremonies. For a thorough-going observance of respect for life, one cannot find a better example in the world than Jainism, particularly among the Jaina monks and nuns. The laity is allowed some latitude.

Chapter VII

THE HETERODOX TRADITION OF BUDDHISM

INTRODUCTION

Buddhism, like Jainism, was mainly a reform movement in India's spiritual life. Like Jainism, it accepted all the gods of the orthodox tradition and rejected the authoritativeness of the Vedas and the utility of sacrifices. It also started, therefore, without any scriptures and began reflecting upon life independently. It disappeared from nearly the whole of India by about the fifteenth century, but it ruled the life of the Indians for nearly two thousand years, from the sixth century BC till then. But unlike Jainism, it allowed more freedom of thought to its followers, so that in India itself quite a large number of Buddhist sects, with new ideas, developed new philosophies out of the few basic doctrines taught by Buddha. In Jainism we find only one system of metaphysics, but in Buddhism many. And when Buddhism disappeared, it was not due to any violent religious conflicts within the Indian religious tradition, but in part to the invasion of Islam, and in part to the gradual development of its own doctrines towards the Upaniṣadic ones, and to the ease with which the developed doctrines could be assimilated and adopted by the philosophies based upon the Upaniṣads. Buddhism never attempted to formulate its own codes of social conduct, allowed the castes to continue as such, and, confining itself to the monasteries, sought only to teach spiritual doctrines and discipline. To be sure, it did not allow caste distinctions within monasteries, and like Jainism, established nunneries for women ascetics. There was no asceticism and there were no convents for women in the orthodox tradition. Now, when the teachings of Buddhism were absorbed by the othodox schools, since Buddhism itself admitted liberality in its doctrines and practices and did not adhere to a fossilized way of thought, it lost the grounds for its separate existence and almost disappeared as a separate institution. Buddha himself was made one of the incarnations of Viṣṇu and his teachings were made an important strand of the philosophical thought of India.

Buddha (the Enlightened), whose original name was Gautama, wrote no book, but taught orally. His followers understood him each in his own way and taught his doctrines as each understood them. Then differences of opinion were noticed and three councils were held by the Buddhists of the country for codifying Buddha's teachings. The first was held one hundred years after his death, the second one hundred years later, and the third another hundred years later. The teachings thus collected were contained in what were called the Three Baskets (*Tripiṭakas*). The first is called *Vinayapiṭaka* or the Basket of Rules of Conduct; the second *Suttapiṭaka*, or the Basket of Sermons; and the third *Abhidhammapiṭaka* or the Basket of Philosophical Disquisitions. On these three Baskets commentaries were written, then expositions and so on until a vast amount of literature grew up. But in these councils there were dissensions and schisms, new schools were formed with their own texts. Finally, the views of the new schools due to the impact of the orthodox ideas, particularly those of the Upaniṣads, became so different form the original teachings, that some of the later schools grouped themselves together under a new name. This great new movement of thought started in the Andhra, but developed in the north and called itself the Great Vehicle (*Mahāyāna*), distinguishing itself from the southern group and calling it the Small Vehicle (*Hīnayāna*). Here vehicle means the carrier to ultimate truth. While for the Small Vehicle (*Hīnayāna*) the Three Baskets (*Tripiṭakas*) are the main scripture, the earliest followers of the Great Vehicle (*Mahāyāna*) composed the *Prajñāpāramitāsutras* (*Aphorisms of the Apex or the End of Knowledge*), on which again different commentaries were written.

The literature of Buddhism is as vast as the number of its schools is great. But all are not philosophically important. Some of them differed from one another merely on a few problems of conduct, like whether a monk could or could not use metal vessels. The development of philosophical doctrines also appeared at various stages in some of the schools. Because of the freedom of thought and practice allowed, some schools accepted elements from different schools, thus forming hybrid schools. It is said that in India alone there were about thirty schools of Buddhism by the time it was absorbed. And if we add to them the schools and sects of the other Asian countries, the number may be very great indeed. We shall deal here only with the more prominent of the schools.

Buddha and Mahāvīra were not myths, but historical personages. While Buddha was a saint and prophet of compassion, Mahāvīra was a saint of austerities. Buddha was so sublimely human and appealed to the masses with such charm that it was easy for Buddhism to spread over the whole of Asia. The emphasis of Buddhism was on wisdom and compassion, from which angle it offered hope and easiness of approach to suffering humanity. The emphasis of Jainism was on austerities and non-injury, which certainly comprehended and went beyond compassion, but the ideal appeared to be too far beyond the reach of ordinary man outside India to attract him.

THE FOUR BASIC TRUTHS

Buddha was not interested in empty metaphysical speculations. He refused to answer such questions as (1) 'Does God exist?' and (2) 'Does the *ātman* exist?' We do not know and cannot define what the words God and *ātman* mean. Then what is the use of asking whether they exist or not? His refusal to answer such questions was taken by his followers as a negative answer. However, it is important to know the answer to questions like (1) 'Why should man strive for salvation?' and (2) 'Is the world a place of perfect happiness? And if it contains misery, what should man do to get over misery?

Buddha, therefore, enunciated the four basic truths, called the *Ārya Satyas* or the Aryan or Noble Truths. The word Aryan had no racial meaning for Buddha, we should remember, but only the meaning of 'the best and the highest.'

1. The first truth is that life is misery. Every experience, even pleasure, contains misery. Old age, disease, and death, through which every life must pass, are misery. To the man who is able to see through life, every activity is misery. This truth is called the truth of misery (*duhkhasatya*).

2. The second truth is called the truth of the cause (*samudayasatya*). Everything arises out of something, i.e. everything has a cause. Misery must have a cause. Then how is misery caused? The three basic miseries are old age, disease and death. The question then becomes: How are these three caused?

The causation of misery belongs to a chain, and this chain, as

Buddhism generallyinterprets it, has twelve links. We shall start from the final effect.

a. Old age, disease and death constitute misery (*jarāmaraṇa*).
b. We are unable to overcome them, because there is rebirth (*jāti*).
c. There is rebirth, because there is the tendency or will in me to be born (*bhāva*).
d. The tendency to be born is due to my clinging to the objects of enjoyment (*upādāna*).
e. The clinging to objects is due to desire or thirst for them (*tṛṣṇā*).
f. There is desire for the object, because there is experience of the object (*vedanā*).
g. There is experience of the object, because there is sense contact with the object (*sparśa*).
h. There is sense contact, because we have sense organs (*ṣaḍāyatana* or six sense-fields). According to the Buddhists, there are six senses, the usual five plus mind.
i. There are the six sense organs, because there is the body-mind (*nāmarūpa*).
j. There is body-mind, because there is the embryonic consciousness (*vijñāna*).
k. There is the embryonic consciousness, because there are the inner drives and impressions (*samskāras*), which are blind and unconscious.
l. And these unconscious drives and impressions are due to my ignorance (*avidyā*) of the truth and to my being rooted in ignorance.

Some words here need explanation. The word *avidyā* is generally translated as Ignorance.[1] This ignorance is said to be the cause of my self, my *vijñāna*, and body-mind. Then before I exist, my ignorance cannot exist. So the Buddhist view implies that this ignorance causes my being itself. Therefore it must be cosmic. For if my being is rooted in ignorance, then I do not know who I am; and then naturally the exhortation, 'Know thyself', has meaning for me. But if this ignorance is subsequent to any existence, it cannot be the cause of my existence.

[1] See the author's *Idealistic Thought of India* (George Allen and Unwin Ltd, London, 1953), pp. 198 ff; for a discussion of Avidyā and *samskāra*, see H. Oldenberg, *Buddha* (Wilhelm Goldmann Verlag, Munchen, 1961), pp. 223 ff.

Thus this ignorance is the cause not only of my future births, but also of the past ones, right from the very beginning of the formation of my individuality, which, according to the Buddhists, is due to ignorance.

The word *samskāras* in Sanskrit covers a wide variety of meanings. It means habits and tendencies produced by actions, impressions left by all experiences, and instincts, impulses and drives inborn with us. For instance, why do mothers love their young ones? Their love is due to *samskāra*. When we see a red rose, why do all of us see it red? The answer is: 'Due to *samskāra*.' Why do you remember an object? Because it left a *samskāra*. Because of the variety of meanings we should understand the word *samskāra* in the above doctrine as meaning the inner drives out of which our initial conscious individuality is born.

The word *vijñāna* means consciousness in Buddhist terminology. But here it means the conscious seed of individuality. The individual is a combination of body and mind, but it is a conscious combination. When I say: 'I am six feet tall', there is the conscious I and its identification with the six-foot-tall body. The Buddhists thought that, before this identification comes into existence, there must have been a seed of consciousness out of which the mind and the body grew.

3. The third truth is called the truth of the cessation of suffering (*nirodhasatya*). As everything has a cause, and is therefore the effect of the cause, the effect can be destroyed if the cause is destroyed. And so misery, i.e. old age, disease, and death can be destroyed, if its cause, ignorance, is destroyed. Destruction here means stopping the functions of the cause. The functions of ignorance can be stopped, if instead of ignorance, we have its opposite, knowledge of the truth. And this has to be done by stopping the functions of the causes from the first of the twelve links. For stopping old age, etc. one should control rebirth; for checking rebirth, one should destroy the tendency to be born and so on till ignorance itself is conquered.

4. The fourth truth is called the truth of the way (*mārgasatya*). Checking the causation of misery is not a physical process, but an ethical one. This process or the Way consists of eight parts.

a. Since ignorance has to be conquered, one should have right knowledge and right views (*samyagdṛṣṭi*). Right knowledge includes the knowledge of the four noble truths also.

b. One should make the right resolve (*samyaksaṇkalpa*). One should make up one's mind that he should follow only truth and so whatever such following implies.

c. This resolve then should express itself in right speech (*samyagvāk*) Lies, slander, harshness, and frivolity in talking should be avoided.

d. Then one should follow the rules of right conduct (*samyakkarma*). One should not destroy life, steal, and indulge in sense gratification

e. One should choose the right type of livelihood (*samyagjīva*). For instance, one should not take to gambling and the like for earning one's livelihood.

f. One should always make the right effort to overcome evil tendencies (*samyagvyāyāma*). Although one makes the resolve to do only good and avoid evil, there will be old tendencies and new temptations. In every case, he should make the right effort to overcome evil.

g. One should be constantly vigilant about evil tendencies and temptations and keep always before his mind the goal he set before himself. This is called right-mindfulness (*samyaksmṛti*). This is important, because very often temptation overpowers us and we either forget our goals and resolves or invent some reasons for breaking our vows.

h. And one should practice the right kind of concentration (*samyaksamādhi*). The ability to concentrate increases as one succeeds more and more in purifying his mind through the above seven practices. The ultimate aim of this concentration is attaining *Nirvāṇa* or absolute placidity of being. And when it is attained, there is no movement towards birth and so towards old age, disease and death.

PHILOSOPHICAL IMPLICATIONS

Buddha's teachings were very simple, addressed to ordinary folk. And since they were not absolutely new in the atmosphere of the philosophical ideas current at the time, but more incisively and clearly put, his listeners accepted them without much difficulty and became his disciples. But later when they and their followers began thinking about them and had to define, explain and defend them in controversies with the followers of the rival schools, the Buddhists were obliged to work out the implications of these four simple truths and formulate them into doctrines. And the doctrines so developed were not all common to all the schools. In this section we shall mention only the common doctrines; and we then discuss some of the important ones on which the schools differed from one another in the following sections.

1. *The Doctrine of Karma.* We have already said that this doctrine is accepted by all the Indian schools except the Cārvākas. We perform actions to obtain pleasures, and we have to be born to enjoy them. But birth means again old age, disease, and death, and so misery. Action, therefore, strengthens the tendency to be born and prolongs misery. The wise man should, therefore, rise above action and obtain Nirvāṇa.

2. *The Doctrine of Momentariness.* Existence in this world is continuous birth, decay and death. The world is a constant flow. The Buddhists developed this idea into the doctrine of the momentariness of all existence. Everything is continually changing, nothing exists even for a moment. Every event is born, stays, and dies in the same moment, according to many Buddhists. Birth, stay, and death are not three moments, but only one. Continuity is only an appearance, not the truth. Every momentary existence leaves its impress (form, *samskāra*, *vāsanā*) in the next, that in its next, and so on. So long as the same form continues, we think that it is the same thing. But in fact, it is only the form that is the same, the being or existence of the thing is different from moment to moment. In Indian philosophy, we should note, there is no difference between Being and existence. Each momentary being of a thing is similar to the preceding and succeeding, because of the transmitted form. When the form itself goes, we say the thing is destroyed.

3. *The Doctrine of the No-Ātman.* Buddha's refusal to answer the question whether the *ātman* existed or not was taken by his followers as his denial of its existence. And to this interpretation the doctrine of momentariness gave additional support. If being itself is momentary, and if the *ātman* has being, i.e. if the *ātman* exists, then it must also be momentary. But those philosophers who defended the reality of the *ātman* did not merely think that it existed only for sometime; they thought that it was eternal. Any eternal being was impossible according

to the doctrine of momentariness. So the Buddhists denied completely any reality of the *ātman*.

But does not every man say that he has an *ātman*, which speaks of itself as the 'I'? The 'I' is not the *ātman*. It is simply the unity of several aggregates that appears as the 'I' and is mistaken to be the *ātman*. On proper analysis the *ātman* shows itself not as a distinct entity, but as an aggregate of five aggregates (*skandhas*).[2] (i) First, there is the aggregate of the physical body, which produces the form (*rūpa*) of the body. This is called the aggregate of form (*rūpaskandha*). (ii) The second is the aggregate of feelings (*vedanāskandha*), consisting of pleasures, pains, sensations, and other kinds of feelings. (iii) The aggregate of ideas (*samjñāskandha*) consists of our perceptions, concepts, and so on. (iv) The aggregate of impressions (*samskāraskandha*) consists of instincts, tendencies, urges, etc., which are both inborn and acquired. (v) Then there is the aggregate of momentary consciousnesses (*vijñānaskandha*), which is a flow or series. If we analyse ourselves, we find only these five aggregates, and we do not find anything beyond them that can be called the *ātman*. Each part of the aggregation is only a momentary existence. Nirvāṇa lies in going beyond this momentariness.

4. *The Doctrine of No-God.* Since the existence of the *ātman* cannot be proved, we cannot prove also the existence of God. If we analyse the world and the nature of our own being, we do not find God anywhere. Nor is it useful to discuss the question how the world is created or whether it is eternal. We have only to realize that the world is a place of misery, and try to get over misery.

5. *The Doctrine of Relative Existence.* Just as what we call the *ātman* has no nature of its own (*nairātmyam*), but is only a unity dependent on the five aggregates, nothing that exists has its own nature, but is dependent on something else. Every momentary being comes into existence, depending upon its preceding momentary being. If the seed, the earth, and water were not there, there would be no tree. So the tree can have no absolute existence of its own, it can have only a relative and dependent existence. Everthing in the universe is, therefore, relative. Nothing has its own nature (*svabhāva*). By itself

[2] *Idealistic Thought of India*, pp. 212 ff.

everything is neither being nor non-being. It is simply *śūnya* (emptiness). This doctrine is called the doctrine of no-own-nature or that of pure relativity.

6. *The Doctrine of Causation.* The Buddhist doctrine of causation has two aspects.[3] (i) Causation is aggregation. Everything we see in the world is an aggregate. It comes into being when the aggregate is formed, and goes out of existence, when the aggregate is destroyed. (ii) Everything comes into being, depending on something else that went out of existence. This is called the doctrine of dependent origination (*pratītyasamutpāda*). Everything is momentary, and so the cause also is momentary. It does not continue in the effect, because, being momentary, it cannot do so. It perishes before the effect is born. But the effect cannot be born without a cause; otherwise, everything must be able to originate out of everthing. So the effect depends on the cause, which only occasions the effect, but does not produce it. The cause is only an occasioning agent, and has nothing more to do with the effect. From the side of the cause, we should say that *causation is only occasionalism*. From the side of the effect, *it is dependent or referential origination*, because the effect originates only with reference to a particular cause.

So with reference to the nature of the world, the metaphysical doctrines of the Buddhists may be summarized thus: (i) Everything is painful; (ii) Everything is momentary; (iii) Everything is without its own nature, or without any *ātman* (self); (iv) Everything is *śūnya* (emptiness), because everything can be analysed away into the others; (v) Everything comes into existence dependent upon something else that precedes it and which is called the cause; and (vi) everything is unique, i.e. itself but without any essential nature.

THE MAIN SCHOOLS OF BUDDHISM

The schools of Buddhism are too many to be discussed in this section. Only a few important ones will be presented here. The first main division is between the Hīnayāna and the Mahāyāna. The Theravāda is one of the main schools of the former, but does not include the Andhakas, who belong to the Hīnayāna thought and whose views are given below.

[3] *Idealistic Thought of India*, pp. 199 ff. See Index also.

The new ideas, which the Mahāyāna introduced are mainly four.

1. The Hīnayāna was more or less a kind of pluralistic metaphysics, accepting a plurality of realities, without making an attempt to unify all of them. But the Mahāyāna was predominantly monistic equating Nirvāṇa, Śūnya (Emptiness) and Vijñāna (consciousness) and the three again to the ultimate Reality. The Mahāyāna schools differed from one another in the emphasis they gave to Śūnya (Emptiness) and Vijñāna (consciousness). One comes across the three concepts in the Hīnayāna writings also, but the tendency to treat them as metaphysical realities is not strong.

2. The ideal in the Hīnayāna is for every man to struggle for his own salvation, i.e. to become an *arhat* (the deserving). But the ideal in Mahāyāna is to become a *bodhisattva* (one whose being is enlightenment, or knowledge itself). Now, the *bodhisattva*, after attaining enlightenment, does not enter Nirvaṇa, but works for the salvation of the other human beings. He would choose to take many more future lives and undergo the miseries of old age, disease and death, if he could thereby help other people working for enlightenment and salvation. And the altruistic spirit of giving away everything one has to others and living for their sake was emphasized in its most excessive and extravagant forms by the Mahāyāna, which, therefore, calls Hīnayāna by the name Khadgayāna, meaning the vehicle of the rhinoceros (*khadga*), because the rhinoceros roams alone in the forests.

3. The Hīnayānists believed that it was not given for everyone to become a Buddha. Only Gautama, the son of Māyādevī and Śuddhodhana, would be Buddha. All the others could only be *arhats*. But the Mahāyānists maintained that everyone who strived for it could obtain enlightenment (*bodhi*) and so could become Buddha (the enlightened one). One could see here the influence of the Upaniṣadic doctrine that everyone can become the Brahman, which is Being, Consciousness, and Bliss (*sat-cit-ānanda*).

4. The Hīnayānists thought of Buddha as only a historical person, who taught a noble doctrine. But by the time of the Mahāyāna, docetism grew among the Hīnayānists themselves. A school called the Lokottaravādins maintained that the body of Buddha was supramundane, and that made of flesh and blood was not Buddha's real body. The Mahāsaṅghikas held that Buddha's body pervaded all directions, and the apparent body was not the real body. The Mahāyāna took over these ideas and developed them further, Buddha had several

bodies. There is the physical body born to his parents. Then there is the body of doctrine (*dharmakāya*), which he taught to his followers. But essentially his body is identical with all reality, and that is his true body. Buddha is essentially Nirvāṇa, Śūnya, Vijñāna. This doctrine gave support to their view that everyone could become Buddha, because everyone could attain the same Nirvāṇa.

1. *The Sautrāntikas*

The Theravāda need not be given a separate treatment in a small book, as it stuck to the four truths of Buddha as such and disagreed with the other Hīnayāna schools.[4]

The Sautrāntikas belonged to the Hīnayāna branch of Buddhism, and derived their name from their claim that they followed the original *sūtras* of the Buddhist scriptures, but not their commentaries. They are a branch of a wider school called Sarvāstivādins (those who hold the doctrine that everything exists). That is, the school of Sarvāstivādins is a branch of Hīnayāna, and the Sautrāntikas are a branch of the Sarvāstivādins. Some of the Sarvāstivādins seemed to have held that eternal atoms existed. But such a doctrine conflicts with the main doctrine of momentariness and is not considered to be orthodox by the other Buddhists. Now, existence also is Being (*sattā*) as opposed to the doctrine of mere flow (change, Becoming, *samsāra*), and, therefore, even the doctrine that everything has existence (*sattā*, *astitā*) was not considered to be in accordance with the original Buddhist teachings.

The Sautrāntikas maintained that, although everything existed and was real, it could not be directly perceived, but inferred. What could be directly perceived were the sensations, ideas, etc., but the real objects were behind them and their existence had to be inferred. Their doctrine of perception is called the representative theory. That is, the ideas we get of objects, when we perceive them, represent them.

2. *The Vaibhāṣikas*

The Vaibhāṣikas also are a branch of the Sarvāstivādins, and derive their name from their claim to follow the commentaries (*vibhāṣās*).

[4] It should be noted, however, that the other Hīnayāna schools claim to be branches of Theravāda and to be equally orthodox. Even the Mahāyāna claims to teach the original gospel of Buddha.

They differ from the Sautrāntikas mainly by asserting that the objects are perceived directly, but not inferred. They uphold the doctrine of direct perception or the presentative theory of perception.

3. *The Andhakas*

The Andhakas constituted an interesting school of Hīnayāna Buddhism, and seem to have contributed much of the growth of the Mahāyāna. It is also said that the *Prajñāpāramitās*, the basic scripture of the Mahāyāna school, was originally composed by the Andhakas. They were bold, original thinkers who attempted to break through the limitations of the early doctrines.

They held (i) that everything, including the physical body, was only mind. It exists when we are mindful of it; otherwise, it is not there. (ii) Secondly, they maintained that, because they were able to continue meditation for a long time, consciousness, as a single state, lasted for a long time. This doctrine violated the original principle, that everything, including consciousness (*vijñāna*), is only momentary. And (iii) they maintained that Nirvāṇa was one of the inborn instincts (*samskāras*) themselves, because it was realizable as being eternally present within us; and the desire to attain Nirvāṇa was an inward pull present in every human being, although appearing only at times as the desire for calm and quietness.

Through these three doctrines, the Andhakas were paving a way for the later appearance of Buddhist idealism and absolutism. If Nirvāṇa is attained through meditation (*dhyāna*), which is conscious, then Nirvāṇa must be conscious. It is placid, unagitated consciousness. And if consciousness can continue for a long time in meditation till it is disturbed, since there is no disturbance in Nirvāṇa, it must be everlasting, undisturbed consciousness (*vijñāna*). Since Nirvāṇa is also an instinct, it always acts on man as an inward pull, as attraction towards itself. And since the body also is mind, everything in the world, appearing as an object is mind only. The Andhakas did not develop the implications of their doctrines; they were developed by later Buddhists.

4. *The Vijñānavādins*

The Vijñānavādins are also called Yogācāras, because they emphasized the importance of Yogic meditation. The Chan and the Zen Buddhism of China and Japan is an offshoot of the Vijñānavāda school. It is a branch of the Mahāyāna.

The founder of the Vijñānavāda school is said to be Maitreyanātha, who belonged to the first century AD. But the greatest exponents of this school were the two brothers, Asaṅga and Vasubandhu, of the fourth century, AD.

Metaphysics. The Vijñānavādins[5] contend that, since Nirvāṇa is the highest happiness without any misery, it must be a conscious state, because without consciousness happiness cannot be experienced. But this state of consciousness (Vijñāna) is without any determination. And it is its indeterminateness that is called Śūnya (Emptiness). Again, although this Vijñāna is something to be attained by man, it is the source of everything determinate. Everything determinate is only a transformation (*pariṇāma*) of this original consciousness (Vijñāna). This Vijñāna, therefore, is the Absolute. Thus by saying that the Absolute is Vijñāna (consciousness), the Vijñānavādins turned Buddhism into Vedānta. But is this Absolute Consciousness eternal? The Vijñānavādins did not like to give a straight answer to the question, and they were not unanimous in their replies. Now, eternity means that the entity concerned lasts forever; it means endless time. But time belongs to Being and there is no Being, according to the Buddhists, without Non-being. Being and Non-being are determinations. But the Absolute Consciousness is beyond all determinations. And so with reference to it, the question has no meaning. But a few of the Vijñānavādins said that the Absolute Consciousness also was momentary. But its moment is not a moment in time, but an eternal moment that has no end. The view that it is not momentary also seems to have been accepted by some Vijñānavādins.

Now, if the Absolute Consciousness is the only reality, what makes it undergo transformation and become the plurality of objects? And if it undergoes transformation, is a part or the whole of it exhausted in the process? The Vijñānavādins said that the transformation was not real; it was only Māyā, like a dream. We think that this world is real;

[5] For the philosophy of Vijñānavāda, see Asaṅga, *Mahāyānasūtrālaṅkāra*, ed. by Sylvain Levi (Librarie Honore Champion, Paris, 1907); Vasubandhu, *Trimsikavijñapti*, ed. by Hermann Jacobi (W. Kohlhammer, Stuttgart, 1932); G. N. Jha: *Tattvasaṁgraha of Śāntarakṣita* (Oriental Institute, Baroda, 1937–9).

but it is only a creation of Māyā or Avidyā, the principle of the Unconscious in us, which creates not only our own finite being, but also the objects around us. At this point, the Buddhists took over the Upaniṣadic ideas of Māyā (illusion) and Avidyā (the Unconscious, Ignorance, Nescience) and developed them. Our ignorance of the original truth is due to our being rooted in the principle of the Unconscious.

Epistemology. The Vijñānavādins developed an epistemology that accorded with their metaphysics. They accepted perception and inference as the valid sources of knowledge, but added that the ultimate truth, viz. the Absolute Consciousness, can be directly known only by intuition, because mere reason, which is used in inference, always ends up in self-contradictions and cannot take a decision upon the existence of the absolute truth (*paramārthasatya*).

Regarding the question of the validity of knowledge, the Vijñānavādins maintain that ultimately both perception and inference, in fact all cognitions of external objects, are false. All cognition of external objects is false, because there are no external objects, only Vijñāna (consciousness) is real. Through Māyā or Avidyā, this Vijñāna takes on the form of external objects, and we see them not as forms of Vijñāna – which they really are – but as different from Vijñāna. So taking the classical Indian example of illusion, the rope seen as a snake, the cognition of the snake is of course false, but the later cognition of the rope as rope also is false. So not only what we regard as false cognition, but also what we regard as true cognition, which reveals the falsity of the first cognition, is false. Thus every cognition is false by itself (*svatah aprāmāṇyam*). But a cognition may be made true by the pragmatic criterion. That is, if the object of cognition serves the purpose for which it is meant (*arthakriyākāritā*), then it is made true. Thus a cognition is made true not by itself, but by a non-cognitive process (*paratah prāmāṇyam*), i.e. by action.

It should be remembered that for all the Indian schools, the world is a world of action. A few schools, like the Vijñānavādins, maintained that the world is false. Even then the world is true for action (*karma*). These schools say that, although the world is false, since it is a world meant for action, its truth lies in its instrumentality for activity. So the cognition of every object in the world, although false by itself, is made true by the activity which it serves. But those schools also that maintain that the world is real, regard the world as a world of action; so generally they say not that action *makes* a cognition true, but it *confirms* the truth of that cognition.

The criterion of empirical truth for the Vijñānavādins is therefore that of serving the purpose for which the object of cognition is meant (*arthakriyārkāritā*). But this criterion is meant only for mundane truth, which is not the ultimate truth (*pāramārthasatya*). This truth is known not by ordinary cognition at all, but by supra-rational intuition. Such intuition is valid by itself. It is not even possible to contradict it, because at that stage there can be no other cognition. There reality is without a second (*advaya*), without the distinction between subject and object, of Being and Non-being, and of subject and predicate.

Regarding the status of the object of illusion, the Vijñānavādins maintain that it is only the mind of the subject itself (*ātmakhyāti*). Mind takes the form of the snake. Here the word *ātman* in *ātmakhyāti* should not be mistaken for the *ātman* of the Vedānta. *Ātmakhyāti* means self-cognition, the self here standing for the subject. The subject projects itself as the snake of the above example and cognizes it. Indeed, according to the Vijñānavādins, every object and the finite subject are projections of the original Vijñāna. Usually we think that the rope is perceived as the snake; so the rope is the substratum, or locus, of the snake. Now, the Vijñānavādins say that both the rope and the snake are false. If so, what is the substratum of this illusion? What is it that is mistaken as the rope and also as the snake? The Vijñānavādins reply that it is the mind of the subject of the cognitions.

5. *The Mādhyamikas*

Like the Vijñānavādins, the Mādhyamikas form one of the two most important schools of the Mahāyāna Buddhism. And they showed greater logical and dialectical powers than the Vijñānavādins. Nagārjuna, the founder of the Mādhyamika school, lived perhaps a little later than Maitreyanātha and is assigned to the second century AD. Of his works, the *Mādhyamikakārikās*[6] is the most important, in which he showed a dialectical skill not surpassed even today by anyone in the world and he became the source of inspiration to the dialecticians of all the other schools in India. And one may even say that the shock of contradictions which Zen Buddhism developed in China and Japan

[6] Published by Commissionaires de l'Académie Imperiale des Sciences, St Petersburg, 1903 (ed. by Louis de la Vallée Poussin).

had its source in Nāgārjuna's dialectic, which for the first time in the history of world's philosophy tried to show the self-contradictory nature of every concept and doctrine about reality.

Metaphysics. The aim of Nagārjuna is to show that nothing positive or negative can be asserted of reality. It is therefore Śūnya (Vacuity, Emptiness). Even to think of it as Śūnya is a mistake, because the concepts, vacuity and emptiness, are understood with reference to fullness. Then there will be two opposites, vacuity and fullness; but the Śūnya is beyond all opposites, as, otherwise, it cannot be Nirvāṇa and the goal of life; and so reality should not be called by the name Śūnya also. Yet, we call it Śūnya, because we have to denote it, not connote it, by some word.

But Nagārjuna's dialectic goes deeper, and the linguistic analysts can find much that interests them in it.[7] Let us take vacuity. What is vacuous is something devoid of everything. Is vacuity devoid of space also? If it is not devoid of space, it is not vacuous. If it is devoid of space, then it contains a reference to space, in fact, a reference to all the things of which it is devoid. That means, it contains this reference. Then how can it be vacuous?

Let us take another instance. We speak of causes and effects. The cause is that which produces the effect, and the effect that which is produced by a cause. Let us call the cause A and the effect B. Now A is the cause that produces the effect B. But A is called the cause only with reference to B. Then it is B that is the cause for A being the cause. B causes A's being the cause. Then the effect becomes the cause of the cause. So causality is a self-contradictory concept, in which the cause becomes the effect and the effect the cause. Furthermore, how can A be the cause before B is produced? It is only with reference to B that A is the cause. But B is not there when A begins to act. If B is already there, then A does not have to produce B. And suppose B is already there, but somehow A produces it, then it is B that causes A to take on productive activity and to become the cause.

Nagārjuna took up all the concepts and doctrines of rival schools and exposed their self-contradictory nature. He did not spare even the Buddhist doctrines like that of momentariness and even the idea of Buddha himself, and showed that all were self-contradictory and false. Nothing determinate could be true and could express the nature of

[7] See *Idealistic Thought of India*, pp. 242 ff.

reality. Reality is unique, and even the concept of uniqueness is not applicable to it, because uniqueness can be understood only with reference to the non-unique. One can see here the influence of the Upaniṣadic doctrine that reality is 'not this and not that (*neti*, *neti*)'. It is beyond concepts, and beyond speech also, if speech represents concept. But we should note that, although Nagārjuna might have been influenced by the Upaniṣadic idea, it goes to his credit that he was the first to have logically worked out the idea. And his dialectic was later adopted by the Vedāntins themselves.

It was, again, Nagārjuna who first enunciated and worked out the doctrine that the world was never born and is not there (*ajātivāda*), which also was later adopted by some of the Advaita Vedāntins. If everything is false and unreal, am I unreal? Is the pen I am writing with unreal? Nagārjuna says that I am not, nothing is. The world was not, is not, and will not be there. There is no question of the world of action even, because action, like all the other concepts, is self-contradictory and, therefore, false. All is Śūnya, Nirvāṇa.

Then, is there any difference between the Śūnya and the false world we experience? Truth must be different from falsity; then the Śūnya, which is truth, must be different, from this world, which is falsity. Nagārjuna says that the two cannot be different. If they are different, we have to think of two entities; but there are no two entities, all is one. Then is the Śūnya the same as this world? How can they be the same? What is denoted by the word Śūnya is beyond all self-contradictions, but the world is full of contradictions. The two cannot, therefore, be the same. Then one may ask Nagārjuna: 'How am I to understand you?' He will say: 'Leave out understanding, which deals with concepts only.' The Śūnya can be experienced here and now, in this world itself; but it is not this world. It is neither identical with the world, nor different from it, nor both identical and different, nor neither identical nor different.

Thus Nagārjuna ended with the principle of the above four-cornered negation, which, although present in the *Prajñāpāramitā* literature and used by the Vijñānavādins also, was made to play a conspicuous role in the Mādhyamika philosophy. The four-cornered negation became the definition of Śūnya and also Māyā. The Śūnya is what is neither Being, nor Non-being, nor both, nor neither. And Māyā also acquired the same definition. Māyā is a power that makes us see a non-existent object as a real object, i.e. the snake. The world is not an illusion like the snake is illusion. But its metaphysical status is the same, because reality is the Śūnya and it appears as the world including myself. It lasts so long as I do not realize that I am the Śūnya, the Nirvāṇa. What appears as me and my world is Māyā and what disappears when I become the Śūnya is also Māyā. But Māyā is the same as the Śūnya, because I and the world are the appearances of the Śūnya itself.

Nagārjuna does not like to call the Śūnya by the name Vijñāna (consciousness), because to call the Śūnya conscious is to characterize it, but the Śūnya is without any characteristic.

Nagārjuna was called a nihilist by his rivals, both orthodox and heterodox, but wrongly. He repeatedly pointed out that the Śūnya was neither negative nor positive, neither Being nor Non-Being. The Śūnya is not Nothingness. Because he rejected both the alternatives, he called himself a Mādhyamika or Middlepather. Besides, the concept of Śūnya is not without value, it is the source of infinite possibilities. If it is determinate, it will be the source only a limited number of possibilities. Its value can be understood when we apply the idea to arithmetic. Śūnya means the zero also. But is the zero negative? For instance, we have negative and positive numbers.

$$\ldots -5, -4, -3, -2, -1, 0, 1, 2, 3, 4, 5, \ldots$$

The zero stands between 1 and −1. Is the zero itself positive or negative? It is neither, Nagārjuna would say. Yet we cannot say that it has no value. It makes the infinite series of positive numbers and an equally infinite series of negative numbers possible. Similarly, the Śūnya in Nagārjuna's philosophy makes the infinite number of negations or negative characterizations of the world and the equally infinite number of affirmations or positive characterizations possible. It is significant that the word Śūnya is used to mean zero, and it is equally significant that the word *pūrṇa* (fullness) is also used to mean the same number. The *Īśavāsya Upaniṣad* used the word *pūrṇa* to mean the infinite, and says that, if we deduct the infinite from the infinite, the remainder is again the infinite.

Epistemology. Although for empirical purposes, Nagārjuna accepted perception and inference as valid sources of knowledge, he rejected them as sources of the knowledge of ultimate truth (*pāramārthikasatya*).

There is no question of *knowing*, but only of *being* the ultimate truth. The fire of his dialectic burnt out perception and inference also along with the other concepts and doctrines.

Regarding the validity of knowledge, Nagārjuna would say that all knowledge is by itself false, because it presents an object, which is not really there at all. All objectivity is false. But we should not conclude that subjectivity is, therefore, true. There is no subject without an object, and so subjectivity also is equally false. To say: 'I exist' is also false, because to know myself as the 'I' is to know myself as an object, but the 'I' is never known. Even the Vijñāna of the Vijñānavādins is false. They say that Vijñāna (consciousness) knows the blissful state of the Nirvāṇa as having no determinations. But how can the Nirvāṇa, which is the Śūnya, be an object of consciousness? If it is, there will be a subject and an object also in Nirvāṇa. Then it will not be Nirvāṇa, which ought to be without distinctions and without any disturbance by activity. So we cannot characterize it as consciousness. We cannot even characterize it as a blind existence like stones, because to do so also would be a characterization. Thus Nāgārjuna carried the idea of indeterminacy to its most logical extreme.

Then why do we call some cognitions true and others false? Nagārjuna gives the same answer as the Vijñānavādins. He also distinguishes between absolute truth (*pāramārthikasatya*) and empirical truth (*samvṛtisatya*). Empirical truth is that which serves the purpose for which it is meant. So action, which is not the same as cognition, makes some cognitions true; but these cognitions are true only within the world of action.

Regarding the status of the object of illusion, Nagārjuna differs from the Vijñānavādins. He says that the snake in the classical example is only a form of the Śūnya, but not a form of the mind of the subject of cognition. Nagārjuna's doctrine is, therefore, called *śūnyakhyāti* (cognition of the *Śūnya*). It is the Śūnya that appears as the objects, both true and false. After all, the Śūnya is not Nothingness. But should not illusion have a definite substratum, or locus? We think that it is the rope that appears as the snake, but not the Śūnya. Must not falsity have a definite substratum that is true? Nagārjuna replies: 'Why should falsity have a substratum? Why should one thing appear as another in falsity?' In hallucinations and dreams, we see false objects as existing and there are no real objects there that are mistaken for false objects. If one is particular about having a substratum, then the

Śūnya itself is the substratum. But it is not necessary to have a substratum. And the definition of the Śūnya and Māyā holds good for the snake. It is not an existent object. Yet it is not an object of our imagination, because an imagined object does not frighten us, whereas the snake frightens us; we do not imagine it, but perceive it. Therefore it is not non-existent. But it cannot be both existent and non-existent also, because 'existent' and 'non-existent' are contradictory attributes and cannot be true of the same object. Yet it cannot be neither existent nor non-existent, because these are the only two alternatives and there cannot be a third. Hence, the snake of illusion is neither existent, nor non-existent, nor both, nor neither. This four-cornered negation is exactly the definition of Māyā and Śūnya, and was taken over later by the Advaita Vedāntins.

NATURE AND AIM OF LIFE

The Hīnayāna thought of man as an aggregate of the five aggregates, unified and made into a person, living in a world of constant becoming and action. It accepted that the original soruce of man's existence was Avidyā (Ignorance, Unconsciousness), which the Hīnayāna must have conceived as cosmic, but did not raise it to the status of a metaphysical reality. It was concerned with rising above pure Becoming, but what man would be when he succeeded in this was considered by the Hīnayāna to be an unanswerable question.

But the Mahāyāna went further and introduced the idea of an ultimate reality, which transformed itself into the world of becoming. But it would not say – only Asaṅga indeed said it – that what so transformed itself was pure Being, because, according to all Buddhism, Being is included in Becoming. Becoming is the combination of Being and Non-being; it is the process of Being changing into Non-being, and Non-being into Being. So if the highest reality is Being, it cannot be above Becoming. Still, there was the highest reality, which is the ground of man's being and with which he can become one and transcend the world of Becoming.

The aim of life is of course to transcend the world of Becoming, which is misery. We have already referred to the self-centred ideal of the Hīnayāna, which taught that every man should seek his own enlightenment and salvation, and to the *bodhisattva* ideal of the Mahāyāna, which taught that man, after obtaining enlightenment, should live as long as possible for helping all other human beings to obtain enlightenment.

Buddhism seems to be the first to use the word *mārga* (way) as a philosophical principle, indeed as an ethical one. Man is a wayfarer from the world of Becoming to Nirvāṇa. Buddha himself taught the eightfold way; but since enlightenment (*bodhi*) was very heavily stressed, Buddhism gave, particularly in the Mahāyāna, the first place to the Way of Knowledge (*jñānamārga*). It seems that the Mahāyānists were the first to use the word *jñānamārga* in the specific meaning it acquired, as distinct, for instance, from *bhaktimārga* (the way of devotion or love). It should not be surprising also, because the basic scripture of the Mahāyānists was the *Prajñāpāramitās* (*The Other Shore or Apex or Knowledge or Wisdom*). These texts mkae knowledge the highest virtue. *Prajñā* means knowledge or wisdom and *pāramitā* means that which has gone to the end or reached its apex, and came to mean virtue in the language of the Buddhists.

But knowledge is not the only *pāramitā* or virtue, although the highest, according to the Mahāyāna. The *bodhisattva* should possess all the virtues carried to perfection in their logical extreme. The six main virtues are charity (*dāna*), character (*śīla*), patience (*kṣānti*, endurance), energy (*vīrya*), meditation (*dhyāna*), and knowledge (*prajñā*). These virtues become *pāramitās*, when their practice is carried to their logical extreme, without any conditions and reservations. For instance, in charity one should give away all that he has without any limit, his property, wife, children, and his life, when needed. Similarly, the *pāramitā* of knowledge consists in the realization that everything in the world is subject to the principle of four-cornered negation and that ultimate truth lies beyond all opposites. The life of the *bodhisattva* was surrounded by a sweetness and a softness, which in their extreme forms did not accord with the rough realities of the world. The Mahāyāna allowed the monks to marry and live like householders. And the Vijñānavāda school, by introducing the idea that Nirvāṇa, although indeterminate, was positive consciousness, brought with it the idea of a positive, merciful, conscious being supervising human life and giving it hope and promising help. Then the Buddhist way of life and its ideals were gradually absorbed by the orthodox schools, particularly the Vedānta.

Chapter VIII

THE LOGICAL TRADITION OF THE NYĀYA

INTRODUCTION

Gautama (about 400 BC).[1] was the founder of the logical tradition in India. It may be that there were others who developed logic earlier, for we come across words denoting logic in much earlier literature. But he seems to have been the first to have systematized logic and insisted that thinking and all argumentation should proceed according to well-fixed logical forms, and avoid all fallacies. Salvation is the primary aim of man, but we should know that it is a reality, not a false hope. We should, therefore, know the nature of reality as it is. But we should know also how we can know and what it is that we can know. Hence logic and epistemology were as important as metaphysics to Gautama, who must have developed his system of philosophy in order to check false, fallacious and sentimental debates, controversies, and dialectic, each involving many a false philosophy of life. Gautama lived about two hundred years after Buddha and Mahāvīra, the founders of Buddhism and Jainism, who attacked the orthodox Vedic philosophies simply from the side of logic and experience and completely denied the validity of scriptural authority. One may surmise, therefore, that Gautama developed his logic to counter these two philosophies on their own grounds, namely, logic and experience. The controversies between the Nyāya and Buddhism in particular are keen. And in reaction to the Nyāya, the followers of Jainism and Buddhism also competed in developing logic. The influence of Gautama, so far as logic and epistemology go, is very great and salutary on both the orthodox and heterodox systems. In fact, the Nyāya was regarded

[1] Gautama is assigned by some Western scholars to the third century AD – which of course precludes the possibility of any deliberate or unconscious borrowal of Indian logical ideas by Aristotle. But such a late date seems to be unreasonable. However, there is no evidence of borrowing either way.

as an essential subsidiary to the Veda even by many orthodox people.

Gautama expounded the Nyāya philosophy as a system for the first time in his *Nyāya Aphorisms* (*Nyāyasūtras*). A number of commentaries were written on them, and then several independent expositions. About the thirteenth century, Gautama's system came to be regarded as the Old Nyāya, and a new school called the New Nyāya was introduced by Gaṅgeśa and Raghunātha. The New Nyāya's greatest contribution is the fineness of its concepts and distinctions, and the great development of definition, so that books began to be written on subjects like 'The Definition of Definition', 'The Definition of the Determinant' and so on. The New Nyāya differed also from the old on metaphysical categorization, which is, on the whole, not regarded as a very important contribution. The metaphysics of the Nyāya in general became later identified with that of the Vaiśeṣika, and the two schools were combined and called the Nyāya-Vaiśeṣika. We shall study the metaphysics of the Nyāya when we study the Vaiśeṣika school.

EPISTEMOLOGY

The Nyāya and the Vaiśeṣika are thoroughly realistic, and believe in the existence of objects independent of mind and the *ātman*. Every entity that is the object of valid knowledge is real and has an existence independent of the processes of knowledge and the knower. And what is valid knowledge can be ascertained by the valid sources of knowledge. They are perception, inference, comparison,[2] and verbal testimony. Memory (*smṛti*), doubt (*samśaya*), error and illusion (*bhrama*) and *reductio ad absurdum* and conditional proof (*tarka*) including the counter-factual[3] are rejected as valid sources. The last two are rejected not because the object, the reality of which they prove, is necessarily

[2] The Nyāya view of comparison is different from that of the Mīmāmsā and has been given in the chapter on the latter.

[3] The main form of *tarka* is the counter-factual negative conditional and is commonly of the form 'Had x been not y, it would not have been z'. But other forms also are possible: 'Had x been y, it would not have been z'; 'Had x been not y, it would have been z'; and 'Had x been y, it would have been z'. It is such statements that are called *tarkas*. Their use lies in negating the consequent and negating the antecedent. Strictly speaking, *tarka* is not the *reductio ad absurdum* inference, it is not an inference but a statement, which of course can be used for the *reductio ad absurdum* argument. Note the difference from the Jaina conception of *tarka*.

unreal, but because they cannot prove the reality of what is previously unknown, but only of what is already known. Thus the so-called valid sources are really the valid unique sources.

If the mountain has no fire, it cannot have smoke; but it has smoke; therefore, it has fire. The *tarka* proves only what has already been known by the regular syllogism.[4] It proves: 'The mountain has fire,' along with 'Had there been no fire, there would not have been smoke' presupposes 'Wherever there is smoke, there is fire'. *Tarka* may be a help, but not a distinct source of knowledge giving new information. Likewise, memory is rejected not only because it is unreliable, but also because, even when it is true, it cannot give any new knowledge, but can only revive the knowledge of what is already known.

Approaching philosophy from the side of epistemology, Gautama distinguishes sixteen categories or topics which must be understood in order to obtain salvation. They are (1) the sources of knowledge (*pramāṇas*); (2) the objects of knowledge (*prameyas*); (3) doubt (*samśaya*); (4) end or purpose (*prayojana*); (5) example (*dṛṣṭānta*); (6) established doctrine (*siddhānta*); (7) the parts or constituents of the syllogism (*avayava*); (8) the indirect negative argument (*tarka*, counter-factual conditional); (9) determination of truth (*nirṇaya*) or what is meant by Q.E.D.; (10) debate earnestly carried for the ascertainment of truth (*vāda*); (11) mere wrangling for verbal victory (*jalpa*); (12) mere destructive criticism without a position of one's own (*vintaṇḍa*); (13) fallacies of the syllogism (*hetvābhāsas*); (14) ambiguity and equivocation (*chala*); (15) futile and pointless objection (*jāti*); and (16) points for admitting or pointing out defeat (*nigrahasthānas*).

The specific context in which these categories are important is that of two parties discussing the nature of reality and of salvation and trying to have victory over the other by any means, logical or illogical, and even by the use of pointless and irrelevant arguments. All such tendencies should be checked, if we are eager to obtain truth and not merely victory in debate.

It is not possible in an elementary work to devote a section to each of the sixteen categories, many of which can be easily understood by the student. The second category, the objects of valid knowledge,

[4] Wherever there is smoke, there is fire;
This mountain has smoke;
This mountain has fire.

reflects Gautama's chief concern; he names them: (1) *ātman*, (2) body, (3) senses, (4) objects of senses, (5) consciousness (*buddhi*), (6) mind (*manas*), (7) action (*karma*), (8) impurity (*doṣa*), (9) rebirth, (10) the fruit of action (*phala*), (11) pain (*duhkha*), and (12) liberation (*mokṣa*). A few need to be explained.

The Nyāya and the Vaiśeṣika do not understand *buddhi* as reason, as do the Sāṅkhya, Yoga and the Vedānta. It is only an adventitious consciousness that arises like a spark or light, when mind (*manas*) comes into contact with the *ātman*. Mind obtains impressions of the objects through the senses. Impurity (*doṣa*) is of three kinds – attachment, aversion, and ignorance. The fruit of actions are merit producing happiness and demerit producing pain. The *ātman* is by nature without pain and pleasure, and is even without consciousness. Liberation (salvation) lies in freeing oneself from everything including mind and becoming absolutely unconscious and, therefore, without any pain or pleasure.

Perception is the cognition resulting from the contact of senses and objects. According to the Nyāya, it is always of the form 'That is a pot'. It is cognition of the object as characterized by the universal 'pot-ness'. The action of mind (*manas*) is necessary for perceptual process. The eye sees the shape and colour; touch informs us about the hardness of the pot; the ear tells us of its sound. The mind collects all these impressions and carries them to the *ātman*. As soon as mind comes into contact with the *ātman*, consciounsess arises in the latter, and the object is known as 'That is a pot' or 'That is an object characterized by the universal potness'. For instantaneously collecting all the sense impressions together, mind (*manas*) must be atomic in size. An atom only can have infinite speed. If mind has any bigger size, it will take time for moving from one sense to another, and the simultaneity of all the sense impressions will be impossible. And unless all the sense-impressions are cognized together, the object as a single unitary entity cannot be grasped.

The Nyāya has a very elaborate theory of perception, and analyses it from different points of view. First, there is the difference between ordinary and extra-ordinary perception. Ordinary perception is what we usually have, the perception of a pot, a pen, a flower, and so on. But the Nyāya recognizes three kinds of extra-ordinary perceptions, which are not due to the usual sense-contact with the objects and which have each a peculiar kind of contact.

The first is called cognition obtained through contact with the universal (*sāmānyalakṣaṇa*). When I see a pot, my mind, through visual sense, comes into contact with the physical object pot, which is an individual. The perception of the pot is of the form, 'That is an object determined by the universal potness'. In this perception, the universal, potness, also is perceived by the sense, and mind comes into contact with that universal also. Now, through contact with this universal, mind knows the whole class of pots, and knows all the pots in general, because the universal is connected with all individuals. Similarly, we can know 'all men' by contact with them through the universal, man-ness. By knowing a single object, the Naiyāyikas say, we can know all objects of the class, but not certainly through sense contact with all individual objects. In perceiving 'all pots' the contact is first with the universal, potness, and then through it with all the individual pots only as forming a class. This kind of perception the Nyāya treats as perception, but not as inference; it explains how we come to know classes.

The second kind of extraordinary perception is cognition due to cognitive association. Looking at a pigeon, I say 'That is soft', even without touching it. But when I look at it, I see only its shape and colour; softness cannot be seen with the eye. Yet, we think that we are *seeing* softness. This kind of cognition is due to the association, in our mind, of the shape and colour of the bird with the soft touch. And as soon as the shape and colour are seen, the idea of softness also arises in our mind, and we tend to see it in the object. The cognitive association is a contact that is of a different kind from the ordinary sense contact, because here there is no sense-contact with softness.

The third kind of extra-ordinary perception is due to Yoga. A yogi can see even atoms without the aid of his senses. He can see objects hundreds and thousands of miles away, and can look through the minds and thoughts of others. This kind of perception has two stages. In the case of yogis who are not yet perfect but are on the way to perfection (*yuñjāna*), such perception needs the effort of concentration. But in the case of those who are perfect (*yukta*), no such effort is needed, and knowledge is constant and spontaneous. The cognition of both men needs no sense contact at all. Their mind can directly come into contact with the objects. Although it is atomic in size, it belongs to the *ātman*, which is infinite, and it can be present wherever the *ātman* is present. That is, being atomic in size, it needs no time interval at all to move from object to object and contact them simultaneously. Such cognition is called intuition.

Although the above analyses of perception are the important ones, it may be mentioned that the Nyāya drew a distinction between internal and external perception, calling both sense perception. For, the Nyāya treats mind as the sixth sense, along with the usual five senses. Of course, without mind, no knowledge can be obtained through any of the five senses, because mind has to convey each of the sense impressions to the *ātman* before any cognition can arise. But mind, as the sixth sense, has its own objects like desire (*icchā*), aversion (*dveṣa*), effort (*prayatna*), pleasure (*sukha*), pain (*duhkha*), and so forth. Since the mind also has its own special objects as the eye the colours, ear the sounds, nose smells and so on, it is called the sixth sense.

Induction[5] as a separate kind of inference is not recognized, although certain checks and methods have been both explicitly and implicitly recognized for obtaining the major premise. The classical Indian example of inference is of the form:

1 This mountain has fire;
2 because it has smoke;
3 wherever there is smoke, there is fire, just as in the kitchen,
4 this mountain also has smoke that is accompanied by fire;
5 ∴ this mountain has fire.

In this form also, we have the three terms: the major term, fire; the middle term, smoke; and the minor term, the mountain. But we have a fourth term also, the kitchen, supporting the major premise, 'Wherever there is smoke, there is fire'. The major term is called *sādhya* (that which is to be proved); the minor *pakṣha* (the subject about which we are going to prove something); and the middle is called *hetu* (or *sādhana*, the reason). The fourth term, the kitchen in the above syllogism is the example (*udāharaṇa* or *dṛṣṭānta*), which is given by Gautama as the fifth among his sixteen categories.

We have five propositions in the syllogism. The first is called the proposition (*pratijñā*), the statement or hypothesis asserted, that has to be proved. The second is called reason (*hetu*, *sādhana*). The third

[5] As the book is expected to be elementary, I am not discussing the epistemology and logic of the Nyāya in any detail. Interested readers may consult the books given in the note on 'Further Reading', p. 242 ff.

is called example (*dṛṣṭānta*, *udāharaṇa*). The Nyāya insists that the example (*dṛṣṭānta*) should be mentioned along with the major premise (*vyāpti*). The reason for giving this honour to example, and only a secondary place to the major premises, and also the reason for Gautama giving example a place of honour by mentioning it as one of the sixteen categories is twofold. *First*, people formulate imaginary and impossible major premises. And unless it is shown that the major premise holds good in at least one case, the inference is rejected as impossible. For instance,

All devils dance at midnight,
Now is midnight,
∴ The devils of this grave are dancing there now.

But who has seen a midnight in which the devils danced? Where is an acceptable example? Such an inference cannot be accepted. *Secondly*, logic is meant not for abstract reasoning, but to enable us to know the nature of existing things. If logic is inapplicable to reality, then it will be of no use, and we can argue forever both for and against any proposition, making all kinds of assumptions, which need not hold true of reality. If they are to hold true of reality, then there must be an example, to which the major premise is applicable. Of course, to give an example is not enough to make an inference true, as we shall see. But it is one of the necessary conditions for the truth of any inference. The example is insisted upon for avoiding impossible and imaginary inferences and for keeping before mind that logic is meant for application to reality; and its applicability is vouchsafed by example.

Induction is the process of obtaining the major premise (*vyāpti*) of the syllogism. The Indian logicians did not develop elaborate inductive methods like those of the western logicians of the modern period, but gave some and explained the processes.

The major premise expresses the concomitance of the middle and the major terms; that is, wherever the middle is found, the major also must be present. Then only will the major premise be valid. The Nyāya accepted two kinds of such relationship, the causal relationship and the species-genus relationship. Both relationships are universal and give rise to universal propositions, which can form major premises.

But how do we first strike upon a major premise? It expresses a relation not between individuals, but between classes of individuals.

When we say that fire causes smoke, we do not mean merely that this fire is the cause of this smoke, but that every smoke is caused by fire. This relation is expressed by the Naiyāyikas thus: Every object that is characterized by the universal, smoke-ness, is caused by an object that is determined by the universal, fire-ness. Such an expression may look clumsy in the English language; but fireness is the class character of all fires and smokeness is that of all smokes. Neither the class character, fire-ness, causes the class character, smoke-ness; nor the whole class of fires causes the whole class of smokes. If we are to be exact, in our expression – which the Naiyāyikas want to be – we have to say that every object that is characterized by smoke-ness is the effect of an object that is characterized by fireness.

But to know this universal proposition, we have to know the two universals, fire-ness and smoke-ness. The Nyāya says that we know them through contact with the universals themselves (*sāmānyalakṣaṇā pratyāsatti*) when we see the fire and smoke in the kitchen. There itself we establish a relationship between the two universals, the relationship of concomitance. It should not be misunderstood that we treat the two universals themselves as cause and effect, but only as concomitants. To say, 'Wherever smoke is found, fire also is present,' is only to say that smoke cannot exist without fire also being present there; it is not an assertion that fire causes smoke although it is true. Nor is it an assertion that the universal, fireness, causes the universal, smokeness. It asserts only a logical relationship or concomitance.

Thus through the peculiar sense-contact with the universals, fire-ness and smoke-ness, we establish a universal relation between the class of fires and the class of smokes, after seeing the instances of both in the kitchen. The Nyāya does not say that the relation is known after seeing a number of similar instances. One instance itself is enough, because even in a single instance we see the universals and through them know the classes, provided we have checks for determining which is the antecedent and which the consequent.

The Nyāya firmly believes in the doctrine of causation, which plays an important role in the doctrine of inference. It believes also in the possibility of obtaining true universal propositions. Cause is defined by the Nyāya as the necessary, unconditional antecedent, which is not 'otherwise established' (present or related as a condition). There are certain necessary, unconditional antecedents which are present even apart from a particular cause-effect relationship. For excluding them the last clause is added; which is, therefore, important. For instance, every event happens in space, and without being conditioned by space nothing can happen. So space is a necessary unconditional antecedent of everything. Yet it is not to be taken into consideration for determining any particular causation. Similarly, with regard to the principle that fire causes smoke, the fire may be made with a matchbox or borrowed from some other house as the primitives did. But the match-box and the other house do not enter the causal principle.

The cause, according to the Nyāya, is chiefly of three kinds: the inhering cause (*samavāyikāraṇa*), the non-inhering cause (*asamavāyikāraṇa*), and the efficient cause (*nimittakāraṇa*). Taking the example of the pot, the clay with which the potter makes the pot is the inhering cause. It is the material cause (also called *upādānakāraṇa*), the cause that constitutes an object. The relation of contact between the parts of the pot, which the potter brings together, is the non-inhering cause. It may also be called the relational cause. It is called non-inhering, because after the potter brings the parts together and joins them, the relation of contact is no longer available, and we have only one single unit, the pot. The potter himself is the efficient cause.

The Nyāya recognizes other factors of causation. The instrumental cause (*karaṇa*) is the cause that is active (*vyāparavat*). The clay with which the pot is made is not active in producing the effect. But the fire or spark by introducing which we explode gunpowder is an instrumental cause. Without fire, gunpowder cannot be exploded, and it is an indispensable instrumental cause for the effect of explosion. Then there is the directive cause (*prayojakakāraṇa*). If a man asks a goldsmith to make a particular kind of ornament for his wife, then that man is the directing cause. The final cause (*prayojanakāraṇa*) or purpose is the pleasure of the man's wife. But these three kinds of cause are not regarded as important factors of any causal process, although they are present in most of the causal processes involving human action. Unless we accept the position that the world-processes happen under the direction of God in order to enable man to enjoy the fruit of their good and evil actions, we cannot read all the six factors of causation into the impersonal physical causation. The Nyāya accepts such a position, but treats the first three as the primary factors of causation.

Chapter IX

THE PLURALISTIC TRADITION OF THE VAIŚEṢIKA

INTRODUCTION

The Vaiśeṣika tradition, started by Kaṇāda (about 400 BC), is pluralistic, realistic and theistic; it supplied metaphysical theories to the Nyāya and adopted its epistemological and logical theories. The two traditions differ from each other on very minor points, and in time became the hyphenated Nyāya-Vaiśeṣika school. Praśastapāda wrote a commentary on Kaṇāda's *Vaiśeṣika Aphorisms* (*Vaiśeṣikasūtras*) and called it *Padārtha-dharma-saṅgraha* (*Compilation of the Characteristics of the Categories*), which was further commented upon and expounded.

Just as the word *nyāya* means logic, the word *vaiśeṣika* means particularist. *Viśeṣas* are the particulars. One should be careful in translating this word and also in interpreting its meaning. Kaṇāda is accredited with the discovery of the particular (*viśeṣa*), for according to his philosophy all particulars are independent of one another, are infinite in number, and cannot be reduced to anything in common. The Vaiśeṣika philosophy is pluralistic and realistic.

METAPHYSICS

Just as Gautama claims that one who understands his sixteen categories will obtain salvation, Praśastapāda announces that one who understands his seven categories will obtain salvation. Gautama lays stress upon understanding and its methods, whereas Kaṇāda emphasizes the objects of that understanding. His categories are the categories of objects. The seven categories are: (1) substance (*dravya*); (2) quality (*guṇa*); (3) activity (*karma*); (4) universal (*sāmānya*); (5) particular (*viśeṣa*); (6) inherence (*samavāya*); and (7) negation (*abhāva*). The first six categories are positive and the seventh negative.

Substance is defined in two ways. First it is that in which qualities inhere. This is how substance is generally understood, it is the substrate (*ādhāra*) of qualities. Second, it is also defined as that which can come into the relation of contact (*saṁyoga*). It is only substances that come into contact, but not qualities etc. My pen, which is black in colour, can come into contact with my table, which is brown. The relation of contact can have effect on substances, but not upon qualities. We generally say that each substance has impact on the other. But qualities cannot have such impact on one another without the substances.

There are nine kinds of substances: earth, water, fire, air, ether, time, space, *ātman*, and mind (*manas*).

The Five Elements. Of the nine categories, the first five are called elements (*bhūtas*), and constitute the material world, and also the five senses. Earth possesses the property of smell and constitutes the corresponding sense, the nose. Water possesses the property of taste and constitutes the sense of taste. Fire possesses colours and constitutes the eye. To air are due the sense of touch and the qualities of touch. To ether are due the ear and sounds.

The Atomic Theory. Of the five elements – earth, water, fire, air, and ether – the first four only are perceivable. Ether is not perceivable at all. It must be inferred. Every sense-quality belongs, as a property, to a particular substance; sound also is a sense-quality; but it does not belong to the perceivable elements, earth, water, fire and air. So it must belong to a fifth substance, called ether. To be capable of being perceived, the object must have a limited and perceptible dimension, and also colour. Ether does not possess colour, nor has it a finite dimension. It cannot, therefore, be perceived. For the same reason, it is infinite and indivisible. Because colour was laid down as one of the conditions for being perceived, some followers of the Nyāya-Vaiśeṣika thought that air could not be perceived, since it had no colour. But others held that it was not colour, but sense-contact that was necessary for perception; for them air could be perceived, but not ether.

All the elements, except ether, are constituted of atoms (*aṇus*). Ether, being infinite and one, has no atoms. The atoms of the four elements have their specific qualities – the earth atoms have smell, the water atoms taste, the fire atoms colour, and the air atoms touch.

The atoms are indivisible, indestructable, eternal, and imperceptible, and have to be inferred. The yogis can perceive them through their extraordinary perception, but we have to infer their existence. Whatever is indivisible and, therefore, indestructable, is eternal. The atoms are indivisible, because, if they are further divisible, then they will have parts, and each part will then be again divisible. Then both a Himalaya mountain and a mustard-seed will equally be infinitely divisible. In that case, there will be no difference between the sizes of the two, because each can have the same number of parts, i.e. an infinite number of parts. So divisibility must stop somewhere, and that is the atom. We can then say that the Himalaya contains more atoms than the mustard-seed, and is therefore bigger.

But then the Vaiśeṣika reaches a difficult position, saying that the atom has no size. If they have size, they will be divisible. But they are not divisible. Two atoms come together and form a dyad. Even the dyad is not perceivable. Three dyads come together and form a triad. This triad is the minimum perceptible molecule. The Vaiśeṣika does not, and cannot explain how out of sizeless atoms, size can be created. It is as if we would get the number 1 by combining six zeros. This problem could not be solved.

Time and Space. Time (*kālā*) and space (*dik*) are two independent, eternal, indivisible, and all-pervading substances. Time is the cause of our knowledge of the distinction: past, present, and future. Similarly, space is the cause of our knowledge of distinctions like east, west, south, north, up, down, and so on. In reality, time and space are each a separate, single indivisible substance. But we draw the distinctions in them due to certain adventitious limiting conditions (*upādhis*), and think that the distinctions are parts.

Another definition of time is that it is the creator of everything that is born[1] and is the container of all the worlds.[2] This is a more dynamic definition than the earlier.

The Ātman. The *ātman* also is an eternal, all-pervading substance and is the substratum of the quality, consciousness. But this quality is not an essential and inseparable quality of the *ātman*; it is only inci-

[1] See *Dinakarī*, pp. 48–9 in *Kārikāvalī* with several commentaries (Chowkhamba Sanskrit Series, Benares, 1951).

[2] Viśvanātha, *Kārikāvalī* (Guzerati Printing Press, Bombay, 1923), p. 30.

dental and adventitious. The *ātman* by itself, without contact with mind, exists without consciousness. The *ātmans* constitute an infinite plurality, and every one of them is different from the others and also from God. The reality of the *ātman* is self-evident in all such experiences as 'I am', 'I know', 'I act', 'I am happy', and so on. The Nyāya-Vaiśeṣika produces the usual arguments also to establish the reality of the *ātman*. Desire, aversion, volition, knowing, ethical responsibility, etc. cannot be explained, if there is no *ātman*. It is not the body, senses, mind, and the stream of consciousness that can know, desire, and enjoy. Even the mind works for someone else, and that other is the *ātman*. Furthermore, they all need direction and guidance. I direct my body, senses, and mind in a particular way and I possess consciousness and I am conscious of my possessing consciousness. So I am different from all of them. And I am the *ātman*.

God. God is not specially mentioned as a category, but is regarded as one of the *ātmans*, although He is the Supreme Ātman (*paramātman*). While, for all the ordinary *ātmans*, consciousness is only an adventitious and transient quality, for God it is an inseparable quality. The *ātmans* obtain liberation after they are completely detached from consciousness, but God remains eternally conscious. He is omniscient, all-powerful and has all the perfections. He creates, sustains, and destroys the world and causes the cycles of creation and destruction. He does not create the world out of himself, but out of the eternal atoms, ether, time, space, and the *ātmans* that are not liberated, and their minds (*manas*). These substances do not in any way limit his omnipotence.

God is, therefore, not the material cause of the world, but its efficient cause. The material cause is eternal, and does not need to be created. Creation means the building up of the world out of the eternal entities, so that the result can be the field of action (*karma*) for the *ātmans*. In creating the world, God is guided by the accumulated merits and demerits of the *ātmans* that are not yet liberated. Thus what is created becomes a moral world meant for moral action. Destruction means reducing the world to atoms and the other original substances.

The Nyāya-Vaiśeṣika gives a number of arguments for the existence of God.

1. The first is the causal argument. The world is a combination of

atoms and of the eternal, infinite substances. It consists of things that are made up of parts, and they are of intermediate magnitude. That is, they are neither infinitesimal like the atoms, nor infinite like space, time, etc. Such things are compounds made up of parts. But every compound is an effect and needs a cause. And this cause must be intelligent, because it must direct the combinations according to fixed laws, and such a direction is possible, if the cause is intelligent. It must know also the ends which the compounds must serve. And it must be omniscient also, as, otherwise, it cannot bring together infinitesimals like atoms and infinites like time and space into relation with one another. And such a cause is God.

2. The second argument is based upon the principle of *karma*, or the principle of moral merit and demerit, which remain in the *ātmans* in an unseen potential form (*adṛṣṭa*). The world has to be created in order to enable the *ātmans* to work out their merit and demerit, which lies potentially in them, but unseen and unknown by them. Together, merit and demerit, it is said, form a kind of force.[3] But this force by itself is not an intelligent, even if a creative agent, and needs intelligent direction. The *ātmans* themselves do not know even its presence, nor will they like that their demerit should work out its consequences. An intelligent, impartial agent is needed to guide the processes of such an unseen force. Such an agent is God.

3. The third argument is based upon the authorship of the Vedas. The Vedas are absolutely true and authoritative. And they derive their truth and authoritativeness from God. who is their author. No one but God could have understood the nature of the seen and the unseen world, and also of the atomic and infinite substances, about which the Vedas impart knowledge.

4. The fourth argument is based upon the testimony of the Vedas. The Vedas teach only the truth and nothing but the truth. And they tell us that God exists. Therefore God exists.

Mind (*Manas*). Mind is a substance and, as mentioned already, atomic in size. This size is postulated in order to make it swift without lapse of time. That is, it can be present at the same instant at any two different places. But by nature, it is unconscious, and can produce consciousness in the *ātman* by coming into contact with it. It is also

[3] For the Mīmāmsā, merit and demerit constitute an unseen force; but for the Nyāya-Vaiśeṣika, they are only qualities.

the sixth sense, with its own special type of objects like pleasure, pain, and emotion.

Quality. Quality is defined as that which exists in substances through the relation of inherence (*samavāya*), and which itself does not have a quality or movement (*nirguṇa* and *niṣkriya*). Things come into contact when they move; but it is the substances that move, not their qualities. So qualities do not come into contact, but only substances. Further, qualities do not have qualities. The red colour of a rose may be pale; but 'pale' is not a quality (*guṇa*) of red, but its mode (*viśeṣaṇa*). Although we generally think that qualities can have qualities, the Nyāya-Vaiśeṣika thinks that what the qualities have are not qualities, but modes. Sound, for instance, may be loud or not loud, sweet or not sweet, high or low, harsh or soft, etc. But these differences are not called qualities, but modes, by this school.

The Nyāya-Vaiśeṣika enunciates another principle. The first three categories – substance, quality, and activity – have existence (*sattā*, being), but not the other four – inherence, universal, particular, and negation. Yet all the seven are real, and the Nyāya-Vaiśeṣika fights with its rival schools for establishing the reality of all the seven categories. This school had, therefore, to be interpreted as drawing a distinction between existence (*sattā*, being) and reality. In the chapter on the Nyāya, we have noticed that everything that is an object of true cognition is real. The negation of the rose on my table is real, because the proposition, 'There is absence of the rose on the table', is true for me and for every other man. Yet the absence of the rose is not an entity that can exist.

Existence does not belong to the relation of inherence (*samavāya*), particular (*viśeṣa*), and the universal also. Yet these three categories differ from negation in that they belong to the class of positive categories. Thus we find the Nyāya-Vaiśeṣika making a distinction between reality (*satya*), existence (*sattā*), and the positive (*bhāva*). But the other schools identify reality and existence (*satya* and *sattā*), because reality is not significant without existence and the two Sanskrit words are derived form the same root (*sat*). And some even identify the two with the positive also and, as a consequence, deny the reality of every category except that of the first three and say that the rest are only concepts.

The qualities, according to the Nyāya-Vaiśeṣika, are twenty-four in number: (1) colour, (2) taste, (3) smell, (4) touch, (5) sound, (6) number, (7) magnitude, (8) distinctness (*pṛthaktvam*), (9) contact (conjunction, *saṁyoga*), (10) separation (*vibhāga*, disjunction), (11) remoteness, (12) nearness, (13) consciousness (*buddhi*, cognition), (14) pleasure, (15) pain, (16) desire, (17) aversion (hate), (18) effort (*prayatna*), (19) heaviness, (20) fluidity, (21) viscidity, (22) tendency (*saṁskāra*), (23) merit (*dharma*), and (24) demerit (*adharma*). Most of these qualities have subdivisions. There are different kinds of taste, smell, touch, etc. Two main subdivisions of sound are the inarticulate noise (*dhvani*) and the articulate word.

It may be noted that number is a quality according to this school. Distinctness (*pṛthaktva*) also is a quality. It is different from difference, which is a form of negation and which will be explained later. It is different also from separateness, which belongs to objects that are disjoined. For instance, New York and Los Angeles are separate; but the colour and shape of the rose are only distinct. Contact is the result of two objects coming together, which can exist separately. My pen and the table come into contact, but they can exist separately. Separateness is sometimes translated as disjunction, because two things that are in contact can be separated, or disjoined. But this disjunction has nothing to do with logical disjunction. Remoteness and nearness are each of two kinds, spatial and temporal.

Buddhi or consciousness is the same as cognition and has no substantial nature. It is an adventitious quality of the *ātman*. Effort (*prayatna*) is of three kinds: striving towards some desired object, striving away from a disliked object, and the striving for life or the vital process (*jīvanayoniyatna*). Tendency (*saṁskāra*) is of three kinds: velocity (*vega*), elasticity which enables a pressed or expanded object to regain its original state, and the impressions left by experiences, which enable us to remember them and also form our habits.

Action. Action (*karma*) is movement. It has, as already discussed, no qualities, but modes, and action itself does not move. It is substances that move. Again, it is only finite substances with shapes that can move; infinite substances, like space and time, cannot move.

Action is of five kinds: (1) upward movement, (2) downward movement, (3) contraction, (4) expansion, and (5) locomotion.

Universal. The universal is what is common to all the individuals of a class. Yet it is not a group of all the common qualities, because the universal does not belong to the category of qualities. Man-ness or 'being a man' is not a quality of every man; it is what makes every individual of the class a man. It does not exist (has no *sattā*), yet it is real and is cognized when we perceive any man. It is what enables us to know that every individual of the class is a man.

The universal is present in every individual of the class through the relation of inherence. It is one and eternal. The same universal, man-ness, is present in every man. Men are born and die, but the same universal is present in every existing individual.

The Nyāya-Vaiśeṣika upholds the realism of the universals. The universal is not a mere name or concept. The Buddhists, for instance, generally maintain that the universal is a mere name. We call every individual of the class men by the name man, not because there is anything real called man-ness, in every individual, but because the same name is applicable to all, since they possess similar characteristics. The Buddhists say, therefore, that the individual alone is real, and the universal is only a name. Such a view is called nominalism. But some Vedāntins and Jainas say that the universal is only a mental idea, a concept, which we apply to every individual of the class. It stands conceptually for the unity of all the common characteristics, and this unity is a concept. This view is called conceptualism. As against both the doctrines, the Nyāya-Vaiśeṣika maintains that the universal is real.

The Nyāya-Vaiśeṣika does not believe that every word that can be formed by adding '-ness' to a noun stands for a real universal. There are six conditions for determining whether a universal is a real universal or not:

1. If there is only one member belonging to a class, then that class cannot have a real universal. For instance, there is only one space, one time, one God and so on. Therefore space-ness, time-ness, God-ness, etc. are not real universals. But there are many men. So man-ness is a real universal. Indeed, we use the word spatiality, but in a different sense, i.e. in the sense of being extended in space. But 'to be space' or 'being space' is not a universal, like 'being man'.

2. If the individuals referred to by a universal are the individuals referred to by another universal, than both of them cannot be real universals. For instance, the words flower and bloom refer to the same class of individuals. So flower-ness and bloom-ness are not two different universals. Or supposing we accept the two definitions of man: (i)

man is a rational animal; (ii) man is a political animal. Then the universal 'rational animal' and the universal 'political animal' are not two real and different universals, because they refer to the same individuals.

3. The classes referred to by two universals should not overlap. If the universal, 'being a European', includes some Asians and the universal, 'being an Asian', includes some Europeans, then the two cannot be real universals.

4. The postulation of a universal should not lead to infinite regress. Horseness is a universal, because there are many horses. But 'horseness-ness' is not a real universal, because we can form other concepts like horseness-ness-ness', 'horseness-ness-ness-ness' and so on *ad infinitum.*

5. Nothing can have a universal, if by having it, the object's very nature is destroyed. The universal is something common to many. But if there is something x that is not common to anything else but is possessed by only one thing A, then x cannot be a universal; for if it is a universal, then x will be had by some other thing B and the particularity of the first thing A is destroyed. So such ultimate particulars cannot have a universal. That is, the particular (*viśeṣa*) cannot have a universal called particularity. This condition will be explained further, when discussing the category of the particular.

6. When the relation between the supposed universal and the individuals is not possible, there can be no real universal. For this reason, negations do not have a universal. There is absence of the pen on the table. But 'absence-ness' is not a real universal, because between the absence of the pen and absent-ness (absence-ness), there can be no relation. The universal resides in the individuals through the relation of inherence (*samavāya*). Inherence is a positive category, and can, therefore, be found only in positive entities, but not in negative entities like the absence of the pen.

Then what is the nature of ideas like 'absent-ness', particularity, space-ness, time-ness etc.? The Nyāya-Vaiśeṣika says that they are only modalities (*upādhis*), which determine those objects, when we know them. They are not real universals, but concepts.

Real universals are of three kinds: the highest (*para*), the lowest (*apara*), and the intermediate (*parāpara*). The highest universal is Being or Existence (*sattā*), which belongs to substance, quality, and activity. The lowest are like potness, clothness, man-ness, etc. In between belong all the intermediary universals, like substance-ness.

Particular. The particular is not the same as the individual, and the two are very often confused with each other not only in the popular language, but also in the language of some philosophers. The Nyāya and the Vaiśeṣika draw a clear distinction between the two. The individual (*vyakti*) is the origin, the manifester of qualities and actions, whereas the particular (*viśeṣa*) is that which differentiates the ultimate infinitesimals and infinites from one another. It is not the ultimate difference, but that which is the basis of that ultimate difference. The universal (*sāmānya*, *jāti*), which has already been explained, is different from the particular and the individual.

The ultimate infinitesimals are the four kinds of atoms – of earth, water, fire, and air – and the minds (*manases*). The infinites are the *ātmans* (including God), ether (*ākāśa*), space, and time. The atoms of earth are all alike, and are, therefore, indistinguishable. Yet they are different from one another, because of a particular (*viśeṣa*) residing in every one. Similarly, every one of the atoms of every one of the other three classes is different from the others of the same class. The earth atoms, for instance, can be differentiated from the atoms of water, because the former have smell as their specific quality, while the latter have taste as their specific quality. But the earth atoms also are different from one another, although all possess the same specific quality. And they are made different from one another, because every atom possesses a particular.

Similarly, our minds, although atomic in size, are different from one another and are alike in every respect. And their difference from one another is due to every mind having a particular.

The *ātmans* also, although every one is infinite, are different from one another. Every one of them has a particular to differentiate it from the others. Space, time, and ether also, in spite of all being infinite, are different from one another, and have each a particular.

Now, the particular (*viśeṣa*), as the ultimate differentiating category, is alike everywhere. Yet it is not the same for all the infinitesimal and infinite entities. It is a plurality. But the particulars do not have a real universal, called particularity (*viśeṣatva*). If they have a universal in common, they will not be completely dissimilar to one another; and if they are not completely dissimilar, they cannot make the ultimate differentiation among the entities. So particularity is not a real universal, but only a conceptual determinant (*upādhi*) that has no reality corresponding to it. This point has already been explained.

Inherence. Inherence (*samavāya*) is defined as an eternal relation between two entities. The relation between universal and individual, between quality and substance, between activity and substance, and between whole and parts, is inherence. Since none of these entities except the universal is eternal, we have to understand the word eternal (*nitya*) in this definition as inseparability. That is, the universal is inseparable from the individual, quality from substance, activity from substance, and the whole from its parts

Compared to inherence, the relation of contact (*samyoga*) is not a relation of inseparability. It is an adventitious relation between two substances coming together, and disappears as soon as they separate.

Inherence and contact are two of the main relations recognized by the Nyāya-Vaiśeṣika school. To it goes the credit of turning even substances into relation. For instance, although space and time are substances according to this school, it recognizes spatial and temporal relations. It says, for instance, that New Delhi is in Los Angeles through the relation of space and that Emperor Asoka lives in President Kennedy through the relation of time; for these individuals exist in the same space and in the same time. There are many other kinds of relation, but inherence received especial attention from this school.

Negation. By negation is to be understood not the process of negating or denying, but the negative (or as it is sometimes called the negative fact). According to the Nyāya-Vaiśeṣika, it is not the positive that forms the basis of negation, but the negative, which is opposed to the positive. The cognition of the negative takes the form of negation or the negative proposition.

On my table, there is nothing, and I am said to cognize the negation or absence of the pen, for instance. But if there is nothing on the table, why do I not cognize the absence of rose or of the pencil? I cognize only that negation, the counterpart (*pratiyogi*) of which I expect. If I expect to see the pen on the table, then I see the negation of the pen; but if I expect to see the rose, then I see the negation of the rose. If I expect both, then I see the negations of both. So the condition for perceiving a negation is that I should expect its counterpart. 'Had there been a pen on the table, then I would have perceived it': such an anticipation is a precondition of every negation.

Hence, there is no negation without a counterpart (*pratiyogi*). That is, there is no mere negation or 'Nothing'. Negation is always of the form, 'negation of something'. That 'something', of which we say: 'Had it been there', is the counterpart. This school accepts the four kinds of negation explained in the chapter on the Mīmāmsā.

For the reason that distinctness is found wherever mutual negation is found and vice versa, some philosophers think that the two ideas are the same. But most of the followers of the Nyāya-Vaiśeṣika say that the two are different, not only because distinctness belongs to the positive categories, while mutual negation belongs to the negative, but also because the quality of being distinct belongs to a thing by itself without reference to any other, while mutual negation has such reference necessarily. For instance, if I say merely 'The lion is not', the sentence is incomplete and I have to complete it by adding 'a tiger'. But I can say, 'The lion is a distinct (unique) kind of animal' without referring to any other animal. So distinctness, separateness, and mutual negation are treated as different ideas with corresponding realities.

LIFE'S IDEAL

So far as active life goes, the Nyāya and the Vaiśeṣika accept the Mīmāmsā view. But they emphasized from the beginning the importance of salvation also. The Vaiśeṣika maintains that obtaining salvation also is a *dharma* or action according to the Vedic injunctions. Action is due to effort, and effort is of three kinds, as already explained: striving towards the desired object, striving away from the disliked object, and striving to maintain one's life. And every one of the three kinds of effort leads to action. Salvation can be obtained by striving towards the realization of the *ātman's* original nature, and by withdrawing from the world of action, which contains both pleasure and pain. This striving itself is action, which is according to the Vedas, and is therefore a *dharma*.

But the *ātman* in its original nature is not only devoid of pain and pleasure, but even of consciousness (*buddhi*). In salvation, it is completely free from contact with mind (*manas*), and, therefore, with the whole world. There will be no cause for pain then. But the Nyāya-Vaiśeṣika conceived the *ātman* as devoid of all consciousness and so as being similar to a stone.

However, the life of the followers of the Nyāya and the Vaiśeṣika is expected to be not only in accordance with the rules of conduct given by the Mīmāmsā and the ethical codes, but also thoroughly logical and rational.

Chapter X

THE DUALISTIC TRADITION OF THE SĀṄKHYA

INTRODUCTION

The word *sāṅkhya* means exact knowledge, which involves exact discrimination. The word *saṅkhya*, in which the first 'a' is shortened, means number; and the Sāṅkhya philosophy counts a definite number of categories, which are generally twenty-five. The philosophy that is usually known by this name is atheistic, but it is not certain whether the philosophy as originally propounded by Kapila,[1] its founder, was atheistic. Kapila is said to have composed the *Sāṅkhya Aphorisms*, which are lost. Later, Īśvarakṛṣṇa wrote his *Sāṅkhyakārikās*[2], purporting to give the ideas of Kapila. The *Mahābhārata* gives an account of theistic Sāṅkhya, and so did Vijñānabhikṣu, who belonged to this school. But in its restricted usage, the word Sāṅkhya has come to mean the atheistic, but spiritual philosophy of Iśvarakṛṣṇa.

Both Jainism and the Sāṅkhya accept that the *ātmans* are many; but while Jainism treats the material world as a plurality, the Sāṅkhya treats it as a unity and calls it Prakṛti, deriving the plurality of the world not from atoms, but from the unitary Prakṛti. For the Sāṅkhya, time and space have no separate existence; they are only forms in which the plurality of the forms of the Prakṛti appears. The Sāṅkhya made no use of the doctrine of the Brahman. Nevertheless, unlike the Mīmāmsā, it believed in salvation. Later, as already mentioned, Vijñānabhikṣu,[3] in the fifteenth century, turned the atheistic Sāṅkhya into a Vedānta.

[1] His name is mentioned in the *Śvetāśvatara Upaniṣad*, which may have been composed before the fourth century BC.

[2] A fairly reliable translation is made by G. N. Jha. See *Tattvakaumudi*, text and translation by G. N. Jha (Oriental Book Agency, Poona, 1934).

[3] See his *Sāṅkhyadarśana* (Chowkhamba Sanskrit Series, Benares, 1909), and his Commentary on the *Brahmasūtras*.

EPISTEMOLOGY

The Sāṅkhya does not seem to accept verbal testimony with the seriousness with which the Mīmāmsā and the Vedānta accepted it. For the Sāṅkhya, the acceptance meant only its being orthodox, since it accepted the Mīmāmsā doctrine of *dharma* for worldly values. Verbal testimony was given an important place by almost all the Indian traditions mainly to defend the truthfulness of the Vedic statements, which were at that time transmitted orally from tracher to pupil. The Sāṅkhya, as an orthodox school, also defended it, saying that the statements of the Veda were absolutely reliable (*āptavacanas*). Statements are of two kinds: those made by worldly beings (*laukika*), and those made by the superempirical Veda (*alaukika*). The former may be mistaken and are often unreliable, but the latter are absolutely reliable. They are meant for the good of the world, not for deceiving it. However, the Sāṅkhya made little use of the Vedas for building up its system, and made an independent approach in expounding its ideas.

The Sāṅkhya maintains that every cognition is valid or invalid in itself, and not made valid or invalid by something else. We have seen that, according to the Mīmāmsā, every cognition is valid in itself, but is made invalid by something else; according to Buddhism, it is invalid in itself, but made valid by something else. The reason which the Sāṅkhya gives for holding this view is that the object we know is a modification of reason (*buddhi*) – which is ontological in the Sāṅkhya as in the Vedānta – brought about by the mind and the senses, which come into contact with the object. Taking the example of the rope seen as a snake, the snake of the illusion is a modification of reason (*buddhi*), and the form of the cognition is, 'That is a snake'. In this cognition the 'That' and the 'snake' are not perceived as distinct entities, but as one object 'That-snake'. Similarly, when we perceive the object correctly as the rope, the form of the cognition is, 'That-rope', expressed in the form 'That is a rope'. It is thought generally that the latter contradicts the former, because 'That is a snake' and 'That is a rope', have the same 'That' in common, and the 'That' cannot be both a rope and a snake. That is, falsity applies to the predicate of a judgment, but not to its subject. But the Sāṅkhya maintains that the 'That' and its predicate are not distinguishable in cognition. The 'That' is never cognized apart from the predicate. That is, only the snake is cognized or the rope is cognized, but not the 'That and the snake' or the 'That and the rope'. So each cognition as a modification of reason (*buddhi*), is a separate one, and is without reference to the other. Hence the cognition of the snake is invalid by itself, and not made invalid by the cognition of the rope; and the cognition of the rope is valid by itself, and not made valid by anything else.

But reason is the same in both cases; and it is the same reason that has the modification of the snake and also that of the rope. And so the same reason knows the validity and invalidity of the two cognitions. This position of the Sāṅkhya needs a little explanation. The Sāṅkhya lifts the common point of reference from the demonstrative 'That' to reason (*buddhi*) itself, because no 'That' can be separated from the predicate and because the assertion of the presence of the object is made by reason. It is the function of reason to confer existence on the forms perceived, but it is not the function of the mere 'That' to do so. Reason itself should, therefore, know which of its modifications are true and which false, and it knows them through its very modifications.

The Sāṅkhya, in its own way but differently from the Mīmāmsā, adopts a thorough-going realistic attitude. Even the false object, e.g. the snake in illusion, is existent and has being. Non-being not only does not exist, but also is never perceived. How can anyone perceive Non-being with his senses? Non-being is only a concept. But the snake is not a concept. So it is an existent or being. The Sāṅkhya adopts, thereby, the doctrine that the object of illusion is existent (*satkhyātivāda*). But it is not an object perceived somewhere else. There is no remembering or recognizing the snake seen in illusion. It is an individual existing object. Since reason (*buddhi*) is a being, but not a non-being, its assertion, which is its modification, is also a being. If we saw the rope, we could not have seen the snake. So there is non-cognition (*akhyāti*) of the rope. If we see the snake, i.e. if reason is modified as the snake, we cannot see the rope; and similarly, if we see the rope, i.e. if reason is modified as the rope, we cannot see the snake. So the Sāṅkhya says that illusion is the perception of one existent object, and the non-perception of another.

If both the snake and the rope are existent, why do we call the former false? Here the original Vedic (Mīmāmsā) view that the world is a world of action comes to the help of the Sāṅkhya also. The snake does not belong to the world of action and does not serve the purpose for which it is meant. So we treat the rope as real and the snake as unreal. But from a point of view above that of the world of action, every object of cognition is existent and real. For the distinction between logical truth and falsity, the Sāṅkhya, like all other philosophies, accepts the principle of contradiction. But logical falsity, although an error, is not the same as illusion and does not raise the problem of the perception of existence.

METAPHYSICS

The Sāṅkhya attempts to understand even the external world from the stand-point of the inner being of man, because even the external world is a being for the consciousness of man. The question for the Sāṅkhya is: How are we to understand the various forms of experience, including that of the independent objective world, with reference to the conscious being of man? So every division and classification has to be made with reference to the being of man. Man is more certain of his own conscious existence – although he may not be clear about exactly what it is – than of anything else. And for a philosophy of life the stand-point of the inner being of man is more important than that of the external world of matter, which is studied by the different sciences. Such is the attitude of the Sāṅkhya to philosophy.

Before entering into details, the metaphysical chart of the Sāṅkhya may be given.

Puruṣa (Ātman) --------- Nature (Prakṛti)

Nature (Prakṛti)
→ Reason (*mahat*, *buddhi*)
→ Ego (*ahaṃkāra*)
→ Mind (*manas*) | Five sensory organs | Five motor organs | Five subtle elements (*tanmātras*)

Five subtle elements (*tanmātras*)
→ Five gross elements (*mahābhūtas*)

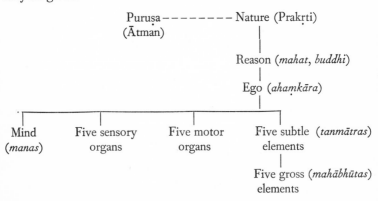

We see in the above chart, there are twenty-five categories (*tattvas*)

including the *ātman*, which is called Puruṣa also. If we exclude Puruṣa, the categories are twenty-four.

The Sāṅkhya, as an atheistic philosophy, rejects the reality of God and advances the usual arguments. They are: (1) God cannot be the cause of the world, because He is said to be eternally perfect and unchanging, but nothing can be a cause, unless it changes itself during the process of causation. (2) God cannot be postulated even as the controller of Nature (*Prakṛti*), which is insentient and blind. For even to control it, God has to act, and in the act He has to undergo transformation. But God is conceived by the theists to be eternally perfect and unchanging. (3) We cannot understand what purpose God can have in creating the world, if he is perfect and complete in Himself, and if there is nothing for Him to desire. (4) A benevolent God could not have created the evil in this world, but God is said to be benevolent. (5) The *ātmans* are all perfect originally and are eternal; there is no need of God to create them.

So it is enough to postulate insentient Nature (*Prakṛti*), with determinate laws of her own. It acts in the same way for every *ātman*, and evolves the world, when the *ātman* so desires; and it withdraws the world, when the *ātman* is no longer interested in her. Prakṛti is like a dancing girl, who shows her postures and forms to those who are interested and retires from those who are not. And she shows herself in the same way to all.

The *ātmans* are of an infinite number, according to the Sāṅkhya. By nature each is pure, existent and conscious. That is, the nature of the *ātman* is existence and consciousness. Unlike the Vedānta, the Sāṅkhya does not attribute bliss to the *ātman*. Bliss belongs to reason (*buddhi*), and is its state. But in the stage of liberation, the *ātman* is freed from reason, and so experiences neither pain nor pleasure.

The so-called proofs for the reality of the *ātman* are the same as those given generally by the other orthodox schools. They are as follows. (1) Every object that is a compound, that is made up of parts, is meant for some other. But every material object is made up of parts. So it is meant for someone else that is not made up of parts. And that someone else is the *ātman*. (2) That someone else must be distinct from all the objects that have parts. These objects are insentient. So the *ātman* must be sentient and without parts. (3) Blind, material, insentient objects in their activities must be controlled and directed by a sentient object, which is the *ātman*. (4) We experience pleasure and pain, and there will not be pleasure and pain without someone who enjoys the pleasures and suffers from the pains. That someone is the *ātman*. (5) Liberation will be meaningless, unless there is an *ātman* that is to be liberated. This argument is directed against the Buddhists, who accept the necessity of liberation, but do not accept the reality of the *ātman* that is to be liberated.

The Sāṅkhya also gives reasons for the plurality of the *ātmans*. (1) Birth, death, and mental and physical capabilities are different for each person. If the *ātman* is the same for all, then birth, death, and the endowments must be the same for all. (2) If the *ātman* is the same, then when one sleeps, the others also must sleep and so on. (3) There are different kinds of sentient beings, gods, men, and birds and beasts. If the *ātman* is the same, these differences cannot be true. But they are true. (4) If the *ātman* is the same, when one *ātman* is liberated, the others also must be liberated. But they are not liberated. (5) If the *ātman* is the same, when one man enjoys the fruits of his action, then other men also must enjoy them.

Prakṛti (Nature) is one and real, and is independent of any *ātman*. Prakṛti is indeed insentient, but we should not equate it with mere matter, which, in western terminology, is what is opposed to mind. For according to the Sāṅkhya, mind also is a product of Prakṛti. The word Prakṛti means the original or original nature, as opposed to *vikṛti*, its form or modification. For instance, we can speak of a man's *prakṛti*, meaning his natural constitution, which may be healthy or unhealthy, weak or strong. Similarly, the *prakṛti* of carbon dioxide is carbon. The basic constituents of any medicine are its *prakṛti*. Prakṛti in any case is the ultimate determining factor. Now, when an *ātman*, which is originally pure and indeterminate consciousness, becomes a personality, what determines it as a personality is Prakṛti. Since the same Prakṛti determines the personalities of all the *ātmans*, there is a basic similarity in the psycho-physical constitution of all of them. Thus Prakṛti is the origin of both the mental and the physical aspects of our being.

However, the Sāṅkhya should not be interpreted as if it knows no distinction between mind and matter. The Sāṅkhya knows the distinction, and goes so far as to abstract sentience so completely that it is treated as having an existence of its own apart from Prakṛti. The Sāṅkhya has also the distinct category of mind, which is one of the twenty-five. The original distinction, for the Sāṅkhya, is not between mind and matter, but between the *ātman*, which is infinite consciousness, but indeterminate and Prakṛti, which is the infinite unconscious, but determinate. It is out of this infinite, but determinate unconscious that the manifold world evolves.

Thus Prakṛti is the original stuff of the psycho-physical world. Yet it is not a chaotic stuff, but something in which everything is in harmony and equilibrium. We cannot attribute order to it, because the concept of order implies a plurality among the members of which definite, fixed relations exist. Prakṛti is originally absolute equilibrium, but completely undifferentiated.

It has three attributes (*guṇas*) – clarity (*sattva*), activity (*rajas*), and darkness (*tamas*) – which remain in equilibrium before the world evolves. There is no consciousness in them. When the *ātman* comes into contact with Prakṛti, and throws its reflection in it, the equilibrium of the three attributes is disturbed, and each begins to dominate over the other two. This disturbance starts the process of the evolution of the world.

The contact between the *ātman* and Prakṛti is not spatial or temporal. And the Sāṅkhya does not explain why and how the two come into contact. Neither can it explain why the *ātman*, even after it is liberated, will not come into contact again.

Evolution of the World

After their equilibrium is disturbed, each of the three attributes of Prakṛti tries to dominate over the other two, and we find the domination in different parts of our being and of the being of the world. In certain things placidity, clearness, purity, and transparence are dominant, and these characteristics are due to *sattva*. In certain others, agitatedness, motion, activity, irritableness, etc., are dominant; these are due to *rajas*. In still others, stupidity, lethargy, opaqueness and dullness are dominant, and these are due to *tamas*. But the three attributes are never completely separate from one another and everything in the universe has the three attributes, but in different proportions. In our character and temperament, in our habits, practices and customs, all the three are found, but again in different proportions. If a man is intelligent and good, is of good tastes and manners, he has the *sattva* dominant in him. If he is irascible, over-active, etc., the attribute *rajas* dominates in him. If he is dull, idle, and stupid, *tamas* is dominant in him. Even the foods one likes can be distinguished accordingly.

After the disturbance is created in the equilibrium of Prakṛti, its *sattva*, as pure and transparent, receives the reflection of the *ātman* and becomes conscious. It is the consciousness belonging to *sattva* that is called reason. The Sāṅkhya uses the words *buddhi* and *Mahat* to denote it. *Buddhi* is reason,[4] and *Mahat* means the Great. It is great in the sense that it is cosmic in significance, it is the Logos, the consciousness of all that is and the existence of that consciousness taken together. The Sāṅkhya gives the highest place for the existential reason, but does not say that it is one and the same for all men. There are as many logoi as there are *ātmans* for whom Prakṛti creates the world. The logos is not only rational, but also ethical and aesthetic.

Thus reason (*buddhi*) is the first evolute of Prakṛti. Out of reason issues the ego (*ahaṁkāra*). In the ego the attribure *sattva* is not as dominant as in reason. *Rajas* gets greater strength; for the nature of the ego is to act, to manipulate, and to appropriate. Out of this ego come the subjective and objective aspects of the world of experience. The ego also has the three aspects, *sattva*, *rajas*, and *tamas*. Out of the *sattva* aspect (*vaikārika*) arises all that belongs to the subject of experience – mind (*manas*), the five senses organs, and the five organs of action; and out of its *tamas* aspect (*bhūtādi*) arises all that is objective – the five subtle elements (*tanmātras*), out of which issue forth the five gross elements. The subtle elements are the stuff of our dream objects, and the gross elements of the material world. The *rajas* aspect (*taijasa*) is responsible for the split into the subjective and objective poles of experience; it is the force that creates the two poles out of the ego.

Reason (*buddhi*), ego (*ahaṁkāra*), and mind (*manas*) are together called the internal organ (*antahkaraṇa*) by the Sāṅkhya, and together correspond to what is called mind in Anglo-American psychology. But they have a metaphysical significance also for the Sāṅkhya. As distinct from the internal organ, the Sāṅkhya treats the five sense organs and the five organs of action as the external organs. But it is not unusual to bring them together into one and call it the external organ (*bāhyakaraṇa*).

The different views of causation in Indian thought concern mainly the material cause. The Buddhists, because of their doctrine of momen-

[4] The concept of *buddhi* or reason in the Sāṅkhya-Yoga and the Vedāntic schools is akin to the concept of the Logos in Neo-Platonism and Stoicism.

tariness, maintain that the effect originates out of the non-being of the cause. As against the Buddhists, the Sāṅkhya, like the Vedānta, says that the effect comes only out of the being of the cause. The Nyāya and the Vaiśeṣika maintain that the effect, before it comes into existence, was non-existent. It was merely Non-being. But the Sāṅkhya finds it difficult to accept that Non-being can become Being, and so contends that the effect, even before it is born, was being. But if the effect was being and existent, how can there be any causation? Causation means the production of something new; and the new is something not already existing. To this objection the Sāṅkhya replies that the effect is only latent in the cause, just as oil is latent in the oil seeds. Producing the effect means making patent what is already latent. Causation is only a manifestation (*āvirbhāva*) of what is already potentially existing. But we have to accept the principle of causation, because we can press oil only out of oil seeds, but not out of sand and stones. There is a definite causal relation between two things like oil seeds and oil. Similarly, a pot can be made out of clay, but not out of water or air.

Thus when Prakṛti produces the world, it simply manifests what it already contains. It cannot manifest what it does not contain. Its nature is thereby fixed. It is this manifestation that is called the transformation (*parināma*) of Prakṛti into the world. This is again the same as the evolution of the world out of Prakṛti.

The human being is thus the subjective pole of the total experienceable world. But essentially his being is not confined to the subjective pole. Even his very ego transcends the distinction between the subjective and objective poles, although it does not transcend the distinction between one ego and another. The ego includes, according to the Sāṅkhya, not only the 'I' that knows and enjoys, but also the 'mine' that is known and enjoyed. So long as the ego lasts, man is subject to the laws of the world of action, is born and dies again and again, and remains in bondage. Salvation lies in being free from the laws of the world of action. For this purpose, man has to realize that he is neither the ego nor even reason (*buddhi*, *Mahat*), but the pure *ātman* itself. And this can be done when the conscious being of man is disentangled from the determinate structure of Prakṛti. And this disentangling is a slow withdrawal of the evolutes of Prakṛti into its original state of equilibrium, when the *ātman* realizes that it is only its reflection in Prakṛti that was really in bondage, but not it itself.

Since the *ātman* then will have no interest in the forms of Prakṛti, it retires and ceases to be active. The withdrawal is a gradual process along the same stages through which Prakṛti evolves the world. It is, therefore, called involution.

The process of involution and the practices nesessary for attaining it are best explained by the Yoga system of Patañjali. The metaphysics on which the Yoga of Pantañjali is based is the same as that of the Sāṅkhya, and the two systems, the Sāṅkhya and the Yoga, are, therefore, often hyphenated and called Sāṅkhya-Yoga. There is only one difference between the two; unlike the Sāṅkhya, the Yoga of Patañjali accepts the reality of God.

Chapter XI

THE YOGA TRADITION OF PATAÑJALI

INTRODUCTION

The Yoga of Patañjali is a meta-psychological technique based upon the philosophy of the Sāṅkhya. Its metaphysics is metapsychology based upon the principle that the outward reality has its roots in the inward and that the realization of the ultimate truth is, therefore, the realization of the most inward being in man, namely, the *ātman*. And by the time the *ātman* is realized, every stage of reality lower than it must have been realized. The Sāṅkhya maintains that everything evolves out of Prakṛti through its first evolute, reason (*buddhi*, *Mahat*). Buddhi is called *citta* by Patañjali. And it is conscious, because it reflects the consciousness of the *ātman*; it is the highest stage of our conscious being, the deepest, and the infinite, since it is the source of all that we are conscious of, including our ego. The world, the Sāṇkya and the Yoga maintain, is due to the evolutionary process of reason, due to its transformation.[1] The bondage of the *ātman* is due to its being entangled in this transformation; its liberation lies in disentangling itself from that process.

We should, again, remind ourselves here that reason is not merely the reasoning or inferring process, but has an ontological significance as in the philosophies of Heraclitus, Pythagoras, Plato, the Stoics and the Neo-Platonists in the West. Otherwise, we cannot understand the significance of the Sāṅkyha and the Yoga.

METAPHYSICS

It has already been said that the metaphysics of the Yoga is the same as that of the Sāṅkhya, except for the former's acceptance of the reality of

[1] Cf. the Stoic view of Nature, Reason, or the Logos, and note the differences also.

God (*Īśvara*). But the Yoga system can stand even without the concept of God, because the concept does not play a necessary role in the Yoga metaphysics. However, the Yoga gives a few proofs for God's existence. (1) The scriptures, or Vedas, say that God exists, and they are infallible. Therefore, God must exist. (2) There is gradation of powers and capabilities in the world. Some men have more strength, more knowledge, and more power than others. And this gradation must reach the highest degree, at which degree the being concerned must have infinite strength, knowledge and power. Such a being is God. (3) The creation of the world is due to the coming into contact of *ātman* and Prakṛti, although they are absolutely disparate entities. Some being must be there to bring them together. That being is God. (4) Prakṛti has to transform itself into the world according to the merits and demerits of the *ātman*. The soul has to take birth, enjoy and suffer in accordance with its own actions. And Prakṛti must create the conditions for such pleasures and pains. The processes of the blind, insentient Prakṛti have therefore to be supervised by an intelligent being. Such an intelligent being is God.

Few people will admit that these proofs are conclusive. Patañjali introduces God only to suggest an easier way to salvation than that of the arduous Yoga technique, which he expounds. God is the infinite, eternal spirit, which is not polluted by ethical and mental impurities. By meditating on Him one can obtain salvation. And meditation on Him is enhanced by complete devotion to Him.

NATURE AND FORMS OF YOGA

The Essence of Yoga

Since everything is due to the transformation of reason (*citta*, *buddhi*), Yoga consists of controlling the transformations. But since everything is a modification of this *citta*, control over *citta* gives the power of control over everything. That is why the yogi is said to acquire supernatural powers, which also are described by Patañjali. The student is advised not to practise Yoga for the sake of supernatural powers, for practically no one is available as a guide and teacher of such practices, and without proper guides the practices may produce mental diseases. Patañjali himself was aware of the difficulties and dangers. And for a true yogi, who is in search of salvation, supernatural powers are temptations and hindrances.

The use of the word reason, although it is associated with the concept of the Logos in Greek philosophy, may mislead the English-speaking reader, and the word *citta* itself will therefore be used. *Citta* has five functions (*vṛttis*) or kinds of modification: (1) Valid cognition (*pramāṇa*) is modification according to perception, inference, and verbal testimony. Through such modifications we know the objects of the world as they exist. (2) Invalid cognition (*viparyaya*) is modification of *citta*, which gives us false knowledge. Corresponding to this modification of the *citta*, there is no object. Such cognitions are illusions. (3) Ideas formed through mere abstraction or verbal or grammatical transformation (*vikalpa*) also have no corresponding existing objects. For instance, 'the hole in the sky', 'the horse's egg', 'the sky-lotus', etc., are only grammatical formations. We understand what the expressions mean, but what they mean is either imaginary or a mere grammatical verbal formation. Again, 'the son of Mr X' seems to convey the idea that, because there is a corresponding object to 'the son' and 'Mr X', there must be a corresponding object to 'of'. But there is no such object. So 'of' has no corresponding object. (4) Memory (*smṛti*) is another modification of *citta*. (5) Sleep (*nidrā*) is also a modification of *citta*. Sleep is a function, it is not the absence of every function, according to Patañjali.

It is the nature of *citta* to be undergoing some modification or other continually without break. The control of *citta* is the control of these modifications. Their control does not mean killing *citta* but, fixing it constantly on something, i.e. making it retain one modification, or object. Such a fixing is concentration. It has five stages. In the first stage (*kṣipta*, the agitated), *citta* constantly moves from one object to another, does not attend to any, and is always agitated. In the second stage (*mūdha*, the torpid), when the attempt is made forcibly to fix it on something, *citta* becomes dull and tends to enter sleep. In the third stage (*vikṣipta*, the distracted), *citta* attends to some object for a moment, then turns to another, and then to still another, and so on. When it attends to one object, the thought of other objects arises, and its attention is violently drawn away. In the fourth stage (*ekāgra*, the focussed), *citta* rests on a particular object for a long time. In this stage, the processes of mind do not completely cease, but are under control. In the fifth stage (*niruddha*, the arrested), the processes are completely stopped, and meditation becomes perfect.

It is not easy for man to reach the last stage, because of five impurities (*kleśas*) that afflict the *ātman*. (1) Ignorance (*avidyā*) prevents him from discriminating between the eternal and non-eternal, and blinds him to the true nature of things. (2) The false notion of one's ego (*asmitā*) makes a man think that he is the particular individual, and say: 'Here I am', as the particular man. (3) Desire and attachment (*rāga*) to pleasures harden his sense of being a particular individual. (4) Hatred of and aversion (*dveṣa*) from pains also contribute to the same end. (5) The instinctive attachment to one's particular being and fear of losing that being in death (*abhiniveśa*) also prevent a man from rising above the particularity of his ego. These five hindrances prevent man from rising above his *citta* in order to control it, and keep him within its processes.

The eight limbs of yoga are the means for the final realization of the *ātman* in the highest trance (*samādhi*) which is essentially free from the forms of *citta*. The earier of the eight lead to the later, but one may attempt to practise all together. But when one starts the practices, the emphasis should be on the earlier ones.

1. The first is self-restraint (*yama*). It consists of (*a*) truthfulness, (*b*) non-stealing, (*c*) celibacy, (*d*) non-injury and (*e*) non-acceptance of gifts from others. The last is emphasized, because people generally think that they can earn merit by bestowing valuable gifts upon yogis. The yogis then become rich, and wealth is one of the greatest temptations. The yogi should keep only what is absolutely necessary to keep his body and soul together.

2. The second limb consists of the observance of certain rules of conduct (*niyama*). (*a*) One should keep both his body and mind pure (*śauca*). He should cultivate all the good attitudes like friendliness, kindness, cheerfulness and indifference to the vices of others. He should keep his body pure not only by taking proper baths, but also by taking only pure food, for certain kinds of food not only affect the body but also the mind. (*b*) The second rule of conduct is the practice of contentment (*santoṣa* cheerfulness). One should be cheerfully content with what one has and should not long for what one does not have. Otherwise, his mind constantly thinks of the ways and means for obtaining such things, becomes agitated, and will be incapable of concentration. (*c*) The third is penance. (*d*) The fourth is the constant study of books on spiritual knowledge (*svādhyāya*). Such a study keeps only good ideas before mind. And (*e*) one should meditate on God (*Īśvarapraṇidhāna*), and surrender oneself to Him.

3. The third limb is the practice of the bodily postures (*āsanas*); it consists of developing sitting postures conducive to long meditation and of exercises for the control of the body and its health. There are many kinds of such postures, a few of which can be easily practised; but the others should be practised only with the guidance of one who knows, as otherwise they will be dangerous.

If a man cannot sit long, and if his limbs give pain, he cannot meditate. So he has not only to select the sitting posture best suited for his body, but also practise it. Again, if he suffers from bodily ailments and irregularities of the involuntary system, he cannot concentrate. For overcoming such irregularities also, certain practices are prescribed. But they should be learnt only from those who have already practised them, for the control of the involuntary system is not easy, and any mistake committed may prove dangerous.

4. *Prāṇāyāma*, or the control of breath, is the fourth limb. It consists of the control of inhalation (*pūraka*), retention (*kumbhaka*), and exhalation (*recaka*). It is to be started with each of the three parts for a short period, gradually prolonging it. Its aim is the control of the vital principle in the body, and also the steadiness of mind. As breath becomes steady, mind also becomes steady. The practice of *prāṇāyāma* also needs the guidance of adepts.

5. The next step in yoga is the withdrawal of the senses from their objects (*pratyāhāra*). This withdrawal is the inward movement of mind from the objects to reason (*Mahat*, *buddhi*, *citta*). In this state, there may be sounds around; but the ear does not hear them; there may be colours in front, but the eye does not see them; for mind is fixed upon something else. The pysical senses are there, but their psychological counterparts are withdrawn into mind and become part and parcel of *citta*.

From this point begins psychological yoga, called *antaraṅgasādhana* (internal practice). The first four are physical yoga, called *bahiraṅgasādhana* (external practice). External practice is only an aid to internal practice, which is of primary importance.

6. *Dhāraṇa* or holding on is the keeping of the object of concentration continually before us. It is uninterrupted attention to the object, without disturbance or agitation. In this state, mind knows only the object of concentration, and nothing else.

7. *Dhyāna* or meditation is the spontaneous flow of the process of *citta* in the pattern of the object of concentration. We have seen that,

according to the Sāṅkhya, the object as cognized is only a modification of *citta*. The nature of *citta* is to be a constant flow, and ordinarily the pattern of this flow changes from object to object. In *dhyāna* the flow sticks spontaneously and without effort to the same object. In *dhāraṇa* also the object is held continually before *citta*, but it is done only with effort. That is, when *dhāraṇa* matures, it becomes *dhyāna*.

8. But when *dhyāna* matures, it becomes samādhi. *Samādhi* is often translated as trance, etc. which does not convey its true significance because of the association these words have in the English language. Literally, the word means, in this context, perfect and complete knowing or placing of mind (*sam* + *ā* + *dhī*). In this state, the contemplating consciousness becomes, as it were, the object con. templated. Contemplation becomes the contemplated, thought becomes the object. In *dhyāna*, *citta* knows itself also when it is conscious of the object. But in *samādhi*, *citta* does not know itself, but only the object; it becomes, as it were, the object.

It should be noted that such a *samādhi* is not the completion of yoga, which is complete cessation of all the functions of *citta*. But since in this *samādhi*, the object is present, and since the object is a modification of *citta*, we cannot say that the functioning of *citta* is completely stopped. Only a strong control of *citta* has been achieved. The functions of *citta* can be said to have completely stopped, only when consciousness goes back to its origin, the *ātman*, or Puruṣa. The cessation of the functions of *citta* depend, therefore, on what object it meditates. If it concentrates on the figure of Christ or Buddha, it becomes, as it were, Christ or Buddha. The phrase 'as it were' is important, because *citta* does not actually become Christ or Buddha, but enters that figure so completely that it becomes unaware of itself. If it does not meditate upon an image, but upon a real object, it enters that real object and can know its internal constitution. If *citta* meditates upon its own inward being, then it will know reality itself.

STAGES OF INWARD CONCENTRATION

Meditation upon inward reality is a gradual process, starting from the gross objects outside and ending with the *ātman* inside. The gradation follows the gradation of the evolutes out of Prakṛti, as given by the Sāṅkhya. It can be best understood by giving a skeletal chart.[2] It

[2] The reader should note that the Chart is not merely classificatory, but gives the stages. The arrow marks show which lower stage leads directly to

should be noted that at every stage there is a *samādhi* (trance). The aim of *samādhi* is to become the object that is meditated upon. But this 'becoming' does not mean that, if consciousness is fixed upon a stone, it becomes the stone, but that it becomes, 'as it were', the stone, in that consciousness forgets itself and enters the being of the stone.

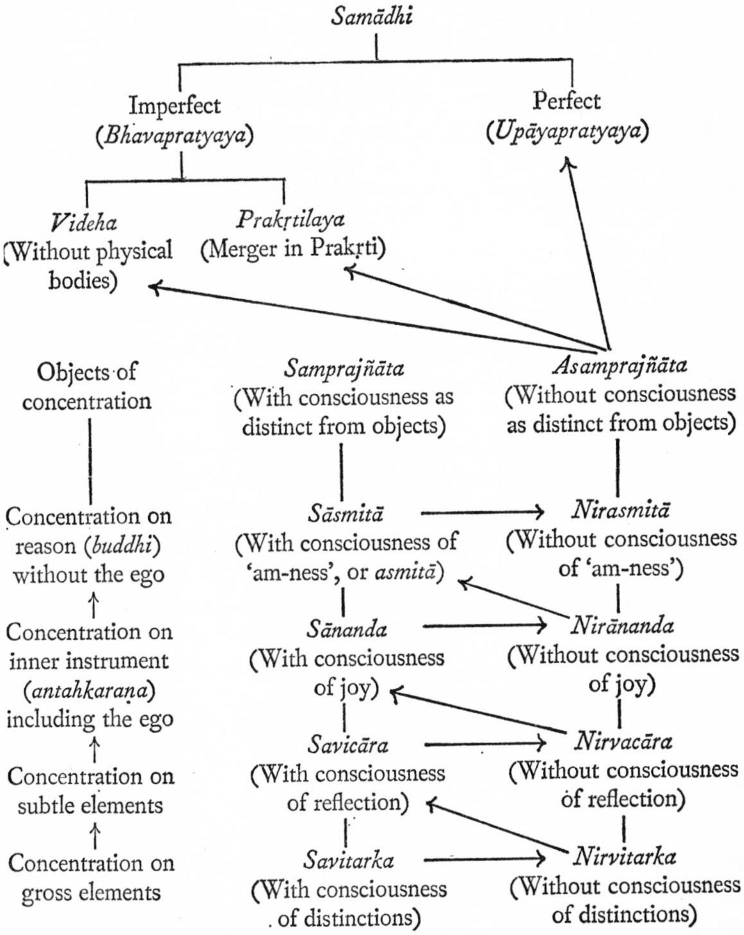

which higher one. From the *nirasmitā* stage, which is one of the *asamprajñāta-samādhis*, one may go to the three still higher stages, of which only one, the Perfect, leads to emancipation.

As the consciousness of man is usually directed externally towards the objects of the world, and because it can be focused easily and can rest upon them for a while, yogic concentration starts with them. The Sāṅkhya and the Yoga do not accept the ultimate reality of atoms, space and time; so there is no concentration on them. According to the Sāṅkhya and the Yoga, atoms are not the finest stuff of the world; it is the subtle elements. But concentration on the subtle elements is the second stage.

When man concentrates on the gross elements, he becomes the elements, as it were, in his *samādhi*. But this *samādhi* is of two kinds: When man, for instance, concentrates on the marble figure of Christ, then he has before him the marble figure, the idea of Christ, and the name of Christ. In the first form of *samādhi*, the consciousness[3] of the object forgets itself, but the three distinctions – object, idea (concept), and name – are present. The distinctions among the three are not lost. This is called *savitarka-samādhi*. But when these distinctions also are lost, *samādhi* becomes complete. There is nothing else in that state than the object, Christ. The marble figure of Christ then becomes alive. The consciousness of man in this *samādhi*, as it were, becomes Christ. But we should not forget that the man does not actually become Christ; he can only know and experience what Christ is. As the distinctions mentioned are not present here, it is called *nirvitarka-samādhi* and becomes one of the forms of *asampraj-ñāta-samādhi*, or *samādhi* without the experience of knowing but only of being the object. It does, however, contain the distinctions in a latent form (*sanskāraśeṣa*). It is called *nirbīja-samādhi* (seedless *samādhi*) also, because the subjective side of this experience, the knowing consciousness, assumes the forms of pure absence, vacuity and the state could not have been attained, if the seeds of the natural impurities of mind were not destroyed.

The next stage of concentration is upon subtle elements, to which *nirvitarka-samādhi* leads. Here again one finds the distinction between the *samādhi* in which the distinctions – object, idea, and name – are found and that in which they are not found. But the distinctions here are more subtle than in the above, as the object is made up of subtle elements. At this stage, the two forms of *samādhi* are respectively called *savicāra* and *nirvacāra samādhis*. Consciousness at the *nirvicāra*

[3] That is, the meditating consciousness is not conscious or aware of itself, but only of the three distinctions.

stage is called *ṛtambhara* (full of truth) as there is here no possibility of the object being false. For man is concerned here with the ultimate constituents of the actual world.

The third stage of concentration is upon the inner instrument (*antahkaraṇa*), i.e. upon reason, ego, and mind taken together, the agent of knowing and acting. At this stage the two attributes, *rajas* and *tamas*, are not transcended or overcome and the feeling of the ego is strongly felt. But the experience at this stage is intense joy or bliss (*ānanda*). At this stage again, the difference between the two kinds of *samādhi*, that with distinctions and that without distinctions, obtains. And the two are called *sānanda* and *nirānanda samādhis* respectively.

The fourth stage of concentration is upon pure reason (*buddhi*, *citta*, *mahat*), in which only the attribute *sattva* without the two other attributes, *rajas* and *tamas*, remains or rather completely suppresses them and which is experienced as the pure 'am' or 'am-ness' without the 'I'. There is no ego experience at this stage. The two forms here are called *sāsmitā* and *nirasmitā samādhis*.

But none of these *samādhis* ends in salvation, because they are not the same as the realization of the *ātman* apart from Prakṛti and its forms. Man in these *samādhis* is still within the sphere of Prakṛti and has to attain higher stages. In all the four *samādhis*, the conscious being of man is not freed from the latent impressions, instincts and forces (*samskāras*) left in him by his past activities and by his involvement in the basic determinism of Prakṛti, and they will surge up again and create for him a new life. Some yogis may be satisfied with these *samādhis* and may not choose to go further; some may enter the being of gods – who are without physical bodies (*videhas*) – and they may continue to be gods until their yogic merit is exhausted, but have to come down again to bodily existence; some others may go a little higher and be contented with merger in Prakṛti, but they also will be reborn; but a few may progress further up to the realization of their *ātman* as completely separate from Prakṛti. The second and the third kinds of *samādhis* are called the imperfect *bhavapratyaya-samādhis*.[4]

For this ultimate realization, man needs faith in what has been achieved and interest in his ideal, enthusiasm for attaining the ideal, and constant mindfulness (*asampramoṣa*) of what he is and what he

[4] *Bhavapratyayasamādhi* is one in which the causes for rebirth (*bhava*) are still dormant. See Patanjali, *Yogasūtras* (Anandasrama Press, Poona, 1932), I, 19.

has to achieve. Lack of faith may be produced by false views of reality and doubts whether what has been achieved is true. Even otherwise, if one has no enthusiasm and power of perseverance, one may be content only with merger in Prakṛti. Furthermore, one should be watchful that his consciousness is not darkened and forgetfulness of his being does not overpower him. He should then constantly discriminate within his being what is the *ātman* and what is Prakṛti. It is through this discrimination that he will be able to realize his pure *ātman*; and this realization will lead to final emancipation after death. This *samādhi* is called *upāya-pratyaya-samādhi*.[5] When he realizes that he is none of the forms of Prakṛti, he will have no future births and deaths.

The discrimination between the *ātman* and Prakṛti is the most important step for salvation. One may attain perfection up to the fourth stage and die. In his next life, he will be born with that perfection and will have only the next stages to go through. The stages in which perfection was attained will need very little effort to be realized again.

Patañjali's yoga was utilized by the followers of the Vedānta also. The *ātmans* may be a plurality, as the Sāṅkhya-Yoga maintains or the same as the Brahman as the Advaita of Sāṅkara maintains: these differences did not preclude the use of yoga. Many Vedāntins accept the plurality of the *ātmans* also; yet they say that the realization of the original state of the *ātman* is the only way for the realization of the Brahman. In every case the methods prescribed by Patañjali and the psychological analyses he gave as the philosophical support of his methods could be usefully incorporated and applied by the other schools also. The Sāṅkhya and the Yoga were, therefore, assimilated by the Vedāntins in particular, and by the Nyāya and the Vaiśeṣika also up to some extent, i.e. so far as the advice about the practices go. In fact every spiritual school, including the heterodox Jainism and Buddhism, has made some use or other of the Yoga of Patañjali.

[5] *Upāyapratyayasamādhi* is one for which the cause is the skilful adoption of means such as faith, enthusiams, and unforgetfulness. See *ibid*., I, 20.

Chapter XII

THE VEDĀNTA AND THE MONISTIC TRADITIONS OF THE SPIRIT

INTRODUCTION

After presenting the activist tradition of the Mīmāmsā, which built up its philosophy on the earliest philosophical ideas about life contained in the Vedas, the heterodox traditions of the Cārvākas, Jainism and Buddhism, which rose as reactions, though in different forms, against the excesses and extravagances of the Mīmāmsā philosophy and the religion, or the way of life it represented, were given; because they represent the counterparts of the Mīmāmsā in active opposition. Following the general practice the Nyāya, Vaiśeṣika, Sāṅkhya, and Yoga traditions, which, though independent, claimed allegiance to the Vedas, were next given. The Vedānta did not rise in conscious, active opposition to the Mīmāmsā. As the philosophy based upon the Upaniṣads, which were the last part of the Veda, the Vedānta originally considered itself to be a completion of the Mīmāmsā, and the Vedāntic philosophy of life a completion and perfection of the Mīmāmsā philosophy of life. The life of the renouncer of the world (*sannyāsin*, ascetic, monk) belonged to the last of the four stages, and was regarded as the culmination of the life of every man. But when the two philosophies of life developed their metaphysical systems, they found themselves to be at opposite poles to each other. The propagation of monastic life by Jainism and Buddhism, and the popularity and respect it obtained made the Vedānta incline more towards the ideal of renunciation than towards that of active life. The gap between the Mīmāmsā and the Vedānta widened. Several attempts were made to reconcile them. The Mīmāmsā in its latest form, accepted the Vedānta, saying that renunciation was only surrender of all our actions to God, but not giving up active life. The *Bhagavadgītā* also made an earnest attempt by asking Arjuna to adopt egoless action. Some of the Vedāntins also made such attempts, as we shall see. But the truth remains that the metaphysics of the Mīmāmsā and that of the Vedānta could not be reconciled.

The basic text on which the Vedānta philosophers built up their systems are the Upaniṣads, the *Brahmasūtras* (*Aphorisms of the Brahman*), and the *Bhagavadgītā*. It is interesting to note that Bādarāyaṇa, the author of the *Brahmasūtras* was a regular householder, but not a monk. The *Bhagavadgītā*[1] is a part of the epic *Mahābhārata*, the authorship of which is attributed to one called Vyāsa and identified with Bādarāyaṇa, because Bādarāyaṇa also had the title Vyāsa (the arranger of a compiled material). But scholars think that the two Vyāsas were different persons, belonging to different ages.

The central doctrines of the Upaniṣads have already been discussed. The Upaniṣads contain four important statements (*mahāvākyas*, the great sentences): 'I am the Brahman' (*aham bhahmāsmi*); 'This ātman is the Brahman' (*ayam ātmā brahma*); 'That thou art' (*tattvamasi*); and 'All this is the Brahman' (*sarvam khalu idam brahma*). When these ideas are added to the main Upaniṣadic doctrines, the result ought to be a kind of monism. This philosophy should not be interpreted as pantheism, according to which the Supreme Spirit is equated to the world, but as panentheism, according to which the world is only part of the Supreme Spirit and the Supreme Spirit is far greater than the world. The *Bhagavadgītā* explains that the world is only one part (*amśa*) of God.

Now, the same Upaniṣads teach how to worship God, how to meditate on Him, and so on. But man cannot meditate on something, unless that something is other than he. Again, the Brahman is spoken of as the origin of myself and the world, as the creator, and as the cause. Then how can the cause of myself be myself? There were a number of religious philosophies, based originally upon Vedic ideas, but assimilating material from local religions and having traditions of their own. The most important of them are Śaivism and Vaiṣṇavism. And they also had to fit the four Great Sentences to their own philosophies. All of them commented on the three basic texts, for expounding their own philosophies. Thus although Vedānta originally meant

[1] Although the Vedāntic commentators regarded the *Bhagavadgītā* as a basic scripture, it is a part of the *Mahābhārata*, one of the epics, and is presented in this book along with the epics, which are regarded as subsidiary to the Vedas, which include the Upaniṣads.

the Upaniṣads, it came to mean later all the systems of philosophy developed by interpreting the three basic texts. We have at least ten schools of the Vedānta, out of which only four – those of Śaṅkara, Rāmānuja, Nimbārka, and Madhva – will be discussed here. In the interpretations, the commentators had to use all their logical, grammatical, etymological, and philological skill in order to extract the meaning they wanted out of the texts. Here we shall deal only with the structures of their philosophies, but not their textual explanations.

The Vedāntic schools name themselves after the relation they acknowledge between the *ātman* and the Brahman. The *Brahmasūtras* say that those who have realized the Brahman (Supreme Spirit) have realized it as their own *ātman* (Spirit).[2] Now, my spirit is within me, and I am essentially my spirit. Is the Supreme Spirit the same as my spirit, or is it something residing in my spirit? What then is their relation? Śaṅkara held the view that there is no difference between the two spirits, they are not two. He is called a non-dualist (Advaitin). The others held that they are two, but maintained different views about the relation between them. They are called dualists (*dvaitins*), dualist-cum-non-dualists (*dvaitādvaitins*), and so on.

If the world is one with the Brahman, in what sense is it one with the Brahman? How has the Brahman created the world? The Brahman, it is said by the Upaniṣads, created the world through the inexplicable energy, called Māyā. Then what is the nature of this Māyā and how is it related to the Brahman and the world? In answering these questions also the Vedāntins differed from one another.

THE VEDĀNTA OF ŚAṄKARA

Śaṅkara is called a non-dualist (*Advaitin*), because he did not accept the ultimate difference between the *ātman* and the Brahman. *Dvaita* means dualism, and *Advaita* means non-dualism. Śaṅkara does not mean that I, the finite being as such, is identical with the Brahman, but that the *ātman* in man is the same as the Brahman. Already even before the time of Śaṅkara, Buddhism developed two ideas: that the ultimate reality is pure consciousness, and that the nature of the world is the four-cornered negation, which is the structure of Māyā. Śaṅkara's grand teacher, Gauḍapāda (about the sixth century AD), took over both the doctrines and wove them up into a philosophy of

[2] IV, i, 3.

the *Māṇḍūkya Upaniṣad*. Śaṅkara developed it further in his own way. He belonged to the eighth century AD, lived only for thirty years, but, as a philosophical genius, wrote commentaries on the Upaniṣads, the *Brahmasūtras*, and the *Bhagavadgītā*, and composed a large number of other works and hymns.

The Brahman and Māyā

According to Śaṅkara, the Brahman is pure Existence, Consciousness, and Bliss (*Sat-cit-ānanda*). Like the Vijñāna of the Vijñānavādins, it is beyond all determinations and characterizations; but unlike their Vijñāna, it is eternal and it is Being itself. It is not Śūnya, which is neither Being nor Non-being. The beings of the world originated out of the Brahman, and the Brahman must, therefore, be Being. Being (or beings) can come only out of Being.

The Brahman is the Absolute and is impersonal; but God is not the Absolute, He is personal. Although God is not the Absolute, He is not a separate being from the Absolute. He is the Absolute facing the world and knowing it as his object. At the level of the Absolute, there is no distinction between the subject and the object, but at the level of God the distinction obtains. The Brahman creates out of itself the world of souls and matter and faces it; as facing it, the Brahman distinguishes itself from the world and becomes God. He is not overwhelmed by the forces of the world; but as facing them, He is free and above them. Yet an element of finitude enters His being, because He distinguishes Himself from something which He is not. The Brahman as God is called *Īśvara* (The Lord, the Ruler of the World).

The concept of Māyā has been variously misunderstood. It is necessary, therefore, to keep in mind its central significance. The Brahman created the world out of itself. Should we then think that the whole or a part of the Brahman is changed and expended in this creation? The Brahman, as the Absolute, is infinite and is eternally present in its perfection. Nothing of the Brahman is expended in the process. The Brahman throws out its mysterious energy (*śakti*) out of itself. The energy as such, apart from the consciousness of the Brahman, is blind, unconscious force, or power. It is this energy that takes the forms of the world. But should we then say that the Brahman has some of its energy spent up in the world and has the rest of that energy left over in it? No, like the Brahman, its energy also is infinite, we may deduct anything from the infinite, the remainder is always infinite. The Brahman never exhausts itself in the process of creation.

Now, we see only the world, which is a transformation of the energy of the Brahman. But we do not see the Brahman. Then, has not the world a separate existence of its own? Is it not able to exist apart from the Brahman? Śaṅkara answers in the negative. The common example to explain this situation is fire and its power to burn, which is fire's energy.[3] Has the power to burn a separate existence of its own apart from the existence of fire? The existence of the power, Śaṅkara says, is the same as the existence of fire. Conceptually, we may think of fire and its power separately; but they do not have separate existence. (The problem here is ontological). We say: 'The rose is', 'I am', 'We are', 'The mountains are', and so on. In all these statements, Being, or existence, denoted by the verbs is the Being of the Brahman itself. And therefore, concludes Śaṅkara, the world has no reality of its own apart from the reality of the Brahman. He does not mean to say that we do not experience the world or that the world is not there around us; he means only that, if we view it apart from the Brahman, the world can have no existence. But indeed, many people think of the world apart from the Brahman. To them Śaṅkara would say what they are thinking of has no existence.

Śaṅkara's answer is not really so simple. Do we not say: 'All the objects around us are there'? Then Śaṅkara says: 'Therefore, you cannot say that the world is non-existent.' But how can it be both existent and non-existent? Śaṅkara answers: 'No, it cannot be both.' Then what else is it? Śaṅkara again, answers: 'It cannot be neither.' because existence and non-existence, being contradictories, are the only two alternatives, and we cannot reject either, i.e. the world cannot be neither. Then what is it? It is inexplicable, it is the inexplicable (*anirvacanīya*) power of the Brahman, *Māyā*. From the standpoint of the Brahman, which is Being, the world, considered apart from the Brahman, is Māyā; it is neither Being, nor Non-being, nor both, nor neither. But considered along with the Brahman – which we do not do – it belongs to its Being and is Being. But Māyā belongs to, and is the Brahman, just as the burning power belongs to, and is fire. Even to say that it 'belongs' is a mistake, because we draw the

[3] Vidyāraṇya's *Pañcadasī* makes a significant use of this example. See any edition. E. von Hartman praises this book highly.

distinction between the burning power which belongs to fire, and fire to which it belongs. They are really one and the same. Māyā loses its unconscious nature when it is realized that it is part and parcel of the Brahman itself. But when viewed as separate, we have to say that it not only has no existence, but also does not belong to the Brahman.

Why then do we view ourselves and the world as apart from the Brahman? It is, again, due to Māyā, that can become an unconscious energy facing the Brahman. In its aspect as the Unconscious, Māyā is called Avidyā and Ajñāna, which are usually translated as Ignorance. Our individual separate existence is rooted in this Unconscious, and we are ignorant, therefore, of our true nature and of the nature of the world. Māyā, Avidyā, Ajñāna mean the same and are used as synonyms by almost all the Advaitins.

Māyā, as apart from the Brahman, has three attributes, each of which is also a power. They are *sattva* (clarity), *rajas* (activity), and *tamas* (darkness). As *tamas*, Māyā conceals the Brahman; as *rajas*, it creates the forms of the world; and as *sattva*, it enables consciousness to appear and know the forms as objects. *Rajas* is also called the projective power (*vikṣepaśakti*), and *tamas* the concealing power (*āvaraṇaśakti*) of Māyā. When we perceive a rose and say: 'That is a rose', the 'is' that is perceived is due to the *sattva*, or pure and transparent aspect of Māyā, through which the Being of the Brahman shines. When I say: 'I am', here also the Being of the Brahman shines through 'am'.

The Being in 'I am' and 'The rose is' is the same as the Being of the Brahman. It is the nature of the power of Māyā to divide itself into the opposites of subject and object. And because Māyā has no separate existence from the Brahman, it is said that the Brahman divides itself into the subject and object. But it should be noted that this division is not a spatial division like the division of a cake into pieces, but creation in which the creator's energy is in no way lessened.

The World

The spatio-temporal world is, therefore, a direct product of Māyā and an indirect product of the Brahman. It consists of the five elements and is governed by causal laws. But if it has no existence of its own, why should we bother about it? In this question, the 'we' refers to us as products of Māyā. We cannot, as products of Māyā, keep ourselves aloof from the objects, which are also products of Māyā. We and our world are correlates. So long as we exist as finite individuals, we have to treat the world as real. If we are real, the world also is real. But ourselves and the world have only relative reality, i.e. reality for the life of action. It is called *vyāvahārikasattā* or pragmatic reality, or existence, for activity. Empirical reality is reality for *vyavahāra* (action).

In this connection Śaṅkara distinguishes four kinds of being. Ultimate Being (*pāramārthikasattā*) is the Being of the Brahman only. Pragmatic or empirical Being (*vyāvahārikasattā*) belongs to the world and to ourselves. The third is the apparent Being (*prātibhāsikasattā*), which belongs to the objects of illusions, hallucinations, and dreams. The fourth is the insignificant Being (*tuccasattā*). It belongs to inexperiencable, imaginary objects, some of which may be self-contradictory or impossible. We can imagine lotus flowers in the sky. Poets generally describe them. There is no impossibility of some lotus flowers being dropped somewhere high up in the skies. But no one has any experience of their existence there. And we may speak of 'the son of a barren woman'. A barren woman cannot have any sons, so the existence of the son of a barren woman is impossible and self-contradictory. Still we think of such self-contradictory objects. One may ask the question: 'What is the nature of the Being of a barren woman's son?' and also 'What is the nature of the Being of the sky lotuses?' Then Śaṅkara and his followers would say: 'It is insignificant Being.' Such Being has no significance for metaphysics, epistemology, and life. But the other three types of Being have significance. Of course, Being is only one, but not many; but it appears at different levels in different forms.

The Ātman

According to Śaṅkara, the *ātman* is the same as the Brahman as involved in the mind, the senses and the physical body; and the Brahman is the same as the *ātman* without that involvement. So when man is able to realize his *ātman* without the mind, etc., he actually realizes the Brahman.

The *ātman*, again, is not the same as the *jīva*. The *jīva* is the ethical soul or personality. It is subject to transmigration and is composed of everything that the finite personality has, except the physical body. The *ātman* does not really experience pleasures and pains, it is the *jīva* that experiences them. The *ātman* is only an onlooker of the experiences of the *jīva*. Essentially, it is not even an onlooker (*sākṣi*). The *ātman* as such is neither the knower nor the agent of actions. Yet the conscious aspect of the *jīva* is due to the *ātman*, and the *ātman* with reference to the *jīva* is the onlooker (*sākṣi*). Without the *ātman*, the *jīva* can have neither consciousness nor even existence.

The *jīva* has three states and three bodies. First, there is the body of the waking consciousness. Secondly, there is the body of dream. Then there is the body of deep sleep, which is called the causal body (*kāraṇaśarīra*), because it contains the roots of our being, which determine what we are. Our body is a vehicle of our finitude and its experiences. The body of deep sleep also is such a vehicle. It is the individual Unconscious. The Vedāntins believed that the *jīva* carries this causal body in transmigration.

According to Śaṅkara, the *ātman* is not the same as the I-consciousness (*ahamdhī*). The I-consciousness is only the ego (*ahaṁkāra*), which knows, acts, and also calls itself the son of so and so, and so on. The ego is only a part of the *jīva*, which has several parts or factors. They are the causal body, apperceptive reason (*citta*), decision making reason (*buddhi*), ego (*ahaṁkāra*), mind (*manas*), the five senses, and the five organs of action. And it may assume the dream body, or the physical body. The function of mind is to synthesize (*saṅkalpa*) and analyse (*vikalpa*). When I perceive an object, e.g. an orange before me, I at first have the sensations of colour, shape, smell, taste, etc. But these belong to different senses. They are unified (synthesized) by mind into the object orange, and the object is separated from the table and other objects around it. This work of combining and separating is done by mind (*manas*). But the object orange is a combination of my sensations, and this 'my' belongs to the ego (*ahaṁkāra*). The ego is the principle in me for appropriating the experiences as my experiences. The object is, therefore, still a subjective form. Then I say: 'That is an orange'. When I say so, I mean that the form I perceive is true not only for me, but also for everyone else. I thereby recognize the independent being or existence of the object, which in its independence is true for every man. The decision I make in fixing it down as an existent orange is the function of *buddhi* (reason). But 'That is an orange' does not stand alone, after being made objective. The orange belongs to the orange tree, that to a grove, that to a person, who pays taxes and so on. The collection of this objectivity together is the function of *citta* (the apperceptive reason).

Just as from the spiritual point of view, the doctrine that the Brahman is realized as one's own *ātman* became important and was variously interpreted; from the metaphysical point of view, the doctrine that the Brahman is the ultimate cause of the world and man became important and was variously interpreted. We have here really two kinds of causation: (1) the causation that obtains within the realm of natural laws; and (2) the causation by the Brahman, which is beyond the realm of natural laws.

Causation

We have seen that the Cārvākas denied the reality of the causal principle, because, since inference can never be adequate to the empirical world, we can never know whether causation exists in the world or not. The structure of inference is a purely formal affair; but if it is to give any knowledge of existing things, it has to be applied to them. For the purpose, we have to have the major premise based upon perception, but we can never get the major premise, since we can never exhaust all the instances. The causal principle belongs to existing empirical objects, and is not merely formal. Since it is always a universal proposition of the form, 'Whenever heat is applied, bodies expand', it can never be known. So the Cārvākas denied causation and said that all was chance (tychism). But all the other schools accepted causation, excepting some of their dialecticians.

The Buddhists understood causation in two ways, as aggregation and as occasioning the effect. In occasioning the effect, since everything is momentary, the cause perishes before the effect is born. The effect is, therefore, born out of the non-being of the cause. So the Buddhist doctrine of causation contains the principle that the actual cause is non-being (*asatkāraṇavāda*). Śaṅkara does not accept this principle, but maintains that the cause is always being (*satkāraṇavāda*). For the Buddhists, there can really be no material cause, and they give the example of the seed and the tree. Unless the seed perishes, the tree cannot be born, and the seed does not exist in the tree. So there is really no material cause. Other instances also have to be explained similarly. But Śaṅkara points to the example of the clay and the pot, and says that the clay is present in the pot and can even be obtained after the pot is destroyed. The pot is only a form, but not being, whereas the clay, which is the material cause, is the being of the pot. So we should say that the material cause is real and existent. Even the seed is existent in a latent state in the tree; the tree is only a form, which the material cause, the seed, takes with the help of water and the materials found in earth. And the doctrine that the cause is existent holds true of the causation of the Brahman also, because ultimately the being of everything is the Being of the Brahman.

Then Śaṅkara distinguishes between two kinds of causation: the first, in which the cause has to transform itself in order to become the effect, and the second, in which the cause, without losing itself in the process, produces the effect. The first is that in which the being of the cause is affected and is called the self-transforming causation or simply change or becoming (*pariṇāma*). Transformation is perhaps not the exact word, because it may mean only change of form, but not of the material. But in becoming and change, the matter along with form is changed. The usual example is the change of milk into buttermilk. After the milk is changed into buttermilk, we cannot get back milk. Similarly, after the seed is changed into the tree, we cannot get back the original seed.

The second kind of causation is that in which the being of the cause is not affected. The example is that of clay and pot, or any metal and the vessel made of it. Now, in the vessel the metal is not lost; and when the vessel is destroyed we can get back the original metal. This causation is called change of form without change of being (*vivartakāraṇa*). We should note that both the seed and the metal are material causes, but they act (change) in different ways for producing the effect.

Śaṅkara says that the Brahman produces the world without in any way affecting its own Being. The world consists only of new forms rising out of the Being of the Brahman. It is, therefore, only a *vivartakāraṇa*. If it were *pariṇāmakāraṇa* (the cause that changes its being also in producing the effect), then the Brahman would lose itself in the process of creation, and so long as the world lasted, there would be no Brahman. But the Brahman is eternally perfect and infinite.

Śaṅkara accepts the other kinds of cause also so far as the empirical world is concerned. They are the efficient cause, the instrumental cause, and the formal cause. Yet these distinctions hold good only in the world of plurality. But the Brahman is without a second (*advaya*), when it creates the world. The Brahman is, therefore, all these causes at once.

Epistemology

Śaṅkara accepts all the sources of knowledge, which the Mīmāmsā accepts. He accepts also the Mīmāmsā theory of the self-validity of knowledge (*svatahprāmāṇya*) and maintains, likewise, that knowledge is made invalid by something else. For him, also, the world is a world of action, and so the cognition of any object belonging to the world must serve the purpose for which it is meant. All objects have a reference to purpose, and the categorization of the world can be divided into the enjoyer (*bhoktā*) and the enjoyed (*bhogya*).

But over the problem of the status of the object of illusion, he differed from the Mīmāmsakas, and maintained that it is an inexplicable entity (*anirvacanīya*). His doctrine is called *anirvacanīyakhyātivāda* or the doctrine that illusion is the cognition of an inexplicable object.

Taking the example of the rope perceived as the snake, we cannot say that it is an object of imagination, because there is difference between imagining and perceiving, and an imagined snake does not produce the fright which the illusory one produces. It appears to us as a being. We cannot, therefore, say that because when we discover the rope, we say: 'There was no snake even when we perceived it', that this backward negative reference meant that it had no Being. And it cannot be both Being and Non-being, which are contradictory opposites. Nor can it be neither, because Being and Non-being are the only two opposites. So the snake has neither Being, nor Non-being, nor both, nor neither. It is inexplicable.

We see that here Śaṅkara has adopted Nagārjuna's view to explain illusion. But he differed also from Nagārjuna. According to Nagārjuna, even the rope is illusroy, and the snake is, therefore, without any real substratum. A cognition is not false with reference necessarily to a true cognition, but by itself. Śaṅkara does not accept this view. If we do not take the rope as real, we have no right to call the snake false. The basis for the distinction between falsity and truth must be found in this world itself; otherwise, we could not have known the distinction at all. Falsity, error, or illusion (*bhrama*) must have truth as its basis (*sadadhiṣṭāna*). So it is the real rope that is mistaken as the false snake.

Yet it is not mistaken for a snake that was experienced in the past and remembered now; it is a new snake altogether that we perceive. Otherwise, when we perceive the snake, the form of our perception will be recognition in the form, 'This is the same snake as that which I perceived on such and such an occasion'. But there is no such recognition at all when we perceive the illusory snake. Here he differs from the Mīmāmsakas, again, who say that the snake is one perceived in the past.

Regarding the criterion of truth, Śaṅkara maintains that it is uncontradictability (*abādhyatvam*). It is not merely uncontradictedness, but uncontradictability. Of course, this is the criterion of absolute truth, i.e. the truth of the Brahman. For even when we see the rope as the rope and say: 'That is a rope', it is still possible to prove that the rope has no absolute being, that by its very nature it depends for its existence on the material with which it is made, on the earth on which it exists, on the person who made it and so on. It can have only relative being. We ignore the fact that it has only a relative being and affirm at once, 'That is a rope.' So even this statement contains an element of falsity, which we do not notice, and we can, therefore, contradict the statement. But in the case of the Brahman, no contradiction is possible, because it is Being itself, the Being that shines through every object.

The Nature and Aim of Life

Śaṅkara teaches that the being of man is essentially the being of the Brahman. But man does not know it, because he is rooted in Ignorance and is born out of Ignorance (*Māyā*, *Avidyā*). This Ignorance is not only the Ignorance that man has, but also the Ignorance that constitutes his foundation. Yet it is through this Ignorance that the 'I' appears as a spark of the Brahman, wihch is being, consciousness, and bliss (*sat-cit-ānanda*). This ignorance is the same as the Unconscious of depth psychology, but is also metaphysical, in that it constitutes the roots of our finite being. It is through this Unconscious that the infinite Brahman appears as the finite 'I'.

The aim of man is, therefore, to realize his true nature, that he is in essence the Brahman itself. But so long as his finitude lasts, the Unconscious cannot be overcome; and finitude cannot be overcome, so long as man considers himself to be a finite subject facing the finite objects of the world and going after them for enjoyment. But man cannot suddenly become the Universal Spirit merely by thinking. He has to realize his essential universality through ethical life and right action. Ethical action purifies the mind by raising it to the universal level.

Śaṅkara accepts all the virtues which the other schools accept. But since it is realization of the Brahman that is the ultimate aim, he treats the way of knowledge (*jñānamārga*) as the highest. He says that devotion to God, leading an active ethical life and surrendering all actions to Him are useful, but they should lead ultimately to the knowledge and realization of the Brahman, which is really the realization of one's essential *ātman* (spirit) and is therefore true self-realization.

But due perhaps to the influence of Jainism and Buddhism, Śaṅkara lays on the whole, less emphasis on the life of action than the other Vedāntins. He says that it is not necessary for man to go through the life of action in order to obtain right knowledge of the Brahman. Action makes man think of the world as a plurality, whereas true knowledge consists of knowing that everything is the Brahman. The two ways, the way of action and the way of knowledge, have opposite goals; we can accept right action only for purifying the mind and then we have to give it up. That is, man has to take to the life of renunciation (*sannyāsa*). And man can take to it as soon as he feels no attachment to the world. He need not necessarily follow the Mīmāmsā teaching of right action (*dharma*) before attempting to know about, and realize the Brahman.

Man can realize the Brahman in this life and body itself. This doctrine is called that of salvation in this life (*jīvanmukti*). By following the prescribed practices, one can realize in this life itself that one's being is the same as that of the Brahman.

But one should prepare oneself for the life of realization. The preparation consists of (1) the ability to discriminate between what is eternal and what is transient; (2) the giving up of all desire for enjoyment here and hereafter; (3) development of the qualities of the control of mind, speech, etc., of detachment, patience and endurance, and the power of concentration; and (4) the desire for salvation. For attaining the ideal of liberation from bondage to the world of action, the life of action prescribed by the Mīmāmsā religion and philosophy is not important, except for purifying the mind.

THE VEDĀNTA OF RĀMĀNUJA

Rāmānuja is a theist. While Śaṅkara's philosophy is called non-dualism (*advaita*), Rāmānuja's is called the non-dualism of the qualified Brahman, or simply qualified, or modified non-dualism (*viśīṣṭādvaita*). Śaṅkara maintained the doctrine of the non-dualism of the indeterminate Brahman (*nirguṇa* or *nirviśeṣa* Brahman); but Rāmānuja upheld the doctrine of the non-dualism of the qualified or determinate Brahman (*saguṇa* or *saviśeṣa Brahman*). The Brahman is not devoid of determinations or characteristics. It is qualified by the *ātmans* and the material world, which together constitute the body (*śarīra*) of the Brahman. The non-duality meant by the Upaniṣads is that of the one-ness of God, the *ātmans*, and the world, like the one-ness of man who is a unity of body and *ātman*.

Rāmānuja belonged to the eleventh century AD, and was a follower of the Vaiṣṇava religion and its Pāñcarātra Āgamas. And he interpreted the three basic texts according to those Āgamas.

The Brahman

Rāmānuja, unlike Śaṅkara, makes no distinction between the Brahman and God. The Absolute, Brahman, is personal and is the same as God. The Brahman is existence, consciousness, and bliss, but these three are its attributes and so qualities. The Brahman has many other great qualities like power, splendour and so on. All these qualities make his nature determinate. Although the world and the *ātmans* constitute the body of the Brahman, it is not affected by the evil present in the world, just as the qualities of the body like white and black do not pertain to the *ātman*. The relation between the Brahman on the one side and the *ātmans* and the material world, on the other, is that of the *ātman*-body relationship (*śarīrātmasambandha*). And although the *ātmans* constitute the body of the Brahman, they are yet different from it. We should not say that the relation is that of both identity and difference, because identity and difference are opposites and cannot be true of the same relationship. The Brahman never exists without the *ātmans* and the material world. Even before creation they stick to him in their subtle form and after creation they assume gross forms. Creation is, therefore, the change (*pariṇāma*) of the subtle into the gross, and dissolution the reverse process of the gross becoming the subtle. Just as the body is different from the *ātman* and has its own being, the *ātmans* and the material world, in both their subtle and gross states, have their own independent being and reality.

Arguments against Māyā

Māyā is the peculiar energy of the Brahman by which he creates the world. It is real and characterizes the Brahman, making it determinate. Rāmānuja does not accept the definition of Māyā given by the Buddhists and Śaṅkara. They say: 'Māyā is neither being, nor non-being, nor both, nor neither.' But if it is not being, it must be non-being; and if it not non-being, it must be being. If it is non-being, it cannot be the cause of the world, because non-being cannot be the cause of anything. It must, therefore, be being. Taking the example of fire and its power to burn, Rāmānuja would say that both have their separate being, and each is as real as the other. The power to burn is a quality, a determinant of fire, which has other qualities also. Nothing is known without a characteristic, and the being that is known and the characteristic through which it is known, are equally real and existent. If the characteristic is false and has no existence of its own, then the object it reveals also may not have its own existence. Even when the Brahman is known, it has to be, and can only be known through some characteristic. Knowledge is always of the form 'S is P', not mere 'S'. Existence as such can never be known. It is known only in the form 'S is P' or 'That is P'.

Ajñāna, or *Avidyā* (Ignorance, Unconscious) is only another name for *karma* (action, latent and actual). The *ātman* forgets its original nature, and acts in order to obtain this or that result. The *ātman* is originally full of bliss and knowledge, which it forgets and becomes active for obtaining pleasure and knowledge. So Avidyā is not the same as Māyā. Rāmānuja criticizes[4] the Advaitin's concept of Māyā and gives several arguments, two of which are important. First, how can Avidyā (the Unconscious) appear in the Brahman, which, according to the Advaitins, is pure consciousness and is the only reality? Does it exist separately and then by some chance overpower the consciousness of the Brahman? But the Advaitins say that it has no existence (being) of its own and that the Brahman is the only reality. Then does it exist in the Brahman or have its being in the Brahman

[4] See his Commentary on *Brahmasūtras*, I, i, 1.

and now and then overpower it? If it does so, then the Brahman will have a power within itself and that power characterizes the Brahman. The conclusion also is not accepted by the Advaitins, who say that the Brahman has even within itself no characteristic other than itself. Secondly, how can this Avidyā produce the world and the *jīva*? If it is the Unconscious, it must be the Unconscious of someone. To be unconscious is to be ignorant, and ignorance cannot exist by itself, but only as belonging to someone. Then does it belong to the Brahman or to the *jīva*? If it belongs to the Brahman, then the Brahman will be characterized and made determinate by it, which view the Advaitins do not accept. Then it must belong to the *jīva*. But how can it belong to the *jīva*? In order to belong to the *jīva*, the *jīva* must exist prior to his being unconscious of his true nature; but according to the Advaitins, the *jīva* himself is a product of Avidyā, and so cannot exist prior to Avidyā. But if he exists prior to Avidyā, then Avidyā cannot have the metaphysical nature attributed to it by the Advaitins; it will only be the absence of knowledge, in the *jīva*, of his true nature. Absence of knowledge is a negative concept, but Advaitins say that Avidyā is a positive metaphysical entity. Rāmānuja concludes, therefore, that the doctrine of Māyā, as expounded by the Advaitins, is self-contradictory and false.

The World

The world, according to Rāmānuja, is real, has its own being apart from that of the Brahman, is a part of the Brahman and is one of its characteristics. Rāmānuja calls it *Prakṛti*. It is unconscious matter. Originally it is subtle and has three attributes – *sattva* (clarity), *rajas* (activity), and *tamas* (darkness). Due to the working of *karma* (action), existing in its subtle form in the *ātman*, the equilibrium of the original subtle *Prakṛti* is destroyed, and the three attributes become separate, act upon one another, and become the world of gross objects. This process was described in detail in the chapter on the Sāṅkhya philosophy, because the Sāṅkhya philosophy was the first to have developed the doctrine. However, *Prakṛti* is part of the Brahman itself, constituting its body. Besides the three attributes, the principle of Limit (*Niyati*) and of Time (Kāla) also belong to *Prakṛti*, according to the Pāñcarātra tradition. But the followers of Rāmānuja give them a place alongside *Prakṛti*.

Since everything is real and has its own being according to Rāmānuja, he does not accept the distinction of the four levels of being, expounded by Śaṅkara. Every object – of the common world, of dreams, and of illusions and hallucinations also – is real and has being. Of course, the insignificant being (*tucchasattā*) does not come into question.

The Ātman

The *ātman*, according to Rāmānuja, is different from the Brahman and is a part of its body. Rāmānuja maintains the view that the *ātman* is atomic in size. But although it is atomic, it has what he calls attribute-consciousness (*dharma-bhūta-jñāna*), which is infinite. The flame of the lamp is very small, but its light spreads in the whole room. Similarly, although the *ātman* is atomic, its consciousness can be infinite. Rāmānuja believes that mind (*manas*) also is atomic.

Forms of Consciousness

Rāmānuja distinguishes between two forms of consciousness, existential conscious (*svarūpajñāna*, consciousness of one's own being) and attribute consciousness (consciousness which one has and therefore forms one's property or attribute, *dharmabhūtajñāna*). When I perceive the rose in front of me, there are three factors in my cognition: (1) the rose of which I am conscious, (2) the consciousness of the rose, (3) and myself as having the consciousness of the rose. The rose is revealed to me by the consciousness I have of the rose; the consciousness of the rose reveals itself through itself to me, but not to itself; and the consciousness of myself reveals itself to itself. The last factor is existential consciousness. It is self-revealing to itself, but only when it knows the object. The consciousness of the rose, which I have, is also self-revealing; but it is self-revealing not to itself, but to the existential consciousness. The existential consciousness is the I-consciousness.

Rāmānuja says that the *ātman* is the same as the I-consciousness. But it is not the same as the ego (*ahaṁkāra*).[5] The I-consciousness, when it identifies itself with a particular form and regards itself as a

[5] See *Śrī Bhāṣya* (Venkateswar Company, Madras, 1909), Vol. I, p. 47.

man or woman, as the son or daughter of so and so, and so on, is the ego. But as pure I-consciousness (*ahamdhī*), it is the *ātman*.

The *ātman* is both the knower and the agent of action, and also the enjoyer of the fruit of those actions. Rāmānuja does not accept the view that the *ātman* is neither the knower nor the doer. He says that experience shows that I am the knower of objects, not my ego, and I am the doer of actions, not again my ego. The I-consciousness is present in knowing and doing. It is the I-consciousness that is in bondage and that has to be liberated. If it is already free, and if it is the ego only that is in bondage, why should I bother about the bondage of my ego, when I am already free?

Causation

Rāmānuja does not accept Śaṅkara's doctrine of causation in which the being of the cause is not transformed into the effect (*vivartakāraṇa*). He accepts only *pariṇāma* or the becoming of the cause into effect. Even the Brahman transforms itself into the world. But then how can the Brahman remain eternally perfect? Rāmānuja replies that this change is the change of the Brahman with its subtle (*sūkṣma*) body into the Brahman with the gross (*sthūla*) body; change, or rather becoming is only a manifestation (*āvirvhāva*) of the subtle in a gross form. It is not the appearance of something new. And in both the states, the subtle and the gross, the Brahman is not affected. But how can the Brahman be not affected by the change, even though it is the manifestation of the subtle as the gross? Rāmānuja says that it is only the body of the Brahman, consisting of the *ātmans* and the material world, that changes; the *Ātman* part remains unchanged in both the states. The followers of Śaṅkara ask: 'If the body is an essential part of the Brahman, how can one part change without affecting the other part?' The answer of Rāmānuja is: In ourselves we find that the body undergoes many changes, but the *ātman* remains the same. But earlier Rāmānuja maintained that the *ātman* is the knower, the doer, and the enjoyer. And it sees, acts, and enjoys through the body. It must, therefore, be affected by the affections of the body. Then how can the *Ātman* part of the Brahman remain unaffected by the changes of its own body? The only answer is that the Brahman has a mysterious power with the help of which it remains unaffected by the changes of its body; and we cannot understand the nature of this power.

Rāmānuja understands all causation, even the causation in material nature as the manifestation of the subtle into the gross. Even the clay, which is the cause of the pot, manifests only what it already contains potentially. Potentially the clay contains the pot and many other things, which become manifest as effects. Rāmānuja accepts the other kinds of cause also, like the efficient cause and the instrumental cause. But the Brahman contains everything.

Epistemology

Rāmānuja accepts three sources of knowledge – perception, inference, and verbal knowledge – and subsumes the others given by the Mīmāmsā under them. He accepts also that all cognition is valid by itself (*svatahprāmāṇya*), and that what we call falsity is generated by something else *(paratah aprāmāṇya)*.

But in expounding this doctrine Rāmānuja goes even further than the Mīmāmsā and Śaṅkara and advocates a position at the opposite extreme of Buddhism, according to which all cognitions are false. Rāmānuja says that every cognition is true, and the objects of illusion also, like the snake in the classical example, are true and have Being (*sat*). This doctrine of illusion is called *satkhyātivāda*, or the doctrine that illusion is the cognition of an existent object. The illusory snake is not a remembered snake, but a new existent snake. But its existence is not a mundane, but a non-mundane (*alaukika*) existence. The world consists of enjoyers (*bhoktās*), or the *ātmans* and the enjoyed (*bhogyas*), or the objects that produce either pleasures or pains. Now, the illusory snake produces fright and anxiety. So it is also like the rope, which is mistaken for the snake. But if any object of cognition is true and existent, why do we make the distinction between the true and the false? We make it, because some of the objects serve the purpose for which they are meant (*arthakriyākāris*), and we call them true; those which do not serve such a purpose are called false. But both of them have existence and are real, and cognition, which belongs to the *ātman*, is never mistaken. Just as from their metaphysical point of view the Buddhists maintain that all cognition of external objects is false by nature. Rāmānuja maintains that all such cognition is true by nature.

In spite of the sweeping assertion that cognition can never be mistaken, Rāmānuja accepts that, from the point of view of the world of action, we do draw the distinction between illusory objects and real objects. He uses also the principle of contradiction to show that the rival doctrines are false, thereby admitting that there is false knowledge.

When explaining the nature of attribute consciousness (*dharmabhūtajñāna*), we explained also the epistemological situation as understood by Rāmānuja. There is no knowledge, according to Rāmānuja, in which the object is not grasped through an attribute. Even direct knowledge of the Brahman is knowledge through an attribute. All knowledge and cognition is of the form 'That is P'. It always contains the distinction between the subject and the predicate. Nothing indeterminate can be the object of knowledge.

The Advaitins maintain that the Brahman is without any determinations or qualities. And direct knowledge of the Brahman, therefore, is knowledge without any determination (*nirvikalpakajñāna*). Similarly, when we perceive an object, first our senses and mind come into contact with it, we know only that there is something, we do not know as yet what it is. This cognition also is called indeterminate knowledge of merely something (*nirvikalpakajñāna*). This is only a stage in cognition, which does not stop, but moves forward till it knows what the object is. Then it arrives at the stage of knowing 'That is a rose'. This stage at which the 'That' is characterized or determined as 'a rose' is called determinate knowledge (*savikalpakajñāna*). In the empirical world, determinate knowledge alone is useful and can be made also the basis of inference.

Rāmānuja also accepts the distinction between determinate and indeterminate knowledge. But while the Advaitins maintain that indeterminate knowledge is formless and qualityless, Rāmānuja says that, since no cognition is without a determination, indeterminate knowledge also, because it is knowledge, has determinations. There is no formless (*niṣprakāraka*) cognition. But the difference lies here: while in determinate cognition, the determinations are universals or class characteristics, in indeterminate knowledge they are individuals. An American boy who does not know anything about an elephant, sees the animal for the first time in his life. But does he not see that the object has a huge body, big trunk and legs, and large ears? These are the characteristics or determinations of the elephant. The boy at that time does not classify the animal, and think of the class or universal, 'huge body', 'big trunk', 'large ears', etc. But when he sees another elephant and remembers the first one, he thinks of the class of elephants, the class of 'huge bodies', etc. Then of course his cognition is determined by the class concept or universal. Indeterminate knowledge is, therefore, knowledge of the individual (*vyakti*), which is characterized by individual determinants, but not by universals. Determinate knowledge is knowledge of objects determined by universal determinants or class concepts.

Creation

According to Rāmānuja, God creates the world of *ātmans* and matter. But creation is only a change of the subtle into the gross. So even matter exists in a subtle form after dissolution and sticks to God. The *ātmans* also are eternal with their attribute-consciousness. Rāmānuja says that, even in their pure state, the *ātmans* have a body, but the body is not made up of Prakṛti, but of a Pure Transparent Substance called *Śuddhasattva*.[6] Thus Śuddhasattva or Pure Sattva is different from the *Sattva* (clarity, transparence), which is a part of *Prakṛti*. *Prakṛti's* Sattva never exists without the other two attributes, *rajas* (activity) and *tamas* (darkness). But Śuddhasattva has no relation with the other two attributes at all. It is very subtle. The *ātman* can regain its pure body by getting over the disturbances of *rajas* (activity), and the impurity of *tamas* (darkness), and trying to be *sattva* (transparence) alone. Then the *ātman* will give up the *sattva* of Prakrti also, and regain *Śuddhasattva*.

Although *sattva*, *rajas*, and *tamas* are called attributes in Indian philosophy, they should be understood as though they are substances (*dravyas*), because they are attributes in the sense in which Spinoza calls mind and matter attributes of God, the Substance. The three can be qualities also of our mind. For instance, our mind may be very calm, pure, and rational, when it is called *sātvika*; it may be very much agitated as in anger, when it is called *rājasika*; and it may be dull and clouded, when it is called *tāmasika*.

Rāmānuja's philosophy is more theological than metaphysical. He believes, like the Jainas, in three kinds of spirits. (1) The eternally liberated *ātmans* belong to demi-gods and angels, and may assume worldly life to help humanity, but are never bound by the laws of the world and of ethical action, because they do not forget their original

[6] Śrīnivāsadāsa, *Yatīndramatadīpikā*, ed. by Adidevananda (Ramakrishna Mutt, Madras, 1949), pp. 79 ff. (For a study of the differences between Śaṅkara and Rāmānuja, see S. M. S. Chari, *Advaita and Viśistādvaita* (Asia Publishing House, Madras, 1961).

nature. (2) The liberated *ātmans* live in the ideal world of God, and, having once been freed from bondage, will never be bound again. And (3) the *ātmans* in bondage have to work for their freedom from bondage.

Way of Life

While Śaṅkara gave the highest place for the way of knowledge (*jñānamārga*), Rāmānuja gave it to the way of devotion (*bhaktimārga*). But he insists that man should lead a life of action until death. The Mīmāmsā life of action holds good as long as man lives. There can be no life without action, and action must always obey the rules of ethical conduct. Rāmānuja does not believe in salvation in this life itself (*jīvanmukti*), and criticizes Śaṅkara for maintaining it. To have this life means not to have been liberated, and to be liberated means not to have this life. The two cannot, therefore, go together. Man lives, so long as he lives, the life of action, and obtains salvation only after death.

But man can obtain salvation, and conquer rebirth, only when he has developed devotion to, or love of God. Rāmānuja defines devotion or love (*bhakti*) not as an emotion, but as continuity of knowledge without break. He gives the example of the girl or boy who cannot get rid of the idea of her lover or beloved, when passionately in love. One may call it passion, but Rāmānuja understands it as the unbroken stream of knowledge. Only to know God is not enough; that knowledge (*jñāna*) must have unbroken continuity. Rāmānuja rejects that verbal and conceptual knowledge of God can bring salvation. It has to be accompanied by meditation (*dhyāna*, *upāsanā*), and this meditation will lead to knowledge and knowledge of devotion. And ethical action is necessary until death for keeping the mind pure and above selfishness.

It is not easy for every man to develop love of God in the sense in which Rāmānuja explains the term. Without God's own responsive help and grace, one cannot attain ideal love. God understands it and helps those who sincerely make the attempt. For this purpose all that man has to do is to take refuge in God (*prapatti*) and take shelter in Him (*śaraṇāgati*). These words mean complete self-surrender. Man should continue leading an active life, but surrender himself and his actions to God, considering himself to be an instrument in His hands for His work in the world.

THE VEDĀNTA OF MADHVA

Śaṅkara was the earliest commentator on the Upaniṣads and the *Brahmasūtras*, if we take into consideration those whose commentaries are available. All the other Vedāntins lived after him and established their name through criticizing him. All of them differed from him and from one another in understanding the relation between the Brahman and the *ātman*, between the *ātman* and the material world, and between the material world and the Brahman. And these Vedāntins mostly belonged either to the Vaiṣṇava or the Śaiva religious tradition. The Vaiṣṇava tradition identifies the Brahman with its highest god, Viṣṇu; and the Śaiva tradition with Śiva. But in some cases, whether the Vedāntin belonged to the Vaiṣṇava (e.g. Rāmānuja) or Śaiva (e.g. Śrīkaṇṭha) tradition, the metaphysical position is the same. They differ only in the forms of worship and, to some extent, of meditation, and also in the name they give the Brahman, which is personified. We shall present only two representative metaphysical positions, one of which is Madhva's.

Madha, also called Pūrṇaprajña, belonged to the thirteenth century AD. He belonged to the Vaiṣṇava tradition and accepted much that Rāmānuja taught. He rejected Śaṅkara's doctrine of Māyā, saying that it is a real power of the Brahman and has its own being. Again, he accepted that the *ātman* is atomic, that it is subservient to the Brahman, that the Vedas were not composed by any person, even by God – a view common to all the Vedāntins – that knowledge is always valid, and that the *ātmans* and the world are different from the Brahman and different from one another. But he did not accept the view that the relation between the Brahman on the one hand and the *ātmans* and the material world on the other is that of the *ātman* and the body. He maintained that they are completely different. The Brahman and the *ātman* are two entities, and form a duality. So his philosophy is called dualism (*dvaita*). But this dualism should not be confused with the dualism of mind and matter found in western philosophy. For him both the *ātman* and the Brahman are spiritual, and yet two. Indeed, matter is also different from both and has its own reality.

Madhava is a pluralist. There is the Brahman, there is an infinite number of *ātmans*, and there is an infinite number of material entities. While Rāmānuja, so far as the explanation of this world goes, is closer to the Śaṅkhya philosophy, Madhva is closer to the pluralism of the

Nyāya, the Vaiśeṣika and the Mīmāmsā philosophies. He even says that the world had no beginning and will have no end, and is real. He accepts five kinds of difference as absolutely real:[7] (1) the difference between the *ātman* and the Brahman; (2) the difference between matter and the Brahman; (3) the difference between one *ātman* and another; (4) the difference between the *ātmans* and matter; and (5) the difference between one material entity and another. He accepts the category of the particular (*viśeṣa*) from the Vaiśeṣika philosophy develops it and says that every entity has a particular (*viśeṣa*), that differentiates it from every other, and explains the particular as the source of the energy or power (*śakti*) which is shown by every object and which is different from the power shown by any other. Unless every object is different from every other object, it cannot show the peculiar energy which it shows, either in the form of resistance or initiative (causal efficiency), and which the others do not show. For instance, one particular seed must have produced this tree; the other seeds, although of the same kind, produce other trees. So every object has its own particular in it. Madhva does not mean merely that every object is a particular, but *has* a particular. He accepts ten categories: Substance, Quality, Activity, Universal, Particular, Negation, Energy (*Śakti*), Similarity, Part, and Whole. These categories are all-pervasive. Madhva classifies all entities under two categories, the independent (*svatantra*) and the dependent (*parantantra*). The Brahman alone is independent and has control over everything else, which is subordinate to it. Māyā is the will (desire, *icchā*) of the Brahman.

One can obtain salvation through love, surrender and service of the Brahman. Madhva is a philosopher, as generally understood, of absolute difference (*bheda*). The unifying principle is the controlling power of the Brahman. Whether this power to control absolutely different entities has any metaphysical basis, except that of Māyā as the will of the Brahman, is not explained.

THE VEDĀNTA OF NIMBĀRKA

Nimbārka is assigned to the thirteenth century and was a follower of the Vaiṣṇava tradition. He also preached the way of devotion. His philosophy is important for its new conception of the relation between the Brahman, on the one side, and the *ātman* and the material world, on the

[7] *Sarvadarśanasangraha*, p. 54.

other. Śaṅkara and Madhva held opposite positions: Śaṅkara emphasized non-difference (*abheda*, identity), and Madhva absolute difference (*bheda*). Nimbārka said that both identity and difference were true. Rāmānuja also attempted to reconcile identity and difference, not by unifying identity and difference into a single relationship, but after rejecting both, and accepting a new concrete form, that of body-*ātman*. Nimbārka does not accept the body-*ātman* relationship, because the afflictions of the body affect the *ātman*; and similarly the evils of the world and the *ātmans* will affect the Brahman. So Nimbārka says that the relation is the complex relation of identity-difference (or identity in difference, *bhedābheda*).

Nimbārka's main argument is simple. The Brahman is the cause of the world, not merely the efficient cause, but also the material cause. Now, the relation between cause and effect is both identity and difference. The clay, which is the material cause of the pot, is identical with the pot. But if it is merely identical with the pot, then there will be no difference between the lump of clay and pot. Hence there is difference also. Similarly, we can show many similarities and differences between the Brahman and the *ātmans* and between the Brahman and the material world.

In answer to the question, whether the identity and difference between the Brahman and the world are both of nature and being, Nimbārka answered that they are only of nature, but not of being. By nature both the Brahman and the *ātman* are identical and also different. They are identical because the ātman is a part (*amśa*) of the Brahman and is conscious like it. But they are different also because the part and whole are not equal to each other. But with regard to being, the two are only different, not identical. The Brahman is supreme and omnipotent, and is the creator of the world, wheras the *ātman* is only a part, finite, and cannot be the creator. So existentially, ontologically or in being, they are only different. Similarly, the material world also has both identity and difference to the Brahman only by nature but not in being. The two words *svābhāvika* and *svārūpya* cannot be exactly translated as 'by being' and 'by form',[8] but as 'by nature' and 'in being'.

[8] The author himself committed the mistake of using the literal translation of these words in his *Idealistic Thought of India*, pp. 150 ff. Just as the thought of a philosopher undergoes modification as he thinks more and more deeply into his concepts, the translation of many of the technical terms undergoes

The problem of the relationship between the Brahman and the *ātman* and the world assumed a new importance in the Vedānta. It was not only the question of reconciliation of identity and difference, but also of the nature of the identity and of difference, that exercised the minds of the thinkers. The Vedāntin to start this problem was Bhāskara[9] (AD 900), who does not seem to belong to the Vaiṣṇava or Śaiva religious tradition in particular, but who wanted to combine the Way of Action and the Way of Knowledge. He maintained that the identity of the Brahman and the *ātman* and the difference between the two were both by nature and in being. But some others like Śrīpati, a Śaiva (AD 1600) said that such a relation exists between the Brahman and the material world also. The literature of these Vedāntic schools is not as exhaustive as that of the schools of Śaṅkara, Rāmānuja and Madhva, and we cannot get answers to all the questions we may like to raise.

change as the translator, who has to be an interpreter also, gets a more and more profound understanding of what he is translating. Very often occasions arise when the translator sees that a particular English term does not fit the system when presented in English; and academic sincerity demands that he should not consider it a loss of prestige to recognize inappropriateness when it is present. It is really important that European writers, many of whom have made admirable contributions to the revival of Eastern philosophies, be very careful in translating technical terms and a long process of re-examination of these translations is needed to prevent false conclusions being drawn from literal translations. This warning applies not only to western scholars, but also to us Indian writers of English.

[9] For a presentation of the central ideas of the other Vedāntins, see the author's *Idealistic Thought of India*.

Chapter XIII

THE EPICS AND THE ETHICAL CODES

THE THREE MAIN WAYS OF LIFE

We have seen that the Mīmāmsā laid all emphasis on action, the Advaita Vedānta, Buddhism and Jainism on knowledge, and the Vedānta of the other schools on devotion or love of God. These three are the main ways of life recognized by Indian thinkers. The Cārvāka or the materialistic and hedonistic way of life is not considered to be noble by the people in general. But there were other ways of life, which were regarded by some thinkers as important ways of God-realization. There were the bio-physical *yoga* (*haṭhayoga*), which consisted in certain practices for controlling the voluntary and involuntary processes of the body and also of the vital principle (*prāṇa*) through control of breath. The *yoga* as taught by Patañjali was meant for controlling all the psychological processes (*pātañjalayoga*) also. This *yoga* made use of the physical *yoga* also. In fact all *yogas* made use of the physical *yoga* and the *yoga* of Patañjali, but treated them as having only instrumental and subsidiary value. Then there was the yoga of drugs (*auṣadhayoga*), which taught that by taking some drugs man could obtain knowledge of the Supreme Spirit. This *yoga* was not considered to be a true *yoga* and was generally ridiculed. It was the practice of alchemy raised to the status of a spiritual way of life with a spiritual philosophy. Next, the *yoga* of the sacred word (*mantrayoga*) taught people that by continuously uttering a sacred word, one could obtain salvation. Although the main *yogas* do not reject it, they think that the uttering of some sacred word is only a help, but cannot directly lead to God-realization, which consists of the direct experience of the Supreme Spirit, but not in uttering its name. The Logos is the Word, but itself is not God. Then there are a few other *yogas*, which are not given even a secondary place; and some of them became degenerate and misleading and were even condemned.

Now, we should note that to talk of a way[1] of life and to talk of a *yoga* have come to mean the same. Although the word Way (*mārga*) has a wider meaning than the word *yoga* – in that a way includes all that a man does directly and indirectly throughout his life with the end of salvation in view, while *yoga* means a definite kind of practice meant directly for obtaining the same salvation, – the two words came to be indifferently used in the same meaning. *Yoga*, as mentioned already, means union, at first, of the finite and the infinite spirits. Then it came to signify the means adopted for having that union. Then it meant the literature and also the philosophy advocating and expounding such a union. Then it came to mean the union of man and any ideal he may have, and also the means and the way he adopts for attaining that ideal. We have seen that the word *yoga* means, in Jaina philosophy the attachment of *karma* to the *ātman*. Because of the many primary and derivative meanings, the word *yoga* came to be used where the word *mārga* also could be used.

Particularly with reference to the three main ways of life, the two words are interchanged. The way of knowledge *(jñānamārga)* is also called the yoga of knowledge (*jñānayoga*); the way of devotion (*bhaktimārga*) the yoga of devotion (*bhaktiyoga*); and the way of action (*karmamārga*) the yoga of action (*karmayoga*).

THE SYNTHESIS IN THE EPICS

The schools did not agree with one another about which way was to be adopted by man, and did not teach also in detail how and when a particular way was to be followed. We have seen that, when attempting to reconcile the truths of the different parts of the Veda, it was left to man himself to choose the way and the corresponding philosophy of reality. It was too heavy a responsibility for man to make the choice. Where some of the greatest thinkers did not agree, it was difficult for the ordinary common man, busy with the many demands on him, to decide. The epics, therefore, made the attempt to teach what every philosophy meant, and how one is to adapt oneself to it. But they did it not through philosophical argument, but through stories, anecdotes, etc., in which the life of men following the way was depicted. And the different philosophies also were presented in the simplest language.

[1] It is interesting to note that the disciples of Christ regarded themselves as the followers of the Way, but not Christianity.

But the heroes of the epics, particularly of the most important ones, were men in active life. So the epics were meant for the majority of mankind, which could draw inspiration from them. And for that reason, they taught mostly the way of action, although they were not opposed to the other ways. But if one wants to know the way of life that comprehends the whole life of man, one can find it only in the epics. And the general view of the epics is that man should lead a life of action throughout, but in complete surrender to God. But for exceptional individuals the way of devotion and the way of knowledge are prescribed. While leading a life of action, the other two ways have to be developed. And when one feels that one is capable enough of renouncing the world and taking to the fourth stage of life, i.e. the life of the monk or nun, then only should one take to the life of pure devotion or of knowledge. But of these two again, the way of devotion is the easier.

The epics are not systematic philosophies. But because they are teachings meant for every man, one gets a full philosophy of life only in the epics, but not in the systems. We should also remember that for the study and the understanding of the Vedas, the study of epics is prescribed as an essential subsidiary. The systems, except the Cārvāka and the Mīmāmsā, are meant to be philosophies for the third and the fourth stages of life, and therefore cannot cover the whole life of man. In this respect, they show a peculiar one-sidedness of interest, which the epics attempt to rectify. But not being systematic philosophies, the epics did not attempt a metaphysical reconciliation of the different metaphysical systems. They are representative of the general outlook and culture of the Indians of the time, and are examples of the fact that any culture is a mixture of several unreconciled philosophical strands – every one of which is emphasized by men at different times and according to circumstances – so that the balance of life can be maintained.

THE SIGNIFICANCE OF THE ETHICAL CODES

The ethical codes are called *dharmaśāstras* or the sciences (*śāstras*) of right action (*dharma*). They were elaborations of what were originally called *dharmasūtras* or the aphorisms on right action, which were not the same as Jaimini's *Mīmāmsāsūtras*, which also were expositions of right action, but applications of Jaimini's concept of right action (*dharma*) to the various detailed situations of social life. But the ethical codes (*dharmaśāstras*) became finally the guides for social duties and the basic texts of jurisprudence for the law courts.

1. The first characteristic of the ethical codes is that they are extensions and applications of the Mīmāmsā concept of *dharma* (right action). They are not systems of ethics or ethical philosophies, but only applications of the idea of right action to concrete social situations. That is why they are called codes. They accept the Mīmāmsā concept of *dharma*. But the Mīmāmsā was interested mainly in the deeper and the transempirical aspects of the concept, explaining the theories underlying the workings of all action, how it produces its effects, what forms it takes for producing them and so on. And because sacrifices and their ritual also have other-worldly aspects, the Mīmāmsā sought to explain them in detail. The ethical codes accepted the Mīmāmsā doctrine of right action (*dharma*), and explained what right action was in society, leaving out the explanation of the sacrifices and their ritual, and of salvation and its theories.

2. The question, 'What is right action?', was answered by the Mīmāmsā, saying, 'It is action according to the injunctions of the Veda.' This answer was enough for the Mīmāmsā, because it was concerned mainly with the transempirical nature of actions. But there are actions which concern mainly the empirical world and society itself. Here, how are we to know what right action is? The ethical codes gave four ways of knowing it: the Veda, the *smṛtis* (the ethical codes, epics, etc.) which are based on the Veda, the example of good men, and what is good to oneself. Of the four, each succeeding criterion has less authority than the preceding one. That is, if there is conflict between the the two, then the preceding one prevails. So in the case of the last, it holds true only when one does not get guidance from the others.

The criterion, the example of good men, made it possible for the authors of the ethical codes to observe the different communities in different places, and determine what was right action. There were people who did not accept the Vedas, there were many non-Aryan tribes with rules of conduct of their own, and even the Aryans who accepted the Vedic way of life understood the Vedas differently in different places and followed ways of life slightly different from one another. All these differences were observed and codified and rules of conduct were fixed. When once the rules were fixed, they became laws and guided not only ethical and social life, but also civil and criminal courts. Obedience and violation of the rules were considered to be as important as obedience and violation of *dharma* (right action) as explained by the Mīmāmsā, because *dharma* consisted in obeying those rules.

3. The rules thus became different in many respects for the different tribes. The Aryan tribes in general had one set of rules, which were different from those of the non-Aryan tribes. For instance, there was the practice of selling their children among some non-Aryan tribes. This was allowed for them; but the Aryans were punished if they sold their children. There was polyandry, and divorces up to ten times among some non-Aryans. But they were illegal among the Aryans.

Besides such differences, there were such different rules laid down for the castes, subcastes, and the stages of life (*āśramas*). Now all such rules are not legal. For instance, it was not legally binding on man to marry or to take to the life of the forest dweller or the monk. But if he once takes to any of these stages, he should obey the rules. But even then, some of the rules are not legally binding. For instance, a man may become a monk, then change his mind, marry and settle down as a householder. Or he may change from one sect to another. Or although as a monk, he is forbidden to touch any money, he may become the head of a monastery, become very rich and lead a luxurious life. In such cases generally, there is only ethical censure, but no legal punishment. The ethical codes thus are not mere legal codes.

But so far as the rules of the castes go, the emphasis was on the members of each caste following its own rules of conduct, and not taking to the professions of others. Even here, there was no legal punishment for violating the rules. Such punishments were very rare. There were Brahmins who took to the duties of the warrior caste and and even started imperial dynasties. Some of them even took to ploughing. The Maurya dynasty, to which Asoka the Great belonged, was of the fourth caste, the Śūdra. The Gupta dynasty, which produced equally powerful emperors and was famous for driving away the White and the Red Huns from India, belonged to the trader caste. Thus although the professions were at first determined by castes, later, in the case particularly of great men and rulers, profession began to determine the caste. But such cases were not very common. People followed their caste rules, as though by inertia. Some kind of a mythological sanction was invented for the formation of the castes, and the mixing up of professions was religiously discouraged. Very few of the lower castes aspired to be Brahmins, because to become a

Brahmin meant the life of priesthood, poverty, penance, purity, etc., which were difficult. Up to the profession of ruling, there was some mixing up and change of professions; but birth still conferred some prestige, not obtained by profession. The orthodox people of course resisted change, to which they had finally to reconcile themselves and invented justification.

4. The ethical codes prescribed legal punishments for the violation of civil and criminal laws. But whenever the violation did not come under those laws and also when the law breaker was able to escape the law, the ethical codes said that such law breakers would reap the fruit of their actions in future lives. They will not only suffer the evil fruit of their *karmas*, but also take a new birth according to the nature of the actions they have performed. That is, action, good and evil, determines future births, good and evil. The doctrine of transmigration or rebirth thus helped the ethical codes in explaining how some good actions go apparently unrewarded and why some evil actions go apparently unpunished. No action goes without consequences; if they are not enjoyed in this life, they will be enjoyed in the next.

5. The causality of ethical actions helped the Indian thinkers to explain the many differences between man and man. Some are born rich, or very intelligent, or healthy, or good, and so on; but others are born very poor, or very dull, or very sickly, or very evil, and so on. These differences are due to the good and evil actions performed in past lives. It should not be understood that society was not allowed to ameliorate the needy and the sick. It is the duty of all those who are happily placed in life to help those who are not so placed. It was not supposed that not to allow the suffering to suffer was a violation of ethical law; otherwise, charity, compassion, etc., would not have been preached. Yet those who were suffering were made a warning to people against evil actions.

6. It is very difficult to prove the doctrine of rebirth and also to prove that the next life will be according to the nature of the actions performed in past lives. Neither is it easy to prove that the doctrine is definitely false. We do not have sufficient evidence for or against the doctrine. Now, we have seen, as early Buddhism taught, birth is due to the tendency to be born, and that again due to our desires and attachments for the objects of this world. The idea of the tendency to be born explains what kind of life will be taken in the next birth.

This tendency is a tendency towards a particular kind of being or living. A hardened murderer, who takes much pleasure in killing people and is quite insensitive to their agonies, has developed a tendency always to be that kind of being. He likes the life of a cruel brute, and will, therefore, be born as a tiger. Thus this tendency is a will that becomes a part and parcel of the man's being and unconsciously works through him. The Mīmāmsakas, it was already mentioned, maintained that every action that has not exhausted itself in its effects takes the form of a latent force (*apūrva*), enters the *ātman* of the agent, and produces for him either later in this life itself or in the other world or in some future life determining conditions for that *ātman* to enjoy the fruit. This unconscious will not only determines the conditions of the man's character and nature, but also has a transempirical nature that determines the conditions of our future lives. It is action (*karma*) in its latent form and has to become kinetic or should manifest itself. And its manifestation lies in those conditions in which the *ātman* enjoys or suffers. Action can thus become a kind of unconscious will that controls the forms of the world, though not its material. This doctrine of the Mīmāmsakas is practically accepted by the ethical codes, which introduced only one modification.

7. The ethical codes call themselves *karmayogaśāstras* or the sciences of the way of action, and they are all theistic, unlike the original Mīmāmsā, which was non-theistic. The modification they introduced is theism, and all that it implies. The world is created by God, who also created the different castes (*varṇas*, colours of skin) and fixed their respective professions. What was originally natural and also determined and fixed by the accidents of history and convention was regarded as having been created by God. Some sub-castes and distinctions of professions were created by man himself through the intermixture of castes. People born into those castes and sub-castes had to follow their prescribed professions without violating God's laws.

The same God now becomes the custodian of the latent forms which our ethical actions take, and dispenses rewards and punishments for good and evil actions. Now, it is not action by itself that creates the conditions for its fructification and exhaustion, but God who supervises our actions.

8. Along with the idea of God, the idea of salvation or liberation from the world of action is accepted by the ethical codes. God can

release an *ātman* from bondage, if the *ātman* is earnest. But man should continue to live an active life, performing actions without attachment to their fruit. This he can do by surrendering himself and all his actions to God and remaining unattached to their fruit. And God sends his grace to those people who sincerely struggle for salvation, but find themselves weak to develop the necessary attitude.

Incidentally, the ethical codes praise the way of devotion and knowledge. But since the codes are meant to guide the life of every person, they teach primarily the way of action. Their main object is to fix the duties of every man according to his station in society, and they thought of society as primarily consisting of castes and sub-castes and of those falling outside the structure of castes and sub-castes.

9. We may conclude that the ethical codes are conservative, not permitting much change. It is the nature of all ethical and legal codes to be conservative, aiming to fix the social structure as they find it. But as conditions of social life change, a need is felt to reformulate the codes. Thus arose several ethical codes in India, the most important of which are *Manu's Ethical Code* and *Parāśara's Ethical Code*.[2] We find difference of views among the codes on certain points.

But none of the codes was against the system of castes and sub-castes. One code[3] permitted the taking back of women and girls, who were by force violated by Muslims, into their original castes. There was also another change, which was not so marked in its observance. The duties of the higher castes were more difficult than those of the lower, and demanded that the higher castes should be more righteous and should follow only noble professions. If a man born in the higher castes was one with evil tendencies, he was considered to be inferior to the men of the lower castes. Similarly, if one belonging to the lower castes was nobler than he was expected to be, he was considered to be higher than the men of the higher castes. But generally he was not allowed to change his caste, although respected and venerated by men of the higher castes also.

The ethical codes thus supplied the rules of social conduct for all the Indians of the time, whatever religion or philosophy they followed. Their philosophical basis is the Mīmāmsā in its theistic forms and

[2] For an exhaustive study of the ethical codes, see P. V. Kane, *History of the Dharmaśāstra*, 5 vols (Bhandarkar Oriental Research Institute, Poona, 1930–62).

[3] *The Code of Devala*, see the above work, Vol. II, p. 399, and Vol. IV, p. 117.

their social basis was the structure of castes and sub-castes, which were considered to be God-given and unalterable. We find some evidence[4] that the ethical writers conceived of the castes in terms of the three attributes – *sattva* (clarity or purity), *rajas* (activity), and *tamas* (lethargy) – just as Plato divided his classes according to the predominance of the rational part, the spirited part, and the appetitive part of the soul. The Brahmin was one in whom purity (*sattva*) dominated; the warrior was one in whom *rajas* (activity) dominated; the trader one in whom activity (*rajas*) and lethargy (*tamas*) dominated, because his function is to acquire and accumulate wealth, which is a mixture of activity and stability; and the Śūdra was one who is dominated by lethargy (*tamas*). But like Plato's principle of division, this principle also is not easily applicable. And besides, except in the hands of the social reformers, it did not result in the fluidity and interchange of castes according to the character indicated.[5] And this acceptance of the castes as final prevented the ethical ideas of the codes from developing into systematic ethical and political philosophies. But all the moral ideas and virtues we find in China and the West are to be found in the Indian ethical codes also.

For social ethics, though it did not develop into systems of thought as in the West, one should turn to the ethical codes. And they are the same for all systems of philosophy – including even Jainism, and Buddhism also for a long time in India – except the Cārvākas, who also could not have violated those rules that were legally enforceable. But ethics and morality are not confined to social and legal codes. Ethics is a science of self-discipline with reference to certain goals; but some of these goals transcend society. For instance, it is not a social concern that I should work for the realization of the Supreme Spirit or even that I should work for heaven after death. But if I have these goals, I have to go through the necessary discipline, and ethics extends over and includes this discipline also. It is here that the different schools of philosophy differ from one another on some points. And all disciplines meant for the realization of our ultimate being or the Buddhist Nirvāṇa are called spiritual disciplines. But we cannot separate ethical disciplines from the spiritual, because they overlap.

[4] See Bhagavan Das, *Science of Social Organization* (Theosophical Society, Madras, 1910).

[5] Dayananda Sarasvati of the nineteenth century introduced this principle into the society he formed, called the Aryasamaj (the Aryan Society).

They have many points in common. For instance, truth-speaking, charitableness, and compassion are both ethical and spiritual disciplines. The two can be distinguished only from the goals they have before them. *Jñānayoga* (way of knowledge) is not mere ethics, but a way of our life. Or we may express the same idea in a different language. Ethical discipline need not be spiritual, i.e. need not have spiritual, but only social goals. But a spiritual discipline cannot be unethical. To give a similar example: politics is not the whole of ethics; but ethics covers political activity also.

Because of the above peculiarity of Indian thought one should not turn merely to the systems of salvation philosophies for studying the ethical ideas of India. One should turn to the Mīmāmsā and the ethical codes. For ideas of spiritual discipline and their differences one should turn to those philosophies. In the light of those philosophies the same ethical ideas obtain a new perspective and a new colouring. And they become part of philosophies of life.

THE PHILOSOPHICAL SYNTHESIS IN THE BHAGAVADGĪTĀ

The *Bhagavadgītā* (the Lord's Song) is a part of the great epic, *Mahābhārata*, which might have been composed and was perhaps only a heroic ballad about 1100 BC, but became reshaped into correct language by about 500 BC, and went on growing perhaps up to AD 300. It is impossible to fix the dates and to say when the *Bhagavadgītā* was composed. Vyāsa is said to be the redactor of the whole *Mahābhārata* including the *Bhagavadgītā*.

In the *Mahābhārata* we read of the Greeks (*Yavanas*, Ionians), Parthians (*Pahlavas*), and Scythians (*Śākas*). It was a time of the contact of the Aryans, the original inhabitants of India, and certain Himalayan and Tibetan races, with several kinds of religion, philosophical ideas, and social forms. The *Mahābhārata* was an attempt to bring them all together under the religion of the Śātvata clan, to which Kṛṣṇa, who is the teacher in the *Bhagavadgītā*, belonged. Kṛṣṇa was identified with the Supreme Spirit of the Universe as its incarnation, and taught Arjuna, his friend and brother-in-law.

The *Bhagavadgītā* is regarded as an epic (*smṛti*), but not as a part of the Veda. But it is supposed to teach the same doctrines as the Veda. Even Śāṅkara, who does not accept the Vaiṣṇava and the Śaiva Āgamas as spiritual authority, accepted the *Bhagavadgītā* as a basic text, although the *Mahābhārata* belonged to the Śātvata religion, which was a branch of Vaiṣṇavism. The *Bhagavadgītā* acquired importance for all schools of philosophy.

The stage for the teaching of Kṛṣṇa was set on the battlefield where the huge armies of the cousins, Kaurayas and Pāṇḍavas, were arrayed against each other. Arjuna, one of the Pāṇḍavas, sees in the rival army his own cousins, uncles, grandfathers and other blood relations and becomes despondent, because he has to kill his own kith and kin. And he prefers the life of an ascetic, retiring to the forest and meditating on the Supreme Being, to destroying his own relations and ruling the kingdom. Thus between the two ways of performing the duties according to his station and of retiring to the forest for meditation after renouncing all actions, he chooses the second because it avoids the necessary bloodshed for reaching the throne. Kṛṣṇa then dissuades Arjuna from giving up the way of right action and from taking to the way of the renunciation of action, and expounds the philosophy underlying that truth. Incidentally he explains also the nature of a number of other ways or *yogas* and their relevance and significance to life's ideal. The *Bhagavadgītā* contains eighteen chapters and each chapter is called a *yoga*. Even the chapter describing Arjuna's despondency is called the 'despondency-yoga'; but it does not mean *yoga* in the ordinary sense, but has to be suitably interpreted. It can be interpreted as meaning the joining of despondency to Arjuna's soul.

The *Bhagavadgītā* may be treated as a great synthesis of the ideas of the impersonal spiritual monism with personalistic monotheism, of the *yoga* of action with the *yoga* of the transcendence of action, and these again with *yogas* of devotion and knowledge. It is not an argumentative work, but a popular one meant to be read by all alike.

The *Bhagavadgītā*, not being an argumentative work, does not discuss epistemology, but only the way of life and the underlying metaphysical theory. And as belonging to the Vaiṣṇava religious tradition, it treats the Brahman as on the whole personalistic. And so far as even the Upaniṣads are concerned, a clearcut distinction between the personal Brahman and the impersonal is not possible; we have to take the distinction as one of emphasis. The Brahman is described as Being, Consciousness, and Bliss. But Being that is also Consciousness is of the nature of 'Am-ness'. We say: 'I am', but 'That is'. In 'That is', there is no implication that the 'That' is consciousness. But in 'I am', there is the implication of its being conscious. So where there is self-consciousness, the consciousness of one's own existence, it is difficult to deny personality. Yet if we understand personality as a self-consciousness that distinguishes itself as necessarily opposed to something else, the Upaniṣads says that there is no such 'something else'. Everything is an element of the Brahman and a part of its Am-ness (conscious Being). Then we cannot attribute personality to it. So the Brahman really transcends the distinction between the personal and the impersonal. But it is the source of personality itself. And Kṛṣṇa speaks of himself as such in the *Bhagavadgītā*. But the commentators fight with one another on this question, emphasizing the one or the other aspect. In interpreting the *Bhagavadgītā* as it is, we have to, and shall avoid the fighting commentators, so far as possible.

The *Bhagavadgītā* treats the question, whether Brahman is personal or impersonal, determinate (*saguṇa*, with qualities) or indeterminate (*nirguṇa*, without qualities), as unimportant. It is *nirguṇa* (without qualities) and yet is full of qualities (*saguṇa*). (Chapter XIII.) It has two kinds of Prakṛti (nature), that which is the source of the material world and that which is the source of the individual *jīvas* (souls). (Chapter VII.) These two are powers or energies (*śaktis*). It has also another power, called Māyā (Chapter IV) and also Yogamāyā (Chapter XV.) Through this power, the Brahman enters the lower Prakṛti (the source of the material world) and creates the world. Both the Prakṛtis and Yogamāyā are real, eternal, and part and parcel of the very being of the Brahman. Yet the Brahman is not merely a neuter gender, it is the Supreme Person (*Puruṣottama*). (Chapter XV.) The *ātman* (or *jīva*) is essentially identical with the Brahman; the Puruṣa (the individual *ātman*) is the great Lord (*Maheśvara*) himself. The *jīvas* (souls) are only parts of the Lord.

The *Bhagavadgītā* does not seem to be inclined toward the view that the unmanifest (*avyakta*) is necessarily the same as the Māyā, or Yogamāyā, or even either of the two Prakrtis.[6] It is the same as the Brahman itself in the originating state of the world of matter and souls, before they become manifest. But it is always, even after manifestation, present in the background (*kūṭastha*). It is unperishing

[6] The word *avyakta* occurs in the text in both masculine and neuter. As masculine it means the Brahman, but as neuter it means the lower Prakṛti, which again is one of the powers of the Brahman.

(*akṣara*). It is the *jīvas* (souls) and material things that are perishing (*kṣara*). (Chapters XV and VIII.) The *jīvas* and the material world issue forth out of the unperishing Unmanifest and enter it again. The Unmanifest is the beginning, the manifest is the middle, and the Unmanifest is again the end of the process of creation (Chapter I). The Brahman, or the Supreme Person, lies beyond the Unmanifest.

The world of the souls and matter is thus a product of the Unmanifest and returns to the Unmanifest. It is real, not an illusion. It is Being, not Non-being. Everything comes out of Being, and what is called destruction or perishing is only a re-entering into the original Being. No being becomes Non-being. To think that destruction is entering Non-being is due to ignorance of the truth.

The lower Prakṛti (producing the material world) has three attributes: *sattva* (clarity), *rajas* (activity), and *tamas* (darkness). These three attributes (*guṇas*) separate themselves from one another, act and react upon one another and produce the world of plurality. They assume the forms of reason (*buddhi*), ego (*ahaṁkāra*), mind (*manas*), the five senses, the five organs of action, and the five elements. The senses are higher than the body, mind higher than the senses, reason higher than mind, and the Brahman higher than reason (Chapter III).

The world-process is a process of the three attributes of the lower Prakṛti, and the souls find themselves involved in that process. The Supreme Person is the controller of this process.

It is difficult to prove what exactly the *Bhagavadgītā* taught about the relation between the *ātman* and the Brahman, whether they are identical, or different, or both identical and different. The main clue to answer this question is: What does the *Bhagavadgītā* say about the *ātman* after it is liberated from the lower Prakṛti? The answer is not ambiguous. The Brahman has two Prakṛtis (natures), one of them is the cause of the material aspect of the world, and the other the cause of its conscious aspect. The soul belongs to the higher Prakṛti and, when liberated, realizes its original nature. But realization of original nature means that the *ātman* now realizes that it is part of the higher Prakṛti of the Brahman. But the *Bhagavadgītā* again says that the *ātman* becomes the Great Lord Himself. So it is possible to say that the *ātman* becomes the Brahman. However, since we know that, according to the general Vaiṣṇava trcdition, the *ātman* is only a part of the Brahman, we may have to give primacy to the former interpretation, since the *Bhagavadgītā* is a part of the general Vaiṣṇava tradition. In any case, it is part and parcel of the Brahman itself, and the Brahman includes and transcends everything. Everything that happens, happens within the Brahman.

The *Bhagavadgītā* is important not so much for its metaphysics as for the synthesis it attempted of all the ways of life or *yogas* current at the time. The main question, as one can easily see, is what action (*karma*) and non-action (*akarma*) mean, when each is extolled as the right path to salvation. Arjuna, whom Kṛṣṇa taught the truth, found it easier to take to non-action (*akarma*), and retire to the forest than killing his own kith and kin, although duty demanded that he should kill them, since they were the evil-doers, depriving him of his right to a share of the kingdom. It was contrary to the duty of a person belonging to the warrior caste to run away from the evil-doer, whether he be a relation or a stranger. But Arjuna found it easy to justify himself in the name of the supposed path of non-action. Kṛṣṇa then showed how Arjuna was mistaken, because he did not understand what non-action meant.

No man can escape action, even when he retires to the forest and gives up everything. To live is to act; at least the bodily needs have to be fulfilled, and they need action. But the whole creation, right from reason (*buddhi*) down to the material elements, is due to the activity of the three attributes of Prakṛti, which is incessantly active and with which the *ātman* has identified itself. So long as man lives, this identification cannot be overcome; but what he has to and can do is to realize that the activity is really the activity of the three attributes. The world process is really the process of the Prakṛtis of the Brahman itself. And man should realize that it is so, and that it is not the *ātman* that kills or gets killed. Even when a man is killed, he does not become Non-being; he originated out of Being and again re-enters Being. The human process (history) is the ethical process of the Brahman, and happens through the individuals. The individual cannot escape it, and should, therefore, act according to it. What we call right action (*dharma*) is action according to the laws of the world process of the Cosmic Person. If an individual tries to go against it by refusing to act, he separates himself from the Brahman and hardens his own separateness and ego. Such non-action does not lead to salvation and realization of oneness with the Brahman.

The laws of the Cosmic Person are good. Evil-doers are born and set the process in the wrong direction. But the Lord takes on an incarnation and sets the process right again. Whether one wishes it or not, knows it or not, the evil and all those who are on its side, perish through the process of the Cosmic Person himself. Not to kill the evil-doers by refusing to act does not prevent their destruction; those who adopt non-action in such circumstances merely act foolishly and harden their separateness from the Cosmic Person.

To the Cosmic Person (*Viśvarūpa*) belong the universal ethical laws governing the world. They can be realized only by raising ourself to the level of reason (*buddhi*). One should surrender oneself to one's reason and act accordingly, whether the result be the death of one's own kith and kin or of oneself. One should act without attachment to the fruits of action (*karmaphalas*). The consideration by Arjuna that his own nearest relations would be killed if he acted according to his station and its duties was his individual, personal, and, therefore, egoistic consideration, not the consideration of the universal reason within him.

Action, therefore, that is not influenced by the egoistic consideration of the fruit is true non-action. Non-action, for instance, the retreat of Arjuna from the battlefield to the forest, lest he should kill his own kith and kin, is not non-action, but wrong action. There is no inaction in the world, but only right actions and wrong actions. True non-action is action without regard for its fruit, and according to the laws of the Cosmic Person (the Logos).

Action without regard for its fruit (*niṣkāmakarma*) is difficult to understand and has been variously misunderstood and misinterpreted. How can one act without regard to the results? Action is always meant for a purpose, and without purpose even the ass does not move. The *Bhagavadgītā* therefore, could not have meant motiveless or aimless action. There is of course involved the principle of duty for duty's sake in the teachings of the *Bhagavadgītā*; but aimless action is not implied by them. What is the aim of action, then, according to the principle, duty for duty's sake? The teaching involves a double aim.

1. The processes of the human world must be kept going. They should not be hindered, but furthered. When evil prevails and the good suffers, the Brahman takes on the appropriate incarnation, destroys evil, and protects the good. But why should the Brahman, which is eternally perfect and for which there is nothing to be desired, take the trouble of incarnating itself as a mundane being, go through the

stages of birth, growth, and death? Why should the incarnation, that knows that it is the same as the eternal Brahman, take the trouble of acting in this world? If it does not act, the world does not survive. If it, as the ideal example of all men, does not act, other men will follow it and the human world will come to an end. But the world-processes, including the processes of the human world, are the two natures (*Prakṛtis*) of the Brahman; and they constitute the good. The good in all circumstances must be preserved. So all men including the divine incarnation have to act.

But action is always prompted by desire, and desires are generated by instinctive urges. What then has man to do? Man should satisfy his desires according to the laws of the Cosmic Person. If desires are killed, there will be no action, and if there is no action, the world cannot be sustained. The *Bhagavadgītā* preaches not the killing of desires, but channelling them.

Sustaining the world (*lokasaṅgraha*) through the satisfaction of desires (*kāma*) according to the laws of the Cosmic Person, which are not subjective but objective, is the ideal action. Kriṣṇa says that he is the desire and enjoyment (*kāma*) in men, that are not in conflict with the principle of right action (*dharmāviruddhah bhuteṣu kāmosmi*). The world of the Indians of the ancient and classical times included matter, men and gods. All in their proper relationships had to be preserved.

But what exactly are these proper relationships? The *Bhagavadgītā* does not discuss them, except saying that sacrifices have to be performed for the gods without any desire for rewards. The gods have to be preserved for the maintenance of the world. So far as actions concerning other human beings go, they are determined by the laws regulating the system of castes and stages of life. For their details one has to refer to the rest of the *Mahābhārata*, of which the *Bhagavadgītā* is a tiny part.

2. The second aim of the teaching is salvation. It is through action without any self-centred motive that one attains salvation, and rises above action. Rising above action means rising above action motivated by one's own egoistic desires, with reference only to one's own interests as an individual, but not as part of the Cosmic Person, for the maintenance of whose order he is meant to be an instrument. The world process goes on – whether one knows it or not – through the activity of the three attributes of Prakṛti, which assume the form of the psycho-physical individual, his reason, ego, instincts, drives,

and so on. The soul should not think that it is itself acting, but only that the three attributes are acting. Man should cultivate this attitude to his actions and the world, and yet continue in his active life. Then true realization will dawn in man's being and he will be liberated. Obviously, the *Bhagavadgītā* teaches that man has to act until death; for to live is to act, life is impossible without action.

But how is man to cultivate the above attitude and attain true realization, viz. that it is only the three attributes of the Prakṛti of the Brahman that are acting in him, but not he himself? How can he know that he is really not the three attributes themselves? To answer this question, Kṛṣṇa teaches Arjuna the various kinds of practice adopted by great men for obtaining the true realization. The rest of the *Bhagavadgītā* is devoted to explaining them. How can one differentiate oneself from all that one is doing and from the world in which one is acting? Man identifies himself with his reason, ego, mind, body, his senses and organs, and all that they do. When he finds it difficult to distinguish himself from them, he should surrender himself and all that he does to the Supreme Person, and say: 'Lord, thy will is done.' This is the *yoga* of devotion (*bhaktiyoga*). But for this purpose, man should surrender himself to his own reason (*buddhi*), by lifting himself to the universality present in his own being.[7] It is not real surrender if it is to do intentional evil, and say: 'Lord, thy will is done.' The *yoga* of knowledge (*jñānayoga*) consists in the discrimination between the true, original nature of the *ātman* and its assumed forms and then acting according to that knowledge.[8] Even these two *yogas* are not easy. Man should use every type of *yoga* as a help. He should use meditation also. And he should learn to distinguish between the unperishing and the perishing, the high and the low, the noble and the mean, the good and the evil, in men, animals, plants, food, etc., and should prefer the former to the latter. Of the three attributes, the *sattva* (clarity) reflects the Brahman clearly; the Brahman can be seen only in those things in which the

[7] One can see the Logos doctrine of the Stoics implicitly accepted by the *Bhagavadgītā*. Man partakes of the nature of the Logos (the way of the Cosmic Person), and should act with the realization that he is partaking of it. True non-action is action according to the Logos, it is right action, not action according to one's own egoistic desires and inclinations.

[8] The purpose of this discrimination is not mere contemplation, but action according to this discrimination. Kṛṣṇa does not teach that discrimination is an end in itself.

attribute *sattva* predominates. Man should, therefore, pay the highest regard for them. Through such practices, and through self-surrender and knowledge, man learns what he truly is. He learns that he is essentially the *ātman*, but not the three attributes of the Prakṛti of the Brahman, and can know what truly action and non-action mean.

We have to conclude that, because the main aim of the teaching of Kṛṣṇa is to make Arjuna act in accordance with the duties prescribed by his station and dissuade him from retiring to the forest and from taking to the life of mere meditation, the *Bhagavadgītā* subordinates all other *yogas* to the *yoga* of action. The work is an exposition of the theistic philosophy of right action and a synthesis of all the *yogas* according to the laws of right action. To act according to the laws of right action and with the proper attitude to it is the same as the transcendence of action. And such action does not bind man to the world of action.

Chapter XIV

THE TRADITIONS AND CONTEMPORARY TRENDS

INTRODUCTION

The Indian traditions (*sampradāyas*) were reflective from the beginning and became philosophies. There were more traditions, but those reviewed here are the most important. It is out of these traditions that contemporary thought arose after the advent of the British. It has several strands. (1) Indian religions were at first severely criticized by the Christian missionaries, who attacked first the external and popular forms, and later began studying the deeper philosophical thought. One aspect of contemporary philosophical thought is its more reflective evaluation of the traditions than was made by Christian religious criticism. (2) After the missionaries began studying the Indian philosophical doctrines, the Vedas, and the Sanskrit language, European scholars like Max Müller, Paul Deussen, A. B. Keith and then a host of others discovered the historical and intellectual significance of this Indian heritage and revealed not only the common religious roots, but also the philosophical similarities between the Indian and European forms of thought. These similarities and common roots have been taken up for study by the Indian thinkers themselves. who began expounding the traditional philosophies in terms of the recent philosophical concepts. Their expositions sound as if they were the old traditions themselves, but they have become richer by the incorporation of new Western developments. (3) The most outstanding of the contemporary thinkers do not take in Western ideas wholesale and indiscriminately, but ask themselves how the traditional philosophies of India are to be oriented towards the new doctrines and the new ideas of reality. These questions enable the philosophers to retain the spirit of traditional systems and yet be conscious of the developments in science and philosophy of the West. (4) Because of the task of the orienting and of the re-orienting of the old and the new, contemporary Indian thought appears to be making little progress; but if philosophy is understood as a way of life, and if the way of thought is to be adjusted to it and has to throw light on it, then philosophy cannot be completely new in any old culture. For although our theories can change quickly, human nature and historical cultures cannot be transformed so quickly. (5) However, it should be observed that some younger philosophers, influenced by communist philosophies, look to the West for liberating Indians from their traditional philosophies, and think that the acceptance of this heritage is due to the backwardness of Indian culture, and that if India is to progress, it has to accept some new materialistic or sceptical philosophy as a guide to life. Such philosophers may perhaps dominate the philosophical circles of India in the future. But the foremost of the Indian thinkers now still think that the traditional philosophies contain important truths and that they can be, and ought to be reconciled with the truths that the new materialistic and sceptical philosophies wish to bring to the forefront.

Contemporary thinkers of India generally belong to the Vedāntic traditions. Some follow a particular tradition explicitly, others cull elements from different traditions. Almost all of them reconstruct the ancient philosophies after incorporating some doctrines from the West. Their work is not merely reaction or reconciliation, but also incorporation. For this purpose a rethinking of the ancient material is encouraged by the Indian Renaissance.

It is not to be expected that the traditions of India differ from one another on every point. So far as the rules of ethical and social conduct go, all the other orthodox traditions – the Nyāya, the Vaiśeṣika, the Sāṅkhya, the Yoga and the Vedānta – in general follow the Mīmāmsā. Yet metaphysically they are different from one another. Jainism, early Buddhism, the Nyāya and the Vaiśeṣika are pluralistic and realistic like the Mīmāmsā. Jainism, the early Mīmāmsā, the Sāṅkhya, and Buddhism are atheistic. The later Buddhism and almost all the Vedāntic schools are idealistic and absolutist, and have influenced one another very much.

India has many religions born in it. Besides Jainism and Buddhism, the two important Vedic religions which have become sectarian are Śaivism and Vaiṣṇavism, both of which are theistic. One may safely say that, in practice, every Hindu is either a Śaiva or Vaiṣṇava. There is really a third group, called Smārta, which does not claim to belong to any sect, does not accept any of the Āgamas of either sect, but follows only the Vedas, and yet attends the temples of both the sects. But not belonging to any sect, its followers are separated from the other two sects and constitute a third sect. They are mostly followers of Śaṅkara, They constitute a relatively small group of intellectuals and philosophers, who are nevertheless of no small importance.[1] What interests a student of philosophy is that the differences between Śaivism and Vaiṣṇavism are not philosophical, but depend, in many cases, on what name one gives the Brahman of the Upaniṣads. The same philosophy serves Vaiṣṇavism, if the Brahman is called Viṣṇu; and it can serve Śaivism equally well if the Brahman is called Śiva. Thus in both Śaivism and Vaiṣṇavism, one finds monism, qualified monism, monism-with-dualism (identity-in-difference), dualism, and pluralism. Hence, a sub-sect of one religion may differentiate itself from the other sects of the same religion only in the name of the system of philosophy it follows; or when the philosophies are the same, one sub-sect may differentiate itself from another by the name it gives the Brahman of the Upaniṣads. There can be differences of ritual, which are not philosophically important.

The traditions, therefore, have to be treated not as fixed but as fluid. And the influences on one another are very great. For instance, there is no strict follower of the Nyāya and the Vaiśeṣika philosophies as religions in the usual sense. Their followers all became Śaivas and in time came to a position very akin to a kind of absolutism like that of Rāmānuja, saying that the eternal atoms, the infinite and eternal substances – the *ātmans*, ether, space, and time – together constitute the body of God. As the body of God, they can be eternal like Him. Without reaching such a position, they cannot have a religion. Similarly, the Sāṅkhya and the Yoga became Vaiṣṇava in religion, although they did not become Vedāntic, except in the hands of Vijñānabhikṣu. And there are few Mīmāmsakas who follow the earlier atheistic teachings of the school, which formed the religion of Brahmanism. As religious philosophies, the Vedāntic schools got the upper hand, and absorbed almost every other school and incorporated it in some form or another. So far as the current philosophies of life go, the cross influences of the traditions are very great; and they are influenced not only by the two heterodox religions, Jainism and

[1] Their families may call themselves *smārtas* even without knowing what the word means.

Buddhism – which themselves are influenced by the orthodox traditions – but also by Islam and Christianity, which gave rise to some reform movements within the so-called Hinduism. And philosophically Christianity contributed to the revival of some of the ancient theistic forms and accentuated them.

M. K. GANDHI

Mohandas Karamchand Gandhi (1869–1948)[2] was not an academic philosopher, and one may doubt the propriety of including him in a book on philosophy. But we have been treating philosophy as a philosophy of life, and Gandhi is much more representative of the general Indian spiritual outlook than many an Indian academic philosopher in the universities. In fact, one may doubt whether the university philosophical circles are nowadays really representative of the thought and culture of the communities around them, whether the country be India, England, or America. It is often said that educated India is not representative of India in general. But one cannot be very wrong in doubting whether nowadays the philosophical circles of some of the leading universities in England and America are representative of the outlook of their countries. It is said that the university circles should bring the thought of the community to a clear focus, show its defects and merits, and lead it forward into something better and higher. But it is open to doubt whether most of the academical philosophers have still before them any aim of that kind.

However, in Gandhi's life and writings, one can find the general Indian outlook reflected more concretely than in purely academic philosophies. Of course, Gandhi was claimed to be a true Buddhist, a true Jaina, a true Muslim, a true Christian, even an incarnation of Christ prophesied long ago; he was considered also as a follower of Tolstoy, as a utopian socialist, and so on. He was called the Mahātmā (the Great Soul) by the Indians, and his techniques of resisting oppression have been adopted by oppressed races and communities all over the world.

Gandhi himself summarized his philosophy in one word, *satyāgraha* (*satya* — truth, *āgraha* — attachment, adherence, sticking to). It is the philosophy of truth in action, the philosophy of *satyāgraha*,

[2] See the author's *Idealistic Thought of India* for the philosophy of Gandhi.

which is misleadingly translated as passive resistance, non-violent resistance, etc. But the original basic word has neither the meaning of 'passive' or 'non-violent' nor that of 'resistance'. Indeed, resistance and non-violence are important for Gandhi, but they are derivatives from the original idea in its application to action.

Gandhi says that in his view God is Truth. His philosophy is, therefore, a philosophy of Truth. But it is not epistemology. The term, 'philosophy of Truth', is vague, since every philosophy claims to explain the nature of Truth. What Gandhi means is that man should be faithful to Truth, so far as he understands it, whatever be the consequences. The idea of loyalty to Truth implies two ideas: (1) absolute sincerity to oneself, to one's own idea of Truth, and (2) putting this idea into practice, not keeping it as an intellectual discovery. One's idea of Truth may be false. But Gandhi believes in the essential goodness of man. He believes that Truth is the same for all; and that by purifying his mind, every man can discover it within himself. It is for this purification of mind that Gandhi preached and practised fasting and prayer.

Gandhi's philosophy of *satyāgraha* can be summarized in the following principles:

1. God is Truth and Truth is God, the two are identical. It is safe to believe in God as Truth, for one can deny God, but none can deny Truth. This Truth is not the perceptual or inferential truth, but the inner spirit of man. Man is essentially spirit. What man appears to be is due to Māyā, Ignorance. Indeed, Gandhi never denied the reality of the world, but he never explained what he meant by Māyā. He used the word in the vague sense in which common people in India use it, in the same way as the ordinary Christian uses the idea of original sin. Just as original sin is used by Christians to explain every moral evil in the world, the original ignorance is made to explain all imperfections in the world by Indian thought. And it meant many things for many philosophers.

2. Since God is Truth, Truth is the Law of Life; the Law and the Lawgiver are one.

3. The essential nature of God is love. So the Law of Truth is the Law of Love. God is not a mere concept, but is affective and spiritual by nature.

4. Truth is always the same as reality, and therefore prevails over unreality. Falsity, like falsehood, cannot prevail except temporarily

(*Dharmo jayati*). What finally wins in the conflict between falsity and Truth, and lasts forever, is Truth.

5. So one must abide by Truth. One who abides by Truth is supported by Reality, Being. Falsity leads to non-existence, ultimate destruction and ruin.

6. One should also abide in Love, since Truth is God and God is Love. *Satyāgraha* will then mean abiding in Love.

7. Therefore one must follow the path of non-violence (*ahimsā*). The extreme opposite of Love is hatred, which leads to destruction of whatever opposes us. If one wants to Love, one must at least avoid violence and be non-violent in all circumstances.

8. But the difficulty for practice lies in knowing Truth as it is. Man is finite. As man, he is not omniscient; his power and knowledge are limited, and he can be mistaken in his conception of Truth and in his convictions. He may misdirect his own actions.

9. In being loyal to Truth and in following one's convictions, one should not destroy another. He may himself be mistaken in his views of the true and the right, and should not, therefore, destroy those who hold opposite views. It may be that they are right and he is wrong. Yet this doubt should not prevent him from holding on to what he himself considers to be the Truth, until he is convinced that he is wrong and the other is right. Conflicts are thus, by implication, inevitable. But no conflict should lead to destruction. Truth, whoever has it, will ultimately prevail. Yet the parties of the conflict should love each other, not destroy each other.

10. When Truth prevails, falsity will be destroyed. But God alone has the right to destroy. He alone, in His infinite wisdom, knows for certain what is true and what is false. But since we are finite, and cannot be certain of the knowledge of Truth, we should follow only the Law of Love, which is also God, and leave destruction of evil and falsity to God Himself. God destroys, when He destroys anything, in love, and not in hatred.

The above is, in essence, the spiritual and philosophical basis of Gandhi's practice. *Satyāgraha* is obstinate and unflinching adherence to the Law of Truth and Love, and so to non-violence. Metaphysically, Gandhi is a kind of Vedāntin, but he never expounded his metaphysics. Several traditions of Indian thought got blended in his theory of action. His insistence on non-violence can be traced to Jainism and Buddhism. His ideas that religion lies in the service of humanity may be traced to the Buddhist *bodhisattva* ideal, according to which even the enlightened man does not enter Nirvāṇa, but lives in order to help suffering humanity. It may be traced also to a Vedāntic idea that no individual salvation is possible, but that one has to wait until the whole world is ready for salvation. His idea that God is the ultimate Truth, and also that the Law and Law-giver are one, may be traced to both Buddhism and the Vedānta. That Truth is the inward spirit is also common to both philosophies. That the essential nature of God is love is common to almost all religions including Christianity. But it is difficult to fix the metaphysics of Gandhi as a particular system of thought, although as a way of practical life it is fairly clear.

B. G. TILAK

Bala Gangadhar Tilak (1856–1920) was a great politician-scholar, who evoked the admiration of Max Müller. He was one of the most forceful personalities of the nationalist movement, one of the most important figures of the Indian Renaissance, and a great Vedic scholar. He felt more strongly than anyone else that, for the strength of any nation and the success of any nationalist movement, the people of the country must have a strong activistic outlook, for which the influence of Jainism, Buddhism and certain forms of the Vedānta are unfavourable. People became, through centuries of this influence, passive and resigned to a kind of fate, and lost the tendency to exert themselves for controlling the adverse circumstances, supporting themselves by the idea that this world is not the ultimate reality and is, in any case, imperfect and evil. For counteracting this tendency, Tilak wrote his *Secret of the Bhadavadgītā* (*Gītārahasya*),[3] in which he wanted to prove that the Mīmāmsā way of life is the only way to salvation, and that the other ways are subsidiary to it. He did not reject the Vedānta teachings, but wanted to combine the Mīmāmsā and Vedānta traditions and show that without the way of action (*karmamārga*), no salvation was possible.

Tilak's main contention is that any other doctrine does not fit in with the context of the *Bhagavadgītā*. This work starts with dissuading Arjuna from giving up the battle and ends in making him fight and win the war. So it is action that is taught by the *Bhadavadgītā*, not

[3] Published by Tilak Bros, Poona, 1935–6.

renunciation of action and retirement to the forest and meditation. The other ways, those of knowledge and devotion, are meant to strengthen action according to the law of the right.

Gandhi himself was trained in political activity by sitting at the feet of Tilak. But Tilak taught that, violence or non-violence, one should follow the law of action. Gandhi differed on this point, saying that one should follow the law of action, but without violence. Indeed, obedience to the law of action should be without any personal consideration (*niṣkāmakarma*), according to both. The question is not: 'Does this action benefit me?', but 'Am I or not following the ethical law?' The moral law is objective, and belongs to the nature of the Cosmic Person (*Viśvarūpa*, World Spirit), and has to be obeyed, whatever be the personal considerations.

R. N. TAGORE

Rabindranath Tagore (1861–1941) is more widely known as a poet than as a philosopher. Yet he has written a few philosophical works (*Sādhana*, *Creative Unity*, *Personality*, and *The Religion of Man*)[4] which expound the philosophy underlying his poetry. Like Tilak, Radhakrishnan, Aurobindo Ghose and Bhaganan Das, he was a product of the Indian Renaissance. He contributed greatly to the nationalist movement through his poetry and other writings and even took active part in it for some time.

Tagore never claimed to be an academic philosopher. He belonged to the theistic Brahmosamaj, a reform movement within Hinduism, which introduced the remarriage of widows, abolition of the caste system and of pre-puberty marriage of girls. In philosophy, Tagore has little sympathy for the Advaita of Śaṅkara, and shows appreciation of the devotional forms of Vaiṣṇavism like that of Śrī Caitanya of Bengal, his own native province. It has some similarities to the Vedānta of Vallabha also.

As a Vedāntin, Tagore is more interested in man than in the Absolute (Brahman), saying that, although man may be an appearance of the Brahman, the paintings on the canvas are more interesting than the

[4] See D. S. Sharma, *Hindu Renaissance* (Benares Hindu University, Benares, 1944) for the important contemporary philosophers. See J. E. Thompson: *Rabindranath Tagore* (Oxford University Press, New York, 1921) for Tagore's philosophy.

canvas on which they are painted. He believes that God is the Truth, but He can be known through love, not through knowledge. It is love that unites God and the finite spirit, and knows also the union and the persons united. But knowledge either treats the two as entirely different or, when it unifies them, overlooks the distinction and grasps only the unity. So knowledge has to be transcended in love.

The Brahmasamaj (Society of the Brahman), to one of the branches of which Rabindranath Togare belonged, was started by Raja Ram Mohan Roy, who revived theism through the influence of Christianity. It is wrong to think that India had no theism and that it was given to India by Christianity or Islam; but it is right to say that its modern strong revival was due to Christianity, the missionaries of which criticized what appeared to be pantheism in India. The theistic philosophy of the Brahmosamaj was indeed a reaction to Christian criticisms; but the Indian theism is as old as the Vedānta itself. Ram Mohan Roy said that Hinduism was superior to Christianity, indeed, as a spiritual life and discipline, but needed some reforms.

DAYANANDA SARASVATI

Dayananda Sarasvati (1824–83): As an example of revivalism in face of the criticism of later modes of thought, the Aryasamaj (Society of the Aryans) started by Dayananda Sarasvati, a great Vedic scholar, may be cited. Dayananda's teaching was: 'Back to the Vedas and the Vedic times.' His philosophy[5] is a combination of the Brahmanism of sacrifices with theism. He contends that in the Vedic times castes were formed not by birth, but by character and profession; and the same principle should be adopted in the present. He cites passages from the Vedas to show that there were widow re-marriages and that girls were not married before maturity. It should be said to the credit of the Aryasamaj that its followers show for what they believe the earnestness and zest which characterized the Aryans of the Vedic times.

Although Dayananda Sarasvati was a monotheist and believed in one God, he contended that only the earlier parts of the Veda constituted the real Veda, and that the Upaniṣads were not really a part of the Veda. One may not be too wrong in characterizing his philosophy as a modern theistic form of Brahmanism.

[5] See his *Light of Truth* (*Satyārthaprakāśa*) (Lahore, 1927).

AUROBINDO GHOSE

Aurobindo Ghose (Śrī Aurobindo) (1892–1950) was a great nationalist turned philosopher and yogi. He belonged to the movement that attempted to drive the British away from India by adopting violent means. Its followers believed that, since the British terrorized the Indians into submission, the British should be terrorized into quitting India. Aurobindo Ghose was arrested, and during the trials themselves, a great spiritual change overtook him. He left British India, went to Pondicherry – which was at that time under the French rule – and began practising Yoga and expounding his philosophy.

Aurobindo Ghose was a Vedāntin of his own kind; but he did not follow any of the traditions wholly. As a man practising yoga, he combined several ideas from several traditions that suited him, giving a new interpretation to even the early Vedic hymns, and including from western philosophy also. He criticized almost every ancient school, but expounded a philosophy that can be traced back to some of the schools, particularly the Śaiva and Śākta Āgamas.[6] But he used a new terminology for the traditional concepts. He expounded a new doctrine of the Superman, which is opposed to that of Nietzsche. His Superman is a yogi who surrenders his ego in the Brahman.

According to Aurobindo Ghose, creation is a circular process, a descent into matter from the Absolute Brahman and an ascent from matter to that Brahman. It is the nature of the Absolute to express itself in this circular process. The world is, therefore, not an unreality due to Māyā and Avidyā (Ignorance). Ignorance is one aspect of knowledge itself and is a power belonging to the Brahman, the nature of which is Existence, Consciousness, and Bliss (*Sat-cit-ānanda*). The worlds are created out of this Brahman, out of Bliss itself. They are the play (*līlā*) of the Brahman.

The stages of the descent from the Brahman are: (1) Brahman, (2) the Super-mind, (3) the Over-mind, (4) mind, (5) life, and (6) matter.[7] The opposite movement or ascent starts from matter. What we call evolution is the ascent from matter. But science knows the levels only up to mind. The levels beyond can be attained through yoga. The

[6] For details of his philosophy, see his *Life Divine* (Sri Aurobindo Library, New York, 1949).

[7] For other explanations and details, see Sri Aurobindo: *The Life Divine*. Book I, Chapter XXVII. (Sri Aurobindo Ashram, Pondicherry, 1949.)

yogi, who can reach the higher stages can obtain power over the lower, and become a Superman. Aurobindo Ghose believes that men can become Supermen.

Aurobindo Ghose says that the usual doctrine of evolution is incomplete. It shows only the stages of development from matter to mind, and omits the higher stages. Furthermore, it cannot explain why mind evolves out of matter through life. We can get an explanation only if we postulate that there was a corresponding descent from mind to matter. The ascent, then, becomes a retracing of the original stages of descent. But the starting point could not be mere mind. In mind, will, activity, knowledge, and reality are disjoined. We may will, but may not act; we may know, but our knowledge may not correspond to reality. But in the starting stage of descent, all these – will, activity, knowledge, and reality – must be in a state of unity, which is the Brahman, the *Sat-cit-ānanda*. And between itself and mind, the descent must have passed through the stages of Super-mind, and Over-mind; and in the ascent also these stages should be passed before reaching the Absolute Brahman.

The aim of Aurobindo Ghose's yoga is to reach the highest unity, the Brahman, which is an integrality of everything. He calls his yoga, therefore, integral yoga. One can easily see the similarity between the supernals (super-stages above mind) as given by Aurobindo Ghose and those given by the Pāśupata and the Pāñcarātra traditions and the *Kaṭha Upaniṣad*, although the names are different.[8] Knowledge at the stage of the supernals is not ordinary knowledge, but intuition or integral consciousness. What one has to develop, then, is integrality of personality. But the term, 'integrality of personality' is not an ethical or merely psychological term. It is complete unification of all our being diversified into will, cognition, action and reality.

Aurobindo Ghose is an idealist, absolutist, and monist, who rejects the view that the world is an unreal illusion. His idea of the circularity of evolution from the absolute to matter and back again is not new to Indian thought,[9] but gains added significance through his comparing it with the western doctrines.

[8] See the author's *Idealistic Thought of India*, pp. 299 ff.

[9] Cf. the philosophy of Plotinus.

VIVEKANANDA

Vivekananda (1863–1902) was a disciple of Ramakrishna (1836–86), also called Sri Ramakrishna Paramhamsa, the saint of Bengal. It is Vivekananda who made the name of Ramakrishna known throughout the religious circles of the world. Ramakrishna was an uneducated priest, who practised the yoga of Hinduism, Islam and Christianity for obtaining communion with God, and preached that, whatever be the religion one follows, one can obtain that communion. Philosophically he was an Advaitin (monist). Vivekananda spread his ideas through lectures and writings. But neither was a new system-builder. Their philosophy is the same as the Vedānta of Śaṅkara. Vivekananda applied Śaṅkara's idea that the *atman* is in its essence the same as the Brahman; he thus showed the inner greatness and divinity of man and taught people that service to man is essentially the same as service to God (Brahman). He introduced social service as part of the monastic discipline, and this introduction was due to the influence of Christian missions. Some social service was a part of the monastic life of the Buddhist, Jaina, and the orthodox monasteries. But it was not considered to be essential, since the monk was expected only to practise meditation and teach spiritual truths, and social activities were confined to the life of the householder. Further, the monk was not supposed to handle money and to own property, either personally or in the name of the monastery; and even the property of the monastery was managed by some trusted householder, although this ideal had many violations. Such management involved organization of worldly affairs, but the monk was supposed to be above them. However, Vivekananda introduced the idea of social service for the monks in an organized form. This was an important change in the social relationships between the monasteries and the laity. Philosophically he was a strict follower of the Vedānta of Śaṅkara, to whom all the monks of Vivekananda's order trace their spiritual descent.

RADHAKRISHNAN

Sarvepalli Radhakrishnan (born 1888) is the best known and most influential philosopher of India. He is known for his remarkable ability as a teacher, author, orator, philosopher, scholar, and thinker, and not only as one of the great philosophers but also as one of the great statesmen of the world. His command over eastern and western philosophies is so great that he is called the liaison officer between the East and the West. He occupied many important positions in international bodies and was also the President of the Republic of India.

Radhakrishnan, like the other philosophers mentioned above, is a product of the Indian Renaissance, and in no other thinker has ancient Indian thought come to clearer self-consciousness than in him. But to say that he is only a product of the Indian Renaissance is only half the truth. His thought is as much a product of the West as of the East. For some time he was an admirer of Tagore's thought; but later he became convinced of the truth of Śaṅkara's Vedānta and defended it in many ways, approaching it from different angles. His greatest contribution to Śaṅkara's Advaita is his reinterpretation of the concept of Māyā. Māyā is not illusion for man; it is real. The world is real, not an illusion due to the perversity of man's cognition. It is as real as man himself. As Radhakrishnan himself puts it

'(1) That the world is not self-explanatory shows its phenomenal character, which is signified by the word *māyā*. (2) The problem of the relation between the world and the Brahman has meaning for us who admit the pure being of the Brahman from the intuitive standpoint and demand an explanation of its relation to the world, which we see from the logical standpoint. We can never understand how the ultimate reality is related to the world of plurality, since the two are heterogeneous, and every attempt at explanation is bound to fail. This incomprehensibility is brought out by the term *māyā*. (3) If the Brahman is to be viewed as the cause of the world, it is only in the sense that the world rests on the Brahman, while the latter is in no way touched by it, and the world which rests on the Brahman is called *māyā*. (4) The principle assumed to account for the appearance of the Brahman as the world is also called *māyā*. (5) If we confine our attention to the empirical world and employ the dialectic of logic, we get the conception of a perfect personality, Īśvara, who has the power of self-expression. This power or energy is called *māyā*. (6) This energy of Īśvara becomes transformed into the *upādhis*, or limitations, the unmanifested matter (*avyākṛtaprakṛti*), from which all existence issues. It is the object through which the supreme subject Iśvara develops the universe.'[10]

[10] *Indian Philosophy* (George Allen and Unwin Ltd, London, 1929), Vol. II, pp. 573–4.

These six meanings of the concept of Māyā, which Radhakrishnan discovers in the philosophy of Śaṅkara, show that the world is not an illusion created for man, but that it is not rationally self-explanatory. What is not self-explanatory and yet cannot be denied as an unreality is Māyā. Our rational consciousness is too full of such concepts, which we cannot give up and yet cannot fully explain. If we want to know ultimate reality, we have to transcend rational consciousness and reach the stage of intution, which Radhakrishnan calls integral experience or knowledge in which the distinction between the known and the knower is transcended. That is the stage and the knowledge of the Brahman.

To Radhakrishnan is due a new revival of interest in the concept of intuition. Just as the Brahman is the support of everything in the world, intuition is at the basis of every form of cognition. Without it there can be neither intellectual cognition nor sense perception. But we may not be able to catch it. It is not the same as indeterminate perception (*nirvikalpakajñāna*) that arises at the first stage of sense-object contact. It is the highest stage of all knowledge, its completion and perfection, just as the Brahman is the completion and perfection of all that is. So the problem, intuition *v.* intellect, intuition *v.* sense-percention, etc., is wrongly put, since intuition is not opposed to any of the other forms of cognition, but is present always at their basis. Man may be able to develop extra-ordinary faculties of knowing like telepathy, and they also are called intuitions. Even then they are not opposed to the ordinary forms.

Like Śaṅkara, Radhakrishnan maintains that God (Īśvara), as the Supreme Personal Spirit, is lower than the Absolute (Brahman). The former is called the Lower Brahman (*Aparabrahman*) as distinguished from the latter, which is called the Higher Brahman (*Parabrahman*). In the Higher Brahman all is one without external and internal distinctions; the material world also is part and parcel of the Brahman, in which the material nature is transformed into the spiritual. But for the Lower Brahman, the world remains as an object distinct from Him, although it does not overpower His consciousness. The Lower Brahman is a 'He', not an 'It' like the other. The Lower Brahman continues to exist, so long as the world continues to exist.[11] His existence as a personality depends, therefore, on the existence of the world, although not overpowered by it. The world needs His guidance and control and

[11] See his *Idealist View of Life* (George Allen and Unwin Ltd, London, 1923), p. 333.

He exists, therefore, as a personality facing the world. But when the whole world obtains salvation, i.e. when there is no finite spirit that has yet to obtain salvation, the world becomes one with God and God becomes the Absolute.

In Indian philosophy, even among the followers of Śaṅkara, there are two doctrines of salvation: (1) According to the first, every individual can obtain his own salvation, although the others do not; (2) according to the second, no individual can obtain salvation till the others also obtain it. Radhakrishnan believes in the second and gives his reasons. God and the world form an organic unity, and the world consists of matter and the individual finite *ātmans*. So long as God exists or matter exists or any of the *ātmans* exists, the others also must exist as such. Salvation is becoming one with the Higher Brahman, and that is possible when God becomes one with the Brahman. But God does not become one with the Brahman if a single *ātman* remains without salvation. Therefore the enlightened *ātmans* have to stay at the stage of God, and work with Him for the enlightenment of the other *ātmans*. The enlightened *ātmans* are not bound by the laws of ethical activity; yet they have to help God for the enlightenment of all the remaining *ātmans*.

In the above doctrine as interpreted by Radhakrishnan, a kind of meliorism is present. Every enlightened *ātman* has to help God in making the remaining *ātmans* enlightened. This task is a duty and is in the interests of the enlightened *ātman* itself. It does not, of course, feel the task as a binding duty. It becomes natural for the enlightened *ātman* to work for the salvation of the rest of the world. In the Mahāyāna Buddhism, we have seen, the enlightened individual (*bodhisattva*) does not care for his own Nirvāṇa, but takes as many lives as necessary for helping the others to obtain enlightenment. But it is left to his choice to enter Nirvāṇa or remain a *bodhisattva*. But in the doctrine expounded by Radhakrishnan, the enlightened one has no such choice.

Radhakrishnan also accepts the doctrine of evolution, because it is present in a spiritual form in the Indian traditional thought itself. But he adds that the stages higher than man cannot be left to natural evolution to reach. They depend on the efforts of man himself.

One philosophical activity which Radhakrishnan started in earnest and encouraged is comparative philosophy. Much work was done before him on comparative religion, and scholars were speaking about the subject of comparative philosophy also. But it was he who in his works on Indian philosophy introduced comparisons with Western doctrines wherever possible. And because of the growing interest in, and necessity of mutual understanding of all cultures of the East and the West, the subject of comparative philosophy has begun to obtain a recognition, which it had never before; and the credit for it goes to Radhakrishnan to a greater degree than to anyone else in the world.

Radhakrishnan is a rationalist, a humanist, and a spiritual, absolutistic monist. His final philosophical position is the absolutism of Śaṅkara. Without violating the basic principles of Śaṅkara, Radhakrishnan, by putting together the different aspects of Māyā, has given the concept a new significance, in which the world does not lose its reality for man. Radhakrishnan is a humanist also, in that his interest in man and humanity is strong; and he maintains that philosophy is for the guidance of man and that man is the same everywhere. Yet a self-sufficient humanism cannot justify itself, because it lacks the basic, deeper foundations, which can be found only in a metaphysics of the Spirit. He is a rationalist who goes all the way up to the point to which reason can lead; but still there is something higher than rational consciousness by entering which reason becomes puzzled and which is the same as integral experience or intuition.

BHAGAVAN DAS

Bhagavan Das (1869–1958) also belongs to the Vedāntic tradition,[12] but formulated his philosophy by bringing together some ideas of the Upaniṣads in his own way under the influence of some German idealists like Fichte and Hegel. The Absolute Brahman is one, but it is a unity of two, spirit and matter. The relation between spirit and matter is negation. But this negation is not merely logical; it is a creative force (*śakti*). This creative force (*śakti*) introduces within the one Spirit the distinction between spirit and its other, which is matter. Matter has no reality without this distinction, and yet the Spirit also never exists without this distinction.

Bhagavan Das is less of a metaphysician than a social philosopher. He is better known as a new interpreter of *Manu's Ethical Code* (*Manudharmaśāsıra*). He contends that the caste system was based on a really good principle, viz. that of character and profession. It is not

[12] See *Idealistic Thought of India*, pp. 311–22.

related to birth. One cannot belong to a higher caste by being born in it. Whatever be the caste in which a man is born, if his character is good and if intellect predominates in it, he is a Brahmin. In him, as the Sāṅkhya and the *Bhagavadgītā* say, the attribute of *sattva* (clarity, purity) predominates, and he will take to a profession that suits his aptitudes. Similarly, if a man's character is dominated by the attribute *rajas* (activity), if he is by nature irascible, of hot temper, courageous, etc., he is a *kṣatriya* (warrior), and he takes to a profession that suits him. If a man's nature is dominated by *tamas* (darkness), if he is dull, lethargic, etc., he is a *śūdra* (the fourth caste), and takes to activities that are always guided by someone else. The third caste, namely, of traders (*vaiśyas*) has a combination of *rajas* (activity) and *tamas* (darkness), and their profession suits them. Bhagavan Das utilizes this principle of the diversion of castes for interpreting *Manu's Ethical Code.*

J. KRISHNAMURTI

Bhagavan Das was a theosophist, a great admirer of Annie Besant and Krishnamurti, and remained so till death. Jiddu Krishnamurti[13] (born 1895) is a spiritual genius discovered by Mrs Annie Besant and acclaimed by her as an incarnation. He was brought up in the Theosophical Society and given western education. But later he not only disclaimed his being an incarnation, but also severed his connections with the Theosophical Society. He says that he is a human being like any other, but working hard for spiritual realization.

He does not belong to any of the ancient classical traditions, except that he believes in the reality of the Spirit. He goes further, and says that it is impossible for anyone to lead another to God and show Him. So to follow a tradition or a teacher is misleading. One can realize the truth only within oneself. Spirit is not an object. If one says: 'I saw God', then one is foolish and mistaken. If Spirit is by nature never an object to be known, then, no intellectual argument, no conceptual tradition, and no teacher can lead a man to it. Man has to depend entirely upon himself.

Another view which Krishnamurti maintains is that evolution itself is leading man to perfection. It is impossible for humanity, even if it wishes, to remain foreover in ignorance of ultimate truth.

[13] Krishnamurti's writings are scattered in the form of lectures published separately. For a connected account, see D. S. Sharma, *Hindu Renaissance.*

MUHAMMAD IQBAL

Although Muhammad Iqbal (1873–1938)[14] is now regarded as a philosopher of Pakistan, he was a philosopher of united India and had admirers among both the Hindus and the Muslims. He came from a family of Brahmins converted to Islam, was at first a nationalist, but later a communalist. He was better known, like Tagore, as a poet than as a philosopher. He was greatly influenced by the Sufi mysticism of Persia (Iran), which became strong in India also, because of the similar mystic trends of the Vedānta.

Iqbal's philosophy is a kind of theistic mysticism. The world is real and man should take interest in it. Yet reality is spiritual; matter consists of spirits of a low order. Everything is a part of a process; and all is preserved in it, nothing is lost. Iqbal believes in intuition and love for realizing God. But curiously enough, he says that we can force God into the relationship of love. He exhorts man to be the viceregent of God on earth, and have control over the elements. Such a viceregent is a Superman. If man can be a master of himself, he can carry on war even with Heaven – which indeed is not necessary, because fortune always smiles on such a man.

OTHER TRENDS

There are other philosophers like K. C. Bhattacharya, Hiralal Haldar and P. N. Srininasachari, who attempt to establish one or the other of the Vedāntic positions from different standpoints adopted by the Western philosophers. K. C. Bhattacharya takes Kant's agnosticism,[15] that we cannot know God, as his starting point and attempts to show that God is knowable, but through a different kind of knowledge, viz. intuition, advocated by the Vedānta. Hiralal Haldar[16] is a great scholar of European idealism and approaches it from the theistic Vedānta of the Brahmosamaj. Srinivasachari[17] is a follower of Rāmānuja's Vedānta and shows how it completes some of the Western

[14] Md. Iqbal, *The Reconstruction of Religious Thought in Islam* (M. Ashraf, Lahore, 1944).

[15] His main work is *Subject as Freedom* (Indian Institute of Philosophy, Amalner, 1930).

[16] His main work is *Neo-Hegelianism* (Heath Cranton Ltd, London, 1927).

[17] He wrote several works. See his *Philosophy of Viśiṣṭādvaita* and *Philosophy of Bhedābheda* (both published by Adyar Library, Madras, 1943 and 1950).

philosophical theories. In all cases, the contemporary trends of Indian thought are no longer the purely ancient or classical Indian ones, but are greatly influenced by Western doctrines also.

To assimilate and absorb Western philosophy in a methodical way without losing the spirit and individuality of India's traditional outlook, philosophy in India has to reflect in a new way, which is the way of comparative philosophy, not merely as a cultural or orientalist study, but as a study of conceptual frameworks with reference to thought and life. The first to do important work on the subject is S. Radhakrishnan. The present author,[18] although as a Vedāntin he is philosophically inclined towards an integral synthesis of phenomenology and existentialism, has been attempting to develop comparative philosophy into a distinct discipline with aims and methods of its own, without leaving the subject at the level of random comparisons, which work without definite aims and methods.

Besides the above trends, one can come across, among the younger generation of philosophers, varieties of Marxists, logical positivists, linguistic analysts, different kinds of realists and idealists, and followers of several other recent western traditions. Of all these new trends, those philosophies that tend overtly to be philosophies of life, covering pervasively somehow the whole life of man, seem to appeal more to the Indian mind in general than mere analytic philosophies, although there is present the tendency to utilize the technique of analysis. One cannot be far wrong in concluding that philosophy as philosophy of life is more characteristic of the eastern outlook as a whole than mere artificial, intellectual constructions and reconstructions, however exact in their methods like pure mathematics. That is why there has been no difference in the East between philosophy and religion.

[18] Under this class come his works *Thought and Reality: Hegelianism and Advaita* (George Allen and Unwin Ltd, London, 1937); *Introduction to Comparative Philosophy* (University of Nebraska Press, Lincoln, 1962, and Southern Illinois University Press, Carbondale, 1970; and *Lectures on Comparative Philosophy* (University of Poona, Poona, 1970).

Glossary of Sanskrit Terms

adharma, demerit, vice, wrong action in the Mīmāmsā; in the same, the potency that produces misery; the principle of rest or immobility in Jainism.
advaita, non-dual, non-dualism, monism.
advaitin, non-dualist, monist.
āgama, that which has come down, sacred scripture accepted by sectarian schools.
ahaṁkāra, ego.
ahimsā, non-injury, non-violence.
ajñāna, ignorance, nescience, the Unconscious as a positive entity for the Advaitins.
ākāśa, space, ether, the source and substratum of sound.
akhyāti, non-cognition, the nature of illusion according to the Mīmāmsā of Prabhākara; note the difference from *anupalabdhi* which is also translated as non-cognition as well as non-apprehension.
ālayavijñāna, the storehouse of ideas, instincts, impressions, and all other forms of consciousness.
anekāntavāda, the doctrine of the Jainas that contrary alternatives can all be true, but from different points of view.
anirvacanīya, the inexplicable, mainly in terms of contradictories like Being and Non-being, 'is' and 'is not'.
anirvacanīyakhyāti, the doctrine of illusion of the Advaitins, according to which the objects of illusion can be explained neither as existent, nor as non-existent, nor as both, nor as neither.
antahkaraṇa, inner instrument; for the Nyāya-Vaiśeṣika, it is *manas*, which is called by them the inner sense organ; for the Sāṅkhya-Yoga and the Vedānta, it includes *manas*, *ahaṁkāra*, and *buddhi*, and *citta* also for the Advaita.
aṇu, atom; the smallest visible particle for Kumārila and the Cārvāka.
anumāna, inference, generally the deductive syllogism.
artha, wealth, one of the four values of life.
asat, non-being, non-existence.
asatkāryavāda, the doctrine of the Nyāya-Vaiśeṣika that the effect had no Being before it is born.
asmitā, 'am-ness'; this is not egoism, but a state reached when the ego is transcended; also the impurity called egoity.
ātman, self, spirit, that which manifests itself as the 'I'; when written as 'Atman', it means the Brahman also.
avidyā, see *ajñāna*.
avyakta, unmanifested, the Unmanifest, used as a synonym for *Prakrti* by the Sāṅkhya.
bhakti, devotion, love.
bheda, difference.
bhedābheda, difference cum identity; identity in difference
bhoktā, enjoyer (of the fruit of actions).
bhrama, illusion, hallucination.
bhūta, element.

bhūtatathatā, suchness of elements, the way of the elements.
bodhi, enlightenment, gnosis, knowledge, widsom.
bodhisattva, one whose being is enlightenment, one on the way to *nirvāṇa*.
brahman, the ever-growing, the ever-increasing; the power of sacrifice which increases thus, the power of incantations; sacrifice; incantation; the Supreme Spirit. From the Upaniṣads onwards, the word means the Supreme Spirit and in some systems even the personal God.
brāhmaṇas, the ritual texts of the Veda, its second part. The word means also the priests who recite the texts at the sacrifice. It means members of the first caste also.
buddhi, consciousness in the Nyāya-Vaiśeṣika; reason in the Sāṅkhya-Yoga and the Vedānta; in the Sāṅkhya etc., *citta*, *vijñāna*, and *Mahat* are its synonyms; in the Advaita of Saṅkara, *citta* is sometimes distinguished from *buddhi* and given a higher place, and *Mahat* is equated to *Mahān* Ātmā of the *Kaṭha Upaniṣad*, Cosmic Reason or Logos. See *manas* and *ahaṁkāra*. *Buddhi* should not be translated by the same English word in all the systems.
darśana, seeing, view, system, school, philosophy.
dharma, merit, virtue, right action and the potency that produces pleasure and happiness in the Mīmāmsā; the principle of motion in Jainism; law, duty; in Buddhism, the doctrine of Buddha, nature, category, quality, and ultimate Reality.
Dharmakāya, the body of law; the cosmic body of Buddha, somewhat corresponding to the Logos of Heraclitus.
duhkha, pain, suffering, misery.
dvaita, dual, dualism.
dvaitin, dualist.
guṇa, quality, attribute.
jīva, soul, the living.
jñāna, consciousness, knowledge.
kāla, *time*.
kāma, love, desire, pleasure, enjoyment.
karma, action, movement.
kevala, alone, pure.
kṣaṇa, moment, instant.
mahābhūtas, the gross elements, as distinct from *sūkṣmabhūtas*, the subtle elements.
mahāvākyas, the great logia, the four principal statements of the Upaniṣads.
māyā, the inexplicable power of the Brahman; illusion, nescience; the principle of the cosmic Unconscious, as distinct from *avidyā* or *ajñāna*; which is the principle of the individual Unconscious, the Unconscious being in either case positive, not negative.
mithyā, false.
mokṣa, emancipation, liberation, release, salvation.
nāma-rūpa, name and form, mind and matter.
nirvāṇa, unagitated, quietude, salvation.
nitya, eternal.
paramārtha, the ultimate, the absolute.
paramātman, the Supreme Spirit.

pariṇāma, change, substantial transformation, transformation of being, evolution; opposed to *vivarta*.

paryāya, in Jainism quality.

pradhāna, the primary, a synonym for Prakṛti in the Sāṅkhya.

prajñā, knowledge, wisdom, gnosis; usually a synonym for *buddhi*.

prakrti, the principle of primeval matter in the Sāṅkhya; the Advaitins equate it to Māyā.

pramāṇa, measure, standard, the means of cognition.

prameya, the object of cognition.

pratītyasamutpāda, dependent origination, origination as occasioned by the cause, in which the cause does not become the effect.

pratyakṣa, perception.

pudgala, the person, the individual, the psycho-physical individual; ordinarily the body.

puruṣa, man, person, *ātman*, Brahman.

rajas, the attribute of activity in the Sāṅkhya.

śabda, sound, word.

sākṣi, witness, the higher *ātman* that only observes the lower *ātman*, but does not act or enjoy.

śakti, force, energy, power.

sat, Being, Existence.

satkāryavāda, the doctrine that the effect had being even before it is born.

sattva, the attribute of transparence or purity in the Sāṅkhya.

satya, true, real, existent.

skandha, aggregate.

smṛti, memory, the remembered, the epics, and ethical codes.

śruti, hearing, ear, that which is heard, scripture, Veda.

śūnya, void, empty, vacuous.

śūnyavāda, the doctrine that reality is the Void, that it has no determinate essence, that it is neither Being nor Non-being.

syādvāda, the doctrine that 'it can be', the doctrine of 'Let it be so'; note its relation to *anekāntavāda* and *nayavāda*.

tamas, darkness, inertia, opaqueness.

tanmātras, subtle elements.

tattva, the true, the real, category.

vāsanā, smell, fragrance, impression, *saṁskāra*.

vijñāna, a synonym for *buddhi*, consciousness, *manas*.

vikalpa, conceptual form or formation, image or image formation in the mind, separation, analysis (as opposed to *saṁkalpa*), determinant.

vivarta, change in form only, assuming a form without change of being, transformation of the material cause without affecting its being.

vyavahāra, activity, customary activity, conventionality, empiricality, pragmatics.

Further Reading

As this book is an elementary one, it seems to be pointless to give a very exhaustive bibliography of Indian philosophy. And it is not likely that Western beginners can read even introductory works in Sanskrit. So no Sanskrit titles are given except a few in translation. For a more exhaustive list, the reader may consult Radhakrishnan and Moore, *A Source Book in Indian Philosophy* (Princeton University Press, Princeton, 1957). Yet even the beginners have to be somewhat informed about the English works listed here, if they wish to proceed for advanced study. The books listed under 'General' contain chapters on different schools and systems.

For listing the various books, the present author is not to be taken as having accepted all the interpretations and the appropriateness of all the English words given in translation by the authors. Yet the books mentioned are largely reliable. The latest editions may be used. As the readers are expected to be beginners, works containing many misleading interpretations and translations are not included – although it is difficult to lay down a strict principle and there can be controversies about the correctness of interpretations and translations – as beginners are not expected to be able to check their correctness.

GENERAL

F. Max Müller, *The Six Systems of Indian Philosophy* (Longmans, New York, 1928).

S. Radhakrishnan, *Indian Philosophy*, 2 vols (George Allen and Unwin Ltd, London, latest edition).

S. N. Dasgupta, *History of Indian Philosophy* Vol. I. (Cambridge University Press, Cambridge, latest edition).

H. Zimmer, *Philosophies of India* (Routledge, London, 1951).

M. Hiriyanna, *Outlines of Indian Philosophy* (George Allen and Unwin Ltd, London, latest edition).

VEDAS AND UPANISADS

H. D. W. Griswold, *The Religion of the Ṛgveda* (Oxford University Press, Oxford, 1923).

A. B. Keith, *The Religion and Philosophy of the Vedas and the Upaniṣads*, 2 vols (Harvard Oriental Series, 1925).

F. Max Müller, *The Upaniṣads* (London, Constable, 1926).

R. D. Ranade, *A Constructive Survey of Upaniṣadic Philosophy* (Oriental Book Agency, Poona, 1926).

R. E. Hume, *The Thirteen Principal Upaniṣads* (Oxford University Press, Oxford, 1923).

MĪMĀMSĀ

G. N. Jha, *Pūrva-Mīmāmsā in its Sources* (Benares Hindu University, Benares, 1942).

A. B. Keith, *The Karma Mīmāmsā* (Oxford University Press, London, 1921).

N. V. Thadani, *The Mīmāṃsā* (Bharati Research Institute, Delhi, 1952).
M. L. Sandal, *The Mīmāṃsā Śutras* (Sacred Books of the Hindus, Allahabad, 1925).

CĀRVĀKA

Dakshinaranjan Sastri, *A Short History of Indian Materialism* (Bookland Private Ltd, Calcutta, 1957).
D. Chattopadhyaya, *Lokāyata* (People's Publishing House, Calcutta, 1959).
A. L. Bhasham, *The Ājīvikas* (Luzac and Co,. Ltd. London, 1951).

JAINISM

Walter Schubring, *The Doctrine of the Jainas* (Motilal Banarasi Das, Delhi, 1912).
M. L. Mehta, *Outlines of Jaina Philosophy* (Jaina Mission Society, Bangalore, 1954).
Satkari Mookerjee, *The Jaina Philosophy of Non-absolutism* (Bharatiya Mahavidyalaya, Calcutta, 1944).
S. T. Stevenson, *The Heart of Jainism* (Oxford University Press, London, 1915).
Nathmal Tatia, *Studies in Jaina Philosophy* (Jaina Cultural Research Society, Benares, 1951).

BUDDHISM

Yamakami Sogen, *Systems of Buddhist Thought* (Calcutta University Press, Calcutta, 1912).
D. T. Suzuki, *Studies in Laṅkāvatāra Sūtra* (Routledge and Kegan Paul, London, 1957).
Bhikshu Sangharakshita, *A Survey of Buddhism* (Indian Institute of World Culture, Bangalore, 1959).
E. J. Thomas, *A History of Buddhist Thought* (Barnes and Nobles, New York, 1951).
P. T. Raju, *Idealistic Thought of India* (George Allen and Unwin Ltd, London, 1953), see the two chapters on Buddhist idealism.
J. B. Pratt, *A Pilgrimage of Buddhism and a Buddhist Pilgrimage* (Macmillan, New York, 1928).
Th. Stcherbatsky, *Buddhist Logic*, 2 vols (Dover Publications, London, 1962).
A. B. Keith, *Buddhist Philosophy in India and Ceylon* (Clarendon Press, Oxford, 1923).
C. A. F. Rhys Davids, *A Manual of Buddhism* (Sheldon Press, London, 1932).
Sir Charles Eliot, *Hinduism and Buddhism*, 3 vols (E. Arnold and Co., London, latest edition).
Edward Conze, *Buddhism: Its Essence and Development* (Philosophical Library, New York, 1954).
A. K. Coomaraswamy, *Buddha and the Gospel of Buddhism* (Harrap, London, 1928).

NYĀYA

A. B. Keith, *Indian Logic and Atomism* (Clarendon Press, Oxford, 1921).
Madhavananda, *Bhāṣāpariccheda* (Eng. transl., Advaita Ashram, Calcutta, 1940).

S. Kuppuswami Sastri, *A Primer of Indian Logic* (P. Varadachari and Co., Madras, 1932).
S. C. Chatterji, *The Nyāya Theory of Knowledge* (Luzac, London, 1950).
S. C. Vidyabhushan, *A History of Indian Logic* (Calcutta University Press, Calcutta, 1921).

VAIŚEṢIKA
A. B. Keith, *Indian Logic and Atomism* (Clarendon Press, Oxford, 1921).
U. Mishra, *The Conception of Matter according to Nyāya-Vaiśeṣika* (M. N. Pandey, Allahabad, 1936).
B. Faddagon, *The Vaiśeṣika System* (K. Müller, Amsterdam, 1918).

SĀṄKHYA
A. B. Keith, *The Sāṅkhya System* (Y.M.C.A. Publishing House, Calcutta, 1949).
G. N. Jha, *Tattvakaumudī* (Eng. trans., Oriental Book Agency, Poona, 1934).

YOGA
S. N. Dasgupta, *Yoga as Philosophy and Religion* (Kegan Paul, London, 1924).
G. N. Jha, *Yogadarśana* (Eng. transl., Bombay Theosophical Publication, Bombay, 1907).
J. H. Woods, *The Yoga System of Patañjali* (Harvard Oriental Series, 1927).

VEDĀNTA
P. T. Raju, *Idealistic Thought of India* (George Allen and Unwin Ltd, London, 1953), see the two chapters on the Vedānta.
G. Thibaut, *The Vedāntasūtras with the Commentary of Śaṅkara* (Clarendon Press, Oxford, latest edition).
G. Thibaut, *The Vedāntasūtras with the Commentary of Rāmānuja* (Clarendon Press, Oxford, latest edition).
D. M. Datta, *Six Ways of Knowing* (Calcutta University Press, Calcutta, latest edition).
H. M. Raghavendrachar, *Dvaita Philosophy and Its Place in the Vedānta* (Mysore University, Mysore, 1941).
T. M. P. Mahadevan, *The Philosophy of Advaita* (Luzac and Co., London, 1938).
P. N. Srinivasachari, *The Philosophy of Viśiṣṭādvaita* (Adyar Library, Madras, 1943).
P. N. Srinivasachari, *The Philosophy of Bhedābheda* (Adyar Library, Madras, 1950).
Śrīnivāsa Dāsa, *Yatīndramatadīpikā* (Eng. transl. by Adidevananda, Ramakrishna Math, Madras, 1949).
B. N. K. Sharma, *Philosophy of Śrī Madhvāchārya* (Bharatiya Vidya Bhaven, Bombay, 1962).
S. M. S. Chari, *Advaita and Viśiṣṭādvaita* (Luzac, London, 1961).

EPICS AND ETHICAL CODES
P. V. Kane, *History of the Dharmaśāstra*, 5 vols (Bhandarkar Oriental Research Institute, Poona, 1932–62).

A. Mahadeva Sastri, *Bhagavadgītā* (Eng. transl., Minerva Press, Madras, 1897).
B. G. Tilak, *Gītārahasya*, 2 vols (Eng. transl., Tilak Bros., Poona, 1935–36).
G. Buhler, *The Laws of Manu* (Sacred Books of the East, Clarendon Press, Oxford, latest edition).
Sir S. Radhakrishnan, *The Bhagavadgītā* (George Allen and Unwin, London, 1948).

Index